3rd Edi

MARKETING & SALES
Career Directory

3rd Edition

MARKETING & SALES
Career Directory

The Career Directory Series

Edited by Ronald W. Fry

The Career Press
62 Beverly Rd.
PO Box 34
Hawthorne, NJ 07507
1-800-CAREER-1
FAX: 201-427-2037

The Career Directory Series

Marketing & Sales Career Directory, Third Edition

Paperback ISBN 0-934829-62-4, $19.95

Copies of this Directory may be ordered by mail or phone directly from the publisher. To order by mail, please include price as noted above, $2.50 handling per order, plus $1.00 for each book ordered. (New Jersey residents please add 6% sales tax.) Send to:

The Career Press Inc.
62 Beverly Rd., PO Box 34,
Hawthorne, NJ 07507

Or call Toll-Free 1-800-CAREER-1 to order using your VISA or Mastercard or for further information on all books published or distributed by The Career Press.

Table of Contents

MARKETING & SALES
Career Directory

Careers In Direct Marketing

Careers In Marketing Research

Careers In Advertising & Promotion

Careers In Public Relations

Section Two: The Job Search Process

Section Three: Job Opportunities Databanks

Section Four: Appendices & Index

Foreword

Getting The Most Out
Of Your Directory

Thank you for purchasing this volume. We have worked long and hard to produce a book that is both as credible and up-to-date as possible. I'm sure you will let us know if we have succeeded!

This *Marketing & Sales Career Directory,* now in its third edition, was specifically created to help *you* break out of the pack hunting for a job in a marketing or sales capacity at a major corporation, market research company, ad or PR agency. It won't just tell you how to get a first job at such a firm—this *Directory* is a compendium of *all* the resources you'll need to make the *series* of decisions necessary to get that first job...or to give you a better understanding of the business so you can move on from your first job.

And it's written by the *pros*—the top people in marketing, sales, marketing research, advertising and public relations today—articles and advice written specifically for this volume and directed specifically to *you*. (For those of you *definitely* interested in working in advertising, or public relations, the fourth editions of both our *Advertising Career Directory* and *Public Relations Career Directory* have also just been published.)

We've attempted to organize this *Directory* in such a way that reading it is a logical, step-by-step, educational progression.

The articles in the first part of this volume offer detailed discussions of the major areas of job specialization and advice from a plethora of top profesionals.

After studying these chapters, you should be well on your way to deciding exactly *what* you want to do—the following chapters will help you figure out *how* to go about getting your first chance to *do* it, including a detailed Job Search Process that will take you through evaluating yourself and potential employers, preparing resumes and cover letters, the interview process, ˜ finally, sifting the job offers.

Our exclusive *Job Opportunities Databank* then lists hundreds of ma᠎ market research companies, ad & PR agencies throughout the United States an᠎ Canada, including information on training programs, key contacts, even actual a᠎

level job openings. This information is exclusive to this *Career Directory*, gathered through our own surveys of these companies.

Finally, two appendices—(A) trade organizations and (B) trade publications. More important information to make sure you get exactly the right first job in marketing & sales.

When we began this project in 1985, students we queried indicated an intense need for a *guide to resources*—articles and advice by the pros out there doing the work, listings of major companies (with then-unavailable information like who to talk to, potential openings, educational requirements, specific titles, etc.), the trade organizations to contact, the trade magazines to read, etc.

The overwhelmingly positive reaction to the first two editions of this volume proved that we had achieved our initial goal: To produce the most comprehensive, all-inclusive guide to the marketing & sales functions for entry-level people ever published.

We feel confident that with this third edition we have succeeded in the more difficult goal we set for ourselves this time: to make the best book on getting into marketing & sales even better.

Most of all, we hope it helps *you* get exactly the job you want in this exciting area.

Good luck!

Section 1

Advice From
The Pros

1

A Career In Direct Sales

Gerald A. Michaelson, Sales and Marketing Consultant
Abt Associates

Of all the career choices open to you, selling offers the best chance for attaining a high level of income. In fact, a good sales record virtually guarantees you a good income.

OK, so sales producers are in demand. How do you get to be one of the good ones (and earn the Big Bucks)?

While many colleges and universities teach marketing, few have courses in selling. But this can work to your advantage, because just about everyone who's competing for the entry-level selling positions has as little experience and training as you! So doing a few basic things to prepare may well give you the competitive edge to win the sales position you want.

Why Is Sales A Great Career?

I believe that selling is the finest thing you can do and the best way to make a living. Why is it such a great career?

Personal Satisfaction—In selling, perhaps more than any other career, you know that when you make the sale, *your* personal effort has been an important contribution to winning.

Giving Service —The word "sell" is derived from the Icelandic word *selja* and the Anglo Saxon word *syllan*—which mean "to give" and "to serve." In direct selling, you are often providing goods and services that make someone's life more enjoyable.

Personal Control—Since your sales record is your "production" record, you can *prove* that you are producing. When you can prove that you are producing, you'll find you have a great deal of flexibility in your personal life.

High Compensation—Salespeople are rewarded directly when they make a sale and *do* make more money than many (if not most) other professions.

The Training You Need To Be Successful

The world is not overflowing with schools that teach selling. It's easier to find courses in sales management than even basic courses in selling.

Since there is no world-renowned academy out there, attendance at which is mandatory for entering the selling profession, all graduates enter the real sales world on an even academic footing.

However, you *can* tip the scales in your favor. There are specific actions you can take that will better the odds of your getting an entry-level sales job and better the odds of your succeeding in that job.

There is an eternal argument about whether selling is an art or a science. The reason the argument continues (and why you should care about it at all) is because if selling is an *art*, then the main ingredient necessary for success is practice—and the more practice you have, the more successful you will become. However, if selling is a *science*, then it can be learned. *Ergo*, the more you learn about the science, the more successful you will become.

The fact is that <u>selling is an art served by many sciences.</u> Success in the art of selling is achieved at the highest levels only by those professionals who understand the underlying science. There *are* successful sales people who *don't* understand the science underlying the art of selling. These people became successful either because they had enormous personal leverage with a few customers or because they stumbled on a few principles that they've applied, without really understanding the basis of their success. (An important point: Since they don't know how *they* became successful, they can't teach *others* to be successful—these people never make the transition to successful sales management. Oh, they sometimes become sales managers, but are never really successful. You can always pick them out—they're the ones who attempt to teach you how to sell by showing you how *they* do it, a business version of "monkey see - monkey do.")

You can prepare for the selling profession by practice and through instruction. Since few of you will have had a chance to get much practice and/or instruction, even a little bit of experience can make a big difference.

Your practice can be acquired through after school, weekend, and summer jobs. These need *not* be selling jobs. These should be the kinds of jobs in the retailing or service industries that place you in contact with people.

You can get your instruction from books. The library is a good source. Start with Dale Carnegie's <u>How to Win Friends and Influence People</u>. Then read anything you can find that tells you how to sell or why people buy.

If you feel the need for more formal learning, there are two worthwhile outside instructional sources. One is the sales school in your market. Explore the Dale Carnegie courses. They will cost money. But showing up at an interview with some kind of sales instruction can be an important differentiator.

The second is to join a Toastmasters Club. The better you are able to think on your feet in front of a large group, the better you'll be able to think when selling one-on-one.

Your reason for joining a Toastmaster's Club should not be because "selling is talking." Too many entry-level salespeople think they must do a lot of talking to make the sale. Selling is *not* talking. Selling is listening. The most successful salespeople listen very carefully, talk very little, but say what the prospect wants to hear. (As you listen, you learn the customers needs and objectives, information you can use to build a case for your product or service. It is understanding the science of the psychology of listening that helps you correctly execute the art of selling.)

The Kinds Of Positions You Can Expect To Find

The world is full of sales opportunities. Selling positions are *not* being lost because of imports. Every product, wherever it's manufactured, needs to be sold. If it isn't, it will soon cease to be manufactured!

A sample listing of opportunities in direct selling would include retail businesses of every kind and extend into real estate, insurance, financial services and a wide range of tangible and intangible products.

There is always room for the competent salesperson somewhere. There is always an opportunity to move on to another company—once you know the skills they are readily transferable. There is always the opportunity to move up into sales management. The opportunity to learn and grow never stops.

Positions in selling pay either a salary, a commission or a combination of the two. As an entry-level salesperson, you will probably be more attracted to a salaried selling position. But as you gain confidence, you will be more attracted to commission plans. My personal advice: Always avoid companies whose compensation plans are salary only. They are not interested in rewarding outstanding performance. To be "the best there is" should be your goal—and if you reach it, you should expect to be compensated accordingly, without the hassle of salary negotiations.

How To Get A Position In Direct Selling

The key to being hired is the interview. Selling yourself is the most difficult sale. Finding the right balance of aggressive self-promotion and self-effacing humility is tough—if you're too brash and talkative, you'll turn off the interviewer; if you're too quiet and reticent, you'll fail to present your case.

In a good interview, each of you should do about half of the talking—the ratio, of course, doesn't need to be *exactly* 50%; allow for variables. Avoid the extremes. If the interviewer does most of the talking, *he* doesn't know how to interview. If *you* do most of the talking, *you* don't learn very much about your prospective employer and *he* may be bored with your monologue. If you need to get the interviewer talking, ask questions.

One of my favorite questions in an interview is "What are the last five books you've read?" All I want to hear is that the candidate is regularly reading *something* that helps them be more successful in their profession.

Similarly, when I ask a more experienced candidate, "How did you learn how to sell?", I'm trying to dig for the educational base of their professional expertise. Certainly, I don't want to hear, "I'm a natural-born salesperson." This poor soul will never get any better, because he thinks his skill is inherited and, since he's already an "expert," there's nothing (and no need) for him to learn.

How Much Can You Expect To Make?

(Money *again*? Well, if you and I weren't interested in money, we wouldn't be in sales in the first place!) The answer varies widely by region and industry. Certainly, depending on your ability, you can expect to make a lot more than most of the people on the payroll.

Different industries have different compensation scales. It is appropriate to ask your prospective employer how much the lowest- and highest-paid salespeople at his company made last year. Find out all you can about the age, geographic location and experience level of the high achievers. The answers can tell you a lot about your opportunity.

You will find that the sales force generally gets more "perks" than anyone else in the company. Most companies make a special effort to keep their sales force highly motivated. This often means the opportunity to win prizes and earn trips. As a sales manager, I've spent weeks in some foreign city while contingents of our national prize winners continually arrived. Show me another profession with that kind of fringe benefit! Oh yes, my spouse came along and so did the spouse (or guest) of each winner.

The Long-Term Opportunity In Selling

Unlike many professions, selling offers several high income career paths.

There is the opportunity for advancement to better selling positions. The experienced salesperson with a proven record gets the most lucrative territories—or just earns the most money because of the contacts that have been developed and nurtured over the years. Prospects turn into customers who become lifelong clients.

There is the opportunity for advancement to sales management. This does not always mean an immediate increase in income. The sales manager is often on the same compensation base as other managers, and earnings may be related more to company performance than to personal performance. In any year, some of the salespeople may make more than the sales manager. So if the top salesperson is selected for sales management, he or she may find that his or her income plateaus until he or she can progress farther up the management ladder.

Your advancement to senior sales management levels may be either:

• Through junior sales management positions; or
• Through a senior sales position where you are responsible for a specific group of important customers—national accounts manager, etc.

There is the opportunity to be in business for yourself. You might find this as an independent real estate agent, an independent insurance agent, a manufacturers representative, etc. These opportunities will become more apparent to you after you enter the selling profession and attain a level of expertise in an industry. From this base, you can either continue on your own or start to build your own professional sales organization.

Some Final Thoughts And Advice

Whatever career path you choose, a great deal of your success will depend on your ability. Unlike many *other* professions where you CAN successfully hide within the corporate body, for years! Your expertise will be judged according to your ability to produce profitable sales.

Selling is a *profession*. It requires training and experience. You must know yourself, your product(s), your customer(s), your market(s). The more you know, the better the base from which you can succeed.

One successful sales manager I know looks for three things in a potential sales person:

1. *A person who understands people.* The decision to buy is an emotional decision, and selling requires that you understand how to work with people. (Please do not enter this profession because you "like people"—that trite statement has no bearing on your success. The foundation must be much deeper.)

2. *A person who likes to work alone.* Much of selling is out of the office, one-on-one with your customer.

3. *A person who likes to read.* You've got to devote time to getting better. How much you read about how you can get better has a lot to do with your success.

Should you consider direct selling as a career path? The answer is an emphatic yes. The rewards are great. It takes a lot of hard work and good luck...but the harder you work, the luckier you will become.

GERALD A. MICHAELSON is a career marketing manager. He has held positions at every level of sales and marketing and has worked and lived in every geographic area of the United States. He has achieved company sales records as a field salesman, as a field sales manager, and as a sales and marketing vice president of Magnavox and North American Philips Consumer Electronics Corp. As a sales vice president, his record increase of over "Sixty Million Dollars" in a single year has been matched by only a handful of executives.

Currently, Jerry is a marketing adviser on the staff of the business strategy group of Abt Associates in Cambridge, Mass. He served as vice president of marketing and sales for the 40,000 members of the American Marketing Association.

Jerry is a worldwide public speaker. He has lectured at marketing management seminars on five continents in cities from Helsinki to Singapore. And he is an author. His articles on sales and marketing have been published by Dartnell and appeared in several issues of *Training, Sales and Marketing Management,* and *Marketing News.* His new book, Winning The Marketing War, has just been published. He is a contributing editor of *Sales and Marketing Management* magazine, for which he writes a monthly column.

2

Getting Started In Industrial (Business-To-Business) Sales

**Theodore G. Johnson, Former Vice-President—Sales and Service
Digital Equipment Corporation**

The implicit job of business-to-business selling is one of developing and managing relationships between two companies.

This implies longer-term contractual and interdependent relationships between two or more entities. It implies strong attention from and involvement with the management of both firms. It implies the probable use of many resources from within and without your own firm that have to be organized and applied to the tasks. Again, the tasks are not just "closing" orders, but also maintaining ongoing customer satisfaction with your company's performance and faith that it will continue to serve the needs of its client customers.

This relationship may depend on the ability of your company to respond to the research and development needs of the customer, who may value many not-so-obvious factors in choosing your company as a supplier. These will include some presumptions about your company's probable strategy, the economic value (to him) of using your products, and the possible marketing leverage or impact of selecting your company. In the case of selling computers to systems contractors, for example, the end user (and customer of your client) is vitally concerned with and may be biased for or against the brand of computer used in the system.

In any selling relationships, you must be prepared to believe not only in your current product, but in your future products and in the integrity and ability of the people in your organizations to perform. You should value your own personal reputation and tie it to an organizations that will enhance your career.

In selling relationships, you are selling trust. Trust in what is expressed in a stream of purchase orders. It is trust in your company and trust in you, including trust that your own position in the company will enable you to perform for your clients.

Company Characteristics

There are all kinds of ways that companies are organized to do business.

The company may be divisionalized, and more than one division may be involved with a particular customer. It may have profit centers or departments with various depths of autonomy and resources.

There may be a corporate-wide sales force, group forces, or a combination of both.

The sales force may have its own technical and support resources or have to draw them from the business center or other parts of the company. Contracts administration will be performed under the watchful eyes of the corporate legal department and the top manager in the business center. All of these resources will have to be assembled, usually by an account manager, sometimes with the business center itself playing a strong lead role in the sale and the negotiations.

Account management and relationship selling have been given a lot of attention in the past decade, and there is a lot of interesting literature on this subject that industrial and technical sales people should read.

For the incoming sales person, companies differ in terms of their orientation. Is the emphasis on technical background? Is there a broader program of training associated with selling, so that it is a stage in a possibly more diversified career, especially up the management ranks? The availability of good initial and ongoing training is a very important opportunity to become more professional and more successful. This training should be looked at in the broader sense—in my view, it includes the way the company continues to relate to the field sales staff and the opportunities they have to be seen and communicate with people at headquarters and within the organization.

A flexible, fluid organization can represent more opportunities for the salesperson to manage resources in a really creative way and get necessary sales support. Each company has its own important attitudes toward the sales function and tends to treat its professionals accordingly. Fortunately, there has been a tremendous amount of progress in the respect the sales function has acquired in the last decade or so, much of it due to the role models set by outstanding companies, particularly those in high technology. I am personally pleased to see such progress and to have made something of a contribution to it through the kind of organization we built at Digital Equipment Corporation.

All companies try to do an effective job, but studying the real differences between them is an ongoing activity for all professionals. The subtle differences in how organizations really function are probably perceived best by the industrial salesman, who has the job of trying to mobilize resources and orchestrate performance of his whole company with another company.

The ability of the people to respond and perform as a team is certainly an important asset for the salesman. The attitudes and willingness at headquarters is very important. Often, this has to do with what is meant by a company being "sales-oriented." Are the people oriented to support the salesman? Does everyone support the selling activity? Do people get excited trying to get the order? More importantly, in the case of industrial selling, do they get excited about winning the commitment and trust of another quality organization.

That trust, by the way, has to emanate from the organization as a whole. It does little good to try to get an order when critical people are still opposed to buying from you or feel they weren't involved in the decision. Yes, industrial selling is a relationship between *companies*, but certainly any such dealings involve the *people* at those companies, sometimes large numbers of people. You want to make sure that you have a solid commitment across the board, from as many people as possible.

What Should You Bring To A Sales Career?

I have tried to sketch out some of the key dimensions of the job of professional selling in an industrial environment. Now let's try to relate that to what you should think about to prepare yourself for success.

In many industrial selling situations, a strong technical background is necessary to absorb product knowledge and relate to the customer. I always believed in what I called "impedance matching" when we staffed for sales. A high level of compatibility, including social and educational compatibility, is very helpful.

I think the job of selling involves a curious mind. It is a daily exercise of learning about people, how to make things happen, how to plan, how to use time effectively, and how to get others—including your teammates and customers—to do what you want. An active interest in current affairs, psychology, economics, etc., is very helpful. It helps to be an interesting person, someone that somebody else would like to have a relationship with.

Above all, however, you have to know your product and be able to help your customers understand how and why it is valuable to them. There is no substitute for highly-honed business skills and a solid conceptual and technical understanding of your product. You can't know too much about your product or your company, unless all of that knowledge is allowed to obscure a grasp of the essentials.

Experience as a user is sometimes very important. And, in the technical area, engineering or product management experience can be very powerful. Sometimes age can be an issue, and it's better to learn what it is like inside a company *before* you try to go out and sell its products. Certainly we had very good experience using technicians, engineers, and others who had considerable experience working internally with the product or with some aspect of product or applications support *before* they entered the field force. In many cases, this experience gave a clear advantage to the selling team and to the person's ultimate career.

Competence is the goal, and that involves learning on-the-job. Education always helps, but it is not a ticket to success in the tough and complex world of selling. If you hope to be able to sell to top managers and executives, you have to be accepted for your competence and, to some extent, for your style. People like to deal with peers, so you must be perceived as successful and able.

The talents you might have to apply are unlimited. But I think the most important talent of all is the ability to listen and generate trust. In the broader sense, you should have a talent for communicating and for problem solving, which can be a very creative process or require great persistence, patience and determination. Staying power is critical. Many a sale has been lost by an inadvertent slip or the failure to sense what to do at the right time.

Your talents and skills should include, therefore, a sense of timing and the ability to make concise and clear presentations. Contrary to the common view of what selling is all about, I think the salesman who talks a lot tends to be his own worst enemy. *Selling is listening*, caring to listen, being able to hear what others are really saying.

It is a discipline that requires organized and systematic processes to assure that communications with the client are as clear as possible at all times. To succeed, you have to value these characteristics and really work to develop them to their fullest. Such an effort will pay big dividends throughout your life, since selling is a constant process of learning how to make friends and influence people, as Mr. Carnegie put it.

In the late '60s, a *Harvard Business Review* article noted that the common characteristics of successful salesmen were "ego drive and empathy." I've never found anything better than that brief description. Truly effective communications and relationships hinge on empathy, the ability to feel, comprehend, and then act upon the feelings and orientation of others. It is the basis of good timing—knowing when to make that next call—because of your sense of how the other person is thinking and feeling.

Motivation

Selling can be lucrative. It is, in my view, one of the best ways to get into general management, especially if you've worked with the product as a user or as an engineer (at least in some organizations).

Nevertheless, you probably shouldn't enter sales if you don't really like people. Tom Watson Sr., former chairman of IBM, said that no salesperson could really be effective if he didn't like his customers. You have to have patience, tact, empathy and courage to face situations that can try your patience and your will, but be capable of "coming up smiling" on the other side, with a real interest in building relationships. The desire to form strong alliances and relationships provides the energy and the satisfaction to a good job of industrial selling.

You also should want to achieve a very high standard of excellence and be prepared to work hard and alone for it. A professional makes the job look easy, but no one knows except him or her how much work went into the preparation.

Salespeople want to be recognized for their talents and accomplishments. They want to feel good and make others feel good about them, their company, their products. Being able to go home every night, evaluate the day, and see what you did right and what you did wrong, is the great part of selling. If you are strongly motivated, this can be a tremendous learning experience.

Entering Sales

Before you enter sales, think about how you can best provide the grounding you will need to be successful. If you want to move into management, what other experiences could you benefit from before you commit a stretch of valuable time to selling? It can be hard to go back later and get that other experience.

I've suggested the importance of training opportunities. If you can get into a program with a top company, you will have made a good move towards establishing a solid base for your career. Picking the company is key. Find a product you are interested in, a field that is exciting to you, and then people that you can respect and work with. Show a desire to learn how to be a real professional, not just your eagerness to "get out and sell;" the company will be making an investment in you. Plan to be in a strong position in three to five years. Show a willingness to be flexible and a strong desire to learn. You will be asking for an opportunity to manage relationships for an important company. You will have to earn that opportunity.

It is difficult to generalize about how you will be spending your time as a new sales-person. Your initial assignments may be in headquarters roles, including sales support, where you will spend a lot of time on the phone, finding answers to problems and questions and organizing information and support activities for customers.

In the field, you may be an apprentice to a senior salesman and be given either missionary selling chores or assigned to support a relatively stable account that requires little senior sales intervention.

You can expect to spend time with the account and in your office—preparing proposals, answering calls, coordinating information, etc. You should spend a considerable amount of your time in purposeful learning; the more you organize for results and skill development, the better off you will eventually be.

Compensation

I would urge you to put considerations of compensation, at least your *initial* compensation, off to the side. It is most important that you pick a company you can feel good about, one that will give you an opportunity to learn and to grow, which is a combination of the training and subsequent work environment, associates, etc. Be intelligent about choosing the first company you work for. Each company has its own internal structure that must be honored. Look for the quality of the opportunity—lower initial pay may reflect greater eventual opportunity.

I joined a small computer electronics company as a sales engineer right out of Harvard Business School and Cal Tech. I accepted $6,500—straight salary—half as much as some larger companies had offered. I ended my sales career as the head of a 3,000 person sales force. Obviously, I was in the right place at the right time. But the *quality of the opportunity* turned out to far surpass any issue of compensation. And that's something I hope you keep in mind as *you* get ready to start out on what will hopefully be your own successful sales career.

After receiving a BSEE from California Institute of Technology in 1956 and an MBA from Harvard in 1958, **THEODORE G. JOHNSON** joined Digital Equipment Corporation, where he spent the next 25 years. He was the first sales engineer they hired and moved up over the course of his career to Western regional sales manager (1959), North American sales manager (1964), vice president - worldwide sales and service (1965), vice president-sales and international (1978) and vice president-corporate marketing (1980). He left the company at the end of 1982.

Since that time, he has served on the board of directors of six companies and two nonprofit organizations, as president of Prelude Management Inc. and as chairman and co-founder of Cambridge Applied Systems Inc.

He is married with two adult children and is an accomplished pianist and enthusiastic sportsman.

3

So You Want To Be A Business-To-Business Marketer?

Robert H. Randolph, Senior Consultant
International Data Corporation

There are about as many definitions of the marketing function as there are books or articles about it, ranging from the formal definition by the American Marketing Association to the working definition that I personally find useful.

According to the American Marketing Association, marketing is "the performance of business activities that direct the flow of goods and services from producer to consumer or user."

Another definition—from George Stiener's book, <u>Top Management Planning</u>—says that marketing is "the performance of business activities that direct the flow of goods and services from producer to consumer or user in order to satisfy customers and accomplish the firm's objectives. The fundamental distinction between marketing and other functions in a firm is that marketing focuses upon exchange between the company and its customers."

Probably the best definition is by Alfred Oxenfeldt in his textbook, <u>Executive Action in Marketing</u>. His definition places a lot more emphasis on what marketers actually *do*. According to Oxenfeldt, "marketing consists of four general activities:

"(1) identifying and selecting the type of customer that the business will cultivate, and learning his needs and desires;

"(2) designing products or services that the firm can sell at a profit in conformity with customer desires;

"(3) persuading customers to buy the firm's offering;

"(4) storing, moving and displaying goods after they leave the production site.

"Along these same lines is a definition that sees marketing as the management task of strategically planning, directing, and controlling the application of a company's efforts to profit-making programs that will provide customer satisfactions—a task which involves the integration of all business activities (including manufacturing, finance, and sales) into a unified system of action."

My personal definition, and one that is easier to remember, is that *marketing is the context in which the sales of products happen.*

Generally marketing activities are focused on two different types of customers. If the customer is an individual, then that type of marketing is called *consumer marketing.* If the customer is a company, then it is called *business-to-business marketing* or *industrial marketing.*

Consumer marketing focuses on products that individual consumers purchase over and over (which is why it's sometimes referred to as *mass marketing*).

On the other hand, business-to-business marketing concerns itself with marketing products that are used to produce still other goods or services. Examples: manufacturing equipment, computers, building materials, chemicals, etc. In our discussion, we will often use the single word "marketing," though we will actually be referring to business-to-business marketing.

The Marketing Organization

As is the case with most departments or functions within a corporation, the marketing organization exists to solve a problem. That problem, simply stated, is: "Now that we have developed this product (this thinking should be done in advance of the product, of course!), how do we: (1) let people know we have the product for sale, and where it can be bought; (2) ensure that its features make it competitive; (3) price it appropriate to its value; and (4) add new product features for continued sales?"

This organizational problem statement fits the classic model that has been called the "Four P's of Marketing." We may apply this model to summarize our problem statement above as follows:

Let people know we have the product for sale	*PROMOTION*
Where it can be purchased	*PLACE*
Features that make the product competitive	*PRODUCT*
New features for continued sales	
Price the product appropriate to its value	*PRICE*

Typically, in most companies that do business-to-business marketing, there is a "chief marketer," usually an officer of the company with a title like vice president of marketing (unless his or her function includes sales, in which case it will be vice president of marketing and sales).

In smaller companies, the chief marketer may be called the director of marketing. When I took my first senior-level marketing job at a small company, they gave me the title of director of marketing. I was later promoted to vp/marketing, after it became clear that I could create a marketing program and establish marketing policies for the company.

In most companies, the marketing organization is divided into five major subgroups or departments:

(A) Market Research

(B) Market Planning and Development

(C) Marketing Communications

(D) Product Management

(E) Sales

Market Research

The market research function is responsible for the ongoing assessment of what customers think about the company and its products. In addition, the market researchers have to find out from customers what additional products or product features they need and how those product changes are likely to be accepted in the marketplace. The primary responsibility of this function is to provide information about what is happening in the marketplace.

Marketing Planning And Development

This function must establish guidelines (usually long-term) about where the company is heading and how they are going to get there. Their job is to tell the company what new products will be needed and what new product features will be required to expand their current customer base (market) or move to a new set of customers (or markets). They are responsible for taking data from the market research people and turning it into actual strategies and action plans.

Marketing Communications

Marketing communications is responsible for promoting the company and its products. They do everything from selecting the advertising agency needed to create and place product advertisements to producing the brochures that describe the product. Their function is to make sure that through their promotional activities, the sales force is well-received when they make sales calls.

Product Management

This is the group that closes the gap between what the engineers want to develop and what the market researchers, planners and salespeople can sell to customers. Product managers are generally responsible for shepherding the product through the maze of problems that occur from the time it's first conceived to the time it lands in the customers' hands. Product managers must understand the different characteristics of their product and what it will look like over the long term (product trends).

Sales

The sales function is responsible for actually getting customers to spend money to obtain the company's products or services. The sales force can be thought of as the magnetic force that attracts customers. They are clearly the frontline troops. Salespeople must translate the market research (that says *which* customers) and the market planning (that says *what* to sell, *where* and *when)* into actual purchase orders from customers—they must convince those customers that they will receive all the benefits for which they paid.

The Product Marketing Scenario

There are several distinct phases that a product passes through during its development. First is the idea phase, in which all the various ways a specific product can be made are conceived so that it meets the needs of customers. This may entail customer surveys (market research), as well as looking at products already on the market to get a better sense of what features or products are missing.

Once the form of the product has been determined (product management and market planning), the research and development people actually produce it. While it is being developed, the marketing communications group will start developing the materials needed to promote it. If it is a new product, some test marketing will usually be done to help finalize its design.

Once the product is ready, it is officially launched (marketing planning and marketing communications)—that is, it's made available to potential customers via advertising (or, as is the case of many industrial products, at a trade show, where the product can be exhibited and actively promoted).

From this point on, the product enters the sales phase. Sales of the product are carefully monitored to see how well it is being received by potential customers. When product sales drop off for a period of time, then it's time to go back to the drawing board and start the whole process again.

What It Takes To Play In This Arena

Now that we have looked at what marketing is all about, the question is, what does it take to play this game?

About 15 years ago, I asked myself that very question. I was managing a group of technical support people for a large computer manufacturer, but wasn't sure that I wanted to do that the rest of my life. I looked around and it seemed that the marketing people were having the most fun. At that time, I had the same mistaken view of "marketing" many people (still) do—it seemed to me that marketing was the same thing as sales. After building a library of books about marketing (and even reading a few of them), I discovered many of the textbook definitions we discussed earlier. From this research, I found that there was a big difference between marketing and sales.

Through a series of circumstances (not entirely beyond my control), it became necessary to find another job within the company I worked for at the time. The textbook definitions were very helpful. After a long round of interviews with several managers of various corporate marketing groups, I noticed that in our discussions about what I would be doing, there was never any mention of market planning, market research, product marketing, or product management.

In retrospect, that series of interviews was a very profound lesson about the differences between sales and marketing. The jobs these managers were describing to me were primarily sales support jobs—they were looking for someone to travel around the country and help salespeople make key presentations to close sales.

The moral of this story is: When you start your own marketing job search, be wary of quasi-sales or sales support jobs masquerading as "marketing" positions. (Unfortunately, many companies still call their salespeople "marketing representatives" or "marketing specialists;" in the case of the more unenlightened companies, "marketing managers." This just makes it tougher to find a real *marketing* job.) Now you may need to take such a job in order to acquire some of the skills necessary to move into a full-blown marketing or sales position. But be clear about what you are doing and what the next steps are.

Now, after that long-winded discussion, do you still want to play the marketing game? Bravo! Then here's what to do about it.

The M.B.A. Dilemma

There are generally two points of view about the necessary training and knowledge required to get into the marketing field. One says that the way to really make it big in marketing is to major in marketing during your first four years of college, then take two additional years to get a Masters degree in Business Administration (M.B.A.).

The other point of view says that a person doesn't need an M.B.A. to be a clever, creative marketer. Since I am essentially a "self-taught" marketing person without an M.B.A., it would be easy for me to say that you obviously don't need one to be successful in marketing.

The truth of the matter is that an M.B.A. *is* a very useful "door opener." Aside from the learning that it represents, an M.B.A. is often an important selection criteria used by personnel managers and other people (with M.B.A.s) to estimate the potential for success. This is especially true for new people just entering the marketing profession.

So by all means, if marketing is something that you want to do, then I heartily recommend that you plan on obtaining an M.B.A. to enhance your chances for long-term success.

There is, however, a note of caution: You must not allow the pursuit of an M.B.A. to destroy your creativity and your ability to think for yourself. One of the key problems I have seen in working with young M.B.A.s is that they rely too heavily on the business models and analytical tools they learned in school.

While an analytical approach to marketing is very useful, it is not, and should never be considered, the final answer. Marketing often requires a balanced approach, involving both intuition (gut feeling) and analysis. For example, no amount of analysis could have predicted the marketing success of the minicomputer, personal computer or, for that matter, the Pet Rock.

While numbers can be used to test intuition—i.e., to assess the amount of risk in a particular marketing idea—the numbers by themselves can't tell whether commitment to the idea will make a difference in the marketplace.

The Basic Skills You Need

To be successful in business-to-business marketing, you must be well-rounded. You need five important skills: (1) communications skills; (2) interpersonal skills; (3) the ability to learn rapidly; (4) creativity; and (5) the ability to think through and solve problems. If these five skills are acquired and developed in a balanced way, you will have an excellent opportunity to make a contribution to any company engaged in this field.

Another way of looking at what marketing requires is in regard to the characteristics a person should have. The first attribute is that of being critically creative. This means being able to take a number of creative possibilities, choosing those that will make a (positive) difference to your company, rejecting those that will ultimately prove detrimental (despite their "creativity").

You must be committed to a life of continuous learning across a number of subject areas. Industrial marketing demands a wide-ranging knowledge of history, business, psychology, science, technology, sociology and international affairs.

The ideal marketer is both a practical person and a dreamer. The marketer has to stand with his feet firmly planted on the ground, while, at the same time, staring at the stars. In other words, the marketer has the responsibility for the success of the company's current products but also for creating a vision for future products.

Sometimes the marketer will have to take on the qualities of a statesman to get his ideas accepted both inside and outside the company. At other times, he may have to mimic a jungle fighter to establish his marketing vision.

Developing these characteristics and skills is what college (yes, even an M.B.A. program) is for. To learn how to think, take courses in mathematics, logic or philosophy. Learn how to examine ideas. Learn how to create new possibilities, ones that go beyond the available, obvious options. Learn how to get "unstuck" from old ideas, especially old company ideas—"We do it that way because we have always done it that way." And, as I've said before, the thinking has to be critical (don't go for the obvious) and creative (bringing forth new possibilities).

There is a critical demand for excellence in the area of communication. Every business-person you ask. will say that communication is a (if not *the*) most important skill for business success. I would like to take that one step further: Communication skill is the essence of success in marketing. I would estimate that if you looked at the typical day of a marketer, you would find that about 90% of his or her time is spent in some form of communication.

Written communications are the marketer's bread and butter. That means that all the stuff that you didn't like about English grammar or English composition is probably the very stuff that will make a big difference now!

Courses in public speaking are invaluable for developing verbal communication skills. Each time I stand up to make a presentation, I am very thankful for all the things I learned in my college public speaking course.

Marketing Jobs

Here is my view of the different marketing job categories:

Category 1	Sales/Sales support
Category 2	Management of sales/Sales support
Category 3	Market research/Marketing services
Category 4	Product planning/Product management
Category 5	Marketing manager
Category 6	Market segment (industry) marketing manager
Category 7	Head of marketing (director, vice president of marketing)

Within each of these categories. are a set of job titles and classifications that will tend to vary from company to company. When giving advise on careers in marketing, I always try to point out that most of us have a basic orientation towards starting at job 1 and fighting our way to job 7 (vertical growth, climbing the corporate ladder). After all, isn't that the American Dream? For fear of being slightly unpatriotic, I have many friends and acquaintances who have found a great deal of fun, challenge, and satisfaction in one of these particular job categories (horizontal growth). For example. their first job was that of a junior salesperson. After a few years, they found that they really loved sales. From there they progressed to senior sales positions, perhaps eventually to sales management, where they spent the remainder of their careers.

The point is: If you choose marketing as a career, you don't *have* to become the company's chief marketer. There are many jobs in the various categories of marketing to provide an individual sense of accomplishment and satisfaction.

But of all the jobs in a company, marketing can be the most creative, risky, highly visible, challenging, satisfying, and rewarding. Go for it!!

ROBERT H. RANDOLPH has over 20 years of experience in the software/hardware products area, including a variety of marketing, development, and management positions.

Prior to his current position, he served as vice president of marketing for Azrex, Inc., a software products company. Prior to Azrex, he worked for Digital Equipment Corporation as senior product manager-marketing, corporate software product marketing. Other positions held at DEC include manager, applications planning and development for the Commercial Systems Group and senior software product manager for the Large Computer Group.

Prior to joining DEC as a software specialist, he worked as a systems programmer for the Boeing Company, North American Aviation and Douglas Aircraft Company. Mr. Randolph holds a B.A. in mathematics from the University of Missouri.

4

Product Management At Industrial Companies

C. H. Neal, General Manager of EDP Programs,
Government Systems
Control Data Corporation

Product management is not an entry-level position or job. You don't major in it or study "how to" do it. And you *don't* start out in it. Rather, think of it as a goal, a position in which you will eventually be able to merge many related business disciplines and studies into a single profession.

The Concept Of Product Management

Product management may be viewed in a number of ways:

In one sense, it is the intersection of the technical discipline and the marketing discipline, glued together by business and management.

It is and can be an internal entrepreneurial spot for talented people in industrial companies.

Ideally, it's the point out in the marketplace where a corporation's products meet its customers' needs.

Product management drives the company, whether it produces industrial or consumer products. (We'll discuss the differences between these two a little later in this chapter.) All companies, in one way or another, are successful only in so far as they manage the products they sell.

Products are constantly changing, growing, evolving, going up or down. They are dynamic. New products replace old ones and new product features are added. And as a particular product goes (up or down), so, sometimes, does the whole company. Especially in my field—hi-tech. Is it surprising that product management is an equally dynamic profession?

Product Groups

In order to control, at least in some sense, the inherent volatility of products, most companies organize around *product groups.* This allows them to group those products that are aimed at the same market(s) or can be promoted via similar marketing strategies. It is necessary sometimes to simply group products together in a way marketing strategies dictate (e.g., by price) in order to leverage resources.

To a great extent, that's what the auto industry has done. General Motors grouped their many car models and styles (Pontiac, Cadillac, Oldsmobile, Chevrolet, etc.) into three distinct product groups based on price and image—one was aimed at the lower-priced end of the market, one at the middle, the last at the top end. Each product group was headed by a single top product executive, who was responsible for coordinating the marketing, advertising, and promotional strategies and production plans for the group as a whole. All of the technical disciplines were formed into separate, company-wide departments that serviced each product group. Many companies in the computer industry have similar organizational structures.

A lot of companies group products that are of the same general category or "product family." At a well known industrial company, for example, all the commercial sandpaper products are in one group, retail clear tapes in another, and industrial tapes in yet a third. The presidents of some ten to twenty major product groups occupy the management-level positions immediately below the president of the company.

Companies may also group products according to the markets they serve or the way in which they are distributed. For example, a large chemical company might group oil and plastics products together, because the advertising and marketing requirements are so similar. But if your product group were responsible for selling chemicals to the large oil companies, you would not be also selling at the *retail* level; that would be the responsibility of another product group (which didn't sell at the wholesale level. You get the idea.)

Product Life Cycles

The *product life cycle* is defined as the period beginning with a product's initial conception through its production *("profitable life")* until it matures and is withdrawn from production (replaced). Overall management of this life cycle is the responsibility of the *product manager.* Thus product management is sometimes like trying to look into a crystal ball...a very *cloudy* crystal ball. That's because of the length of the "start-up time" that exists between thinking about and designing a product and actually having it out in the marketplace. The longer that cycle, the more things that can go wrong during it and the greater the possibility that technology will overwhelm or supersede it before it even reaches the marketplace. The product cycle in hi-tech industries (computers, electronics, etc.) can be as short as six months. In more mature industries (plastics, steel, etc.), the product life cycle can last for many years.

Products must be introduced correctly—at the right time, in the right way. That, in short, is the responsibility of the product manager. But the product manager is actually responsible for virtually everything short of designing the product itself (and he *may* have a hand in there, too). He or she is responsible for making recommendation to the corporation of what the release and marketing schedule should be, the pricing, whom to sell to, what features to add, and when to withdraw the product. In addition, upper management will look to the product manager for information about every aspect of that product during its entire life cycle.

Consumer Goods Vs. Industrial Products

There are differences in being a product or brand manager at a consumer goods company like Procter & Gamble, General Mills or Anheuser-Busch (and do read the excellent chapter in this volume by the latter's VP-Brand Management, Jack MacDonough) and the same position at an industrial company like my own, IBM, Digital Equipment Corp., etc.

Many of these supposed differences are not really differences in the product management assignment; rather, they are inherent differences between the two kinds of companies, the products they produce, and the markets and customers they sell and/or service. The responsibilities are the same.

Technology is the key word. Industrial companies are driven by technology. All down the line, product management at an industrial company tends to be more technical. There are other avenues into product management in an industrial firm than the technical route, as we'll discuss in the next section, but the driving factor *is* technical. On the consumer side, the drive is marketing.

In an industrial company, you're selling to people who understand what the product should be and what it's supposed to do. They understand it *technically* (and there's something technical there to *understand*). Let's face it—there's not a whole slew of "technical" differences between competing brands of toothpaste or paper napkins!

Alternately, we can differentiate product managers as "inward-looking" or "outward-looking." The inward-looking product manager is the controller-type. He or she is deeply involved with the technical and technological advancement within the company, the "field" from which his or her products grow. Most technology-driven companies (and, hence, most industrial companies) need product managers like this. Their major concern is competitors' introduction of a more advanced product or feature that will compete with *their* product.

The outward-looking product manager is the external marketer-type. He is facing outward, studying the markets in which *his* flowers bloom. Most product managers at consumer goods companies—like our "toothpaste" guy—are this type. His concerns are market share, distribution channels, pricing and promotion.

Needless to say, the two types are quite different in outlook, goals, skills, etc. And they are not interchangeable. The outward-looking manager without technical skills will most likely fail miserably in a technology-driven company. And the trained engineer will not necessarily make it selling toothpaste. It helps to be looking in the same direction as the company you work for.

Unfortunately, you must choose *now*, while you're still in school, the direction you plan to "look," since the focus of your coursework is so different. And the decision will be a lifelong one—it is almost impossible to move back and forth from product management in industrial companies to consumer goods companies, or vice versa. There's a lot of movement within each *category*, but *not* across the boundary line between them. The case of someone like John Sculley —who moved from the executive ranks at consumer-giant Pepsico to technological-giant Apple Computer—is the exception, not the rule.

What Should I Study And How Do I Get In?

As I mentioned earlier, one of the key differences between product management at an industrial company vs. a consumer goods company is that *there are more ways in*. At the consumer goods company, the best avenue in is marketing and/or business administration. At industrial companies, there are three routes: technical, business/administrative, and marketing or sales.

The Three Routes Into Industrial Product Management

A good technical background in a specific discipline is invaluable and probably the easiest way in. And there are a number of possible avenues from within the technical ranks— designers, engineers, analysts, etc. may all make the leap into product management. An M.B.A., a knowledge and understanding of the processes of management, and some background in advertising and promotion is most helpful.

The most ideal candidate, in fact, would probably be someone from the technical side with an M.B.A. that gave him or her the necessary communication, people, marketing and financial skills. Unfortunately, many technical people in the U.S. want to remain "techies" first and foremost, and see little value in these other dimensions; the Japanese, for one, see things quite differently—they place people management on an equal footing with product innovation. Quality—and people's perception of it—is an important factor in their products' life cycles. This has led, in some measure, to their recent success in the hi-tech business area.

The second avenue is out of the marketing/sales force. These people know what the customers need, the price they're willing to pay, and how to sell it to them. But they don't necessarily know how to build or produce the product. While their technical training may be limited, their excellent sales and people skills will make the product successful and, thus, help them make the grade.

The last route into product management is from the administrative side—people, some with M.B.A.s, who move over from finance, distribution, etc. There are far fewer such people in industrial vs. consumer goods companies, since the latter stress finance so much more. After all, it's not whether a toothpaste is particularly good that really counts. (Face it: most toothpastes *are* the same.) It's whether it can be <u>sold</u>, its costs profitably covered, its distribution channel properly managed. So the emphasis at a consumer goods company is on marketing, promotion, distribution, and finance, not the technical side so emphasized by industrial firms.

Qualities Common To All Successful Candidates

If you are planning to get your M.B.A., focus on marketing, but don't overlook the importance of financial and accounting coursework. Make sure you learn about management, organizational structures, and how to set goals and objectives.

Studying advertising and promotion will be helpful.

Majoring in liberal arts is okay. I knew one successful product manager who studied sociology. Though he later got an M.B.A., he never had much technical knowledge. But he understood people.

I personally look for evidence of an understanding of psychology—knowing what makes people tick, what motivates them, how you set up their expectations, how to follow up. After all, product managers must be able to get people to do what they don't necessarily *want* to do, but will do for *them*.

Skills that *must* be developed: people, listening, motivation. Take a Dale Carnegie course or something like it if you can.

While in school, practice consensus gathering. A product manager spends at least 60-70% of his time in meetings, trying to convince others that *his* particular ideas and approaches will benefit everyone else in the room. Remember: Product management is the intersection of a number of disciplines.

Practice organizational activities. As a college student engineer, I didn't like fraternities, but the communication and organizational skills they foster would have been valuable to me at an earlier time in my career.

Practice taking risks. In situations where the consequences aren't life-threatening. Try something novel, even if it's dumb. See what it feels like to fail. It may be your last chance to do so without putting your job on the line! The product manager learns from failures and applies those lessons to achieve future success.

Career Advancement And Money

Whichever route you choose into product management, avoid the staff position at the intersection of lots of products. Focus *somewhere*—salesperson, engineer, programmer, designer, etc.

But don't stop there! There are steps to take within each of the three disciplines (technical, marketing/sales, administrative) in order to move up the ladder and land in product management.

Your next step is to focus on a particular product or specific area and learn as much as you can about it. This is where risk-taking comes in, as you attempt to take on more responsibility.

The third step—to manager of one of the three disciplines.

Finally, on the fourth step, you make it to the product level. The group product level is one more step away.

Entry-level people from the technical side earn beginning salaries in the $20,000-$25,000 range; a unique skill may command a bit more. These salaries will be competitive with other areas in the company (i.e., engineers will be paid as engineers).

Entry-level people in sales/marketing are usually paid a base salary plus incentives. The beginning package may be as high as $30,000 (though not a lot of that is salary). Candidates with M.B.A.s might start as much as $10,000 higher.

On the administrative side, beginning accountants earn between $18,000 and $25,000.

Any of these three people, having moved up to manager of their particular discipline, would earn between $40,000 and $60,000.

Product managers (remember· the fourth step up this ladder) will earn in the neighborhood of $60,000 in salary, with an additional incentive equal to as much as 40-50% of base. Most industrial companies have such incentive plans.

Group product managers are well into six figure salaries plus a lot of incentives/bonuses.

Where All Good Product Managers Go

Noting the vast numbers of relatively young people running major ad agencies, controlling millions of dollars of client's monies, and turning out expensive, celebrity-studded TV commercial extravaganzas, someone once wondered where all the whiz kids went after they turned 40!?

Where do product managers go? Product management is a high risk, high pressure business and profession. And product managers, not surprisingly, either rise to the executive ranks or fall by the wayside. Many of the most successful ones wind up in the executive suites of major corporation. Mr. Amdahl (of the company of the same name), for example, was program/product manager of the 360 line of computers at IBM.

But even successful product managers occasionally fail—that's simply the reality of the job. The *really* successful ones are those who recover from the sometimes inevitable failures. The life cycle of a product manager is intimately tied to the life cycle of his or her product. Often, "success" consists of getting off a decaying product and on to another one! There *was* a product manager for the Edsel, another for the PC jr. But there is also one for the PC AT and for Budweiser beer. There's a product manager for the Boeing 727 (737, 747, etc.). And one for 3M Post-It Notes.

There is a wide range of power, responsibilities and talents. But wherever the product management system is practiced, someone has the unique chance to run his or her own business...with someone else's money! To actually run the profit and loss for these companies' major product lines. What could be more exciting?

Lots of pressure. But lot of rewards, too.

It's a fun career, with daily reinforcement, self-satisfaction, creativity, and challenges. The rewards are tangible and measurable, the feedback and stroking constant.

In his current position, **C. H NEAL** is general manager of business development for Government Systems. He has been with Control Data for 20 years—in two separate 10-year stints. He first went to work for them in 1965 as a programmer (later, systems designer and software engineer). He left for two years to become a product manager with Digital Equipment Corp. He returned to Control Data in 1976 as head of the application product management group.

Prior to Control Data, Mr. Neal was a system designer for the Minnesota Highway Department and a systems analyst at Univac.

He studied aeronautical engineering at Howard University and received a BSE degree in applied mathematics (with a minor in aeronautical engineering) from the University of Minnesota. He has taken further management courses at the University of Minnesota and marketing, marketing management, and product/program management courses at Columbia University.

5

Brand Management In Consumer Products

Jack MacDonough, Vice President—Brand Management
Anheuser-Busch, Inc.

The concept of brand management was first developed at Procter & Gamble more than 30 years ago. If a consumer needed laundry detergent and P&G made *two* detergents, they recognized that each detergent might serve a different market. So they gave marketing responsibilities to separate "brand managers." Since then, this concept has been embraced by almost every consumer product company that has more than one brand in a product category.

A Brand Manager's Responsibilities

The scope of a brand manager's function may vary greatly from company to company, but the essence of the job is to search for the most productive way to build the long-term profitability of a consumer product. This is an appropriate definition for the product manager of "durables" as well as "consumables." The key difference between the two categories is that the "repeat cycle" for consumables (whether goods or services) is much more rapid than for durables.

For example, cars, furniture and industrial machinery are, hopefully, durable enough to not need replacement within a year. But soap, paper diapers, and orange juice are *consumed*, not re-used, so within a week, the purchaser may "repeat purchase" such an item.

Because of this rapid repeat purchase cycle, product sales are rapidly responsive to changes in price, product, packaging, positioning, and promotion of a given product or its competition. Managing and coordinating those variables is the job of brand management. Usually the responsibility for an individual brand variable, such as the physical product itself, resides in a separate department (in this case, manufacturing). The challenge of brand or product management (the two terms are used virtually interchangeably, as I will in this article) is to know the individual business well enough to accomplish two basic tasks. First, to recommend a direction for that business. Second, and often more difficult, to generate a consensus for that direction and "champion" it with what is often a diverse group of functional areas that *don't* report directly to brand management.

This requires a sharp mind, constantly open and searching for better ways to make the product appealing or profitable, and the ability to coordinate the implementation of the chosen direction. A brand manager must be sufficiently knowledgeable to analyze, identify or create a business-building idea and have enough leadership and salesmanship to sell the idea and lead others to implement it.

How does the product manager generate a more appealing or profitable product? Often the most important tools are the means to communicate what makes the product unique, what differentiates it from the competition. Since advertising is usually a key component of that process, a brand manager must understand strategies of advertising communication *as well as or better than* an advertising agency account executive. The brand manager must be experienced in the creation, testing and production of advertising and in its placement in appropriate media. The higher the percentage of a brand's marketing budget that advertising represents, the more time its brand manager will spend directing the resources of an advertising agency. Additionally, the brand manager usually coordinates sales promotion and merchandising. On small brands, these tools may be more important than advertising.

While the brand manager's job function may primarily be that of an advertising and merchandising manager, there are other important tasks that must be accomplished if he or she is to be effective. Often a breakthrough or change in other key areas can move a brand ahead.

Coordinating The Product Itself

The brand manager must fully understand how the product is made and be close enough to the manufacturing, product research and purchasing functions to pursue and recommend product improvements that can potentially yield either higher volume or higher pricing in an effort to achieve higher profit. Sometimes product improvements are necessary merely to match competitive improvements. On the other hand, the "improvement" might consist of finding a way to manufacture the same quality product less expensively. The savings can either be invested directly into profit or indirectly into marketing programs.

Any product improvements or competitive advantages are usually communicated via the marketing and advertising programs. The brand manager is the person to coordinate such changes. An example of such a product change is the often seen "New & Improved" announcement on so many consumer products. Of course, the product manager must ensure that what the company identifies as an "improvement" in the product will be clearly perceived as such by the customer. Sometimes a product change can be dangerous, as it was with the substitution of the New Coke for the old.

Coordinating The Name And/Or Package

This is the aspect of marketing that impacts the consumer far more directly than advertising, because it is what consumers see when they purchase and use the product. "Branding," by definition, is applying an identifier or name to a product that separates it from the rest, a concept born in the days of branding cattle. Sometimes a name change or modification can improve sales. Certainly in the development of a new product, the choice of a name can be the most important decision (after the choice of the product itself).

The brand manager should be open-minded to opportunities to improve the functionality and/or appearance of the package. Sometimes a more expensive package will provide enough "added value" to induce the consumer buy more of or pay more for the product. Other times, a change can save costs. Some packaging innovations have been so effective that they forced competitive reactions, e.g., the "crush-proof" cigarette box and "easy-opening" pop-tab cans for soft drinks and beers.

Improvements in the appearance of the package often impact on sales. Again, it is the brand manager's responsibility to work with package designers, legal advisors, purchasing, and manufacturing to coordinate the improvements and incorporate the changes into the entire marketing mix.

Coordinating Price And Price Promotion

This aspect of the job requires close coordination with the sales organization. Pricing communicates as much about a product as any other aspect of the product. Price differences may have been the initial reason the product was developed in the first place. Most product segments are based on segmentation of price into low price/cheap brands, normal price brands and expensive brands. A good brand manager will recommend pricing adjustments that properly position the brand against its competition. Alternatively, the brand manager can recommend the use of couponing, refunds, price-off deals, or similar marketing tools.

Coordinating Distribution And Sales

This usually falls within the responsibility of the sales department, which may have a number of brands to sell. The good brand manager ensures that the sales force has the motivation, knowledge and incentive to sell his or her brands as aggressively as possible. Creation of sales materials, meetings, incentive programs, and personal persuasion are all important tasks for the brand manager.

Operational Responsibilities

In addition to the thinking and planning necessitated by all the previous considerations we've discussed, brand managers are also responsible for certain operational functions, such as inventory planning, keeping an expenditure budget, and analyzing sales and profit trends for the brand and its competition in as much detail as required. The job may require the selection of sales channels and, sometimes, even entail establishing manufacturing facilities or calculating capital projects. The more exhaustive the list, the more the job expands from a marketing manager to a general manager. For that reason, general managers are often drawn from the ranks of brand management.

The range of a brand manager's function varies from company to company, and sometimes *within* the same company, according to the availability, expertise, and scale of corporate ancillary groups (marketing research, inventory control, etc.) and the profit importance of the individual brand. Generally, the bigger the brand, the more attention ancillary groups automatically provide. And the less flexibility the brand manager will have to implement change, since the financial impact of any changes in a major brand on the whole company will be more profound.

The level of experience needed for a brand manager is usually three to five years as a *marketing assistant* and/or *assistant product manager* (working for a brand manager). A brand organization may consist of as few as one manager, as many as five or more, depending on the size and complexity of the brand and the sophistication of the ancillary specialized groups.

The most common route to a "starting" position in a brand group is via a sales or advertising agency background, though many companies hire people into brand group training positions directly from business school M.B.A. programs. While there have been many successful brand managers who have *not* had M.B.As, the degree *is* almost a requirement at some companies. If you are considering earning an MBA primarily to get into brand management, make sure a sufficient number of companies recruit entry-level brand management personnel at the school you're planning to attend. Once you enter a company's brand management program, upward or outward opportunities will become available.

Salary And Career Development

Starting salaries for entry-level positions vary from $30,000 to $50,000, depending on the size of the company and its brand management organization, as well as the experience and educational level of the individual. Brand managers' compensation varies widely by industry, but generally within a range of $50,000 to $90,000. Bonuses are common, stock options unusual.

Increasing responsibilities carry a variety of titles. A brand group may report to a *group brand manager, marketing director, group brand director*, etc. The next level might be *vice president—brand management, VP—marketing*, or *vice president/general manager*.

You need not, however, consider rising through the brand management ranks your only course. The business training in most companies is usually complete and broad-based enough to qualify a brand manager for moves into other areas within the company, including sales management, new venture development, etc. Executive recruiters, with opportunities to join other companies' marketing organizations in hand, offer still another advancement alternative. Advertising agencies and management consulting companies also recruit experienced brand management personnel.

JACK MACDONOUGH graduated with an engineering degree from Cornell University. After one year's experience in manufacturing management at Procter & Gamble, he entered Stanford Business School with a desire to work in brand management. He was recruited by General Mills, which, at the time, hired more than 20 MBAs a year into "starting level" brand management jobs. He gained experience on a number of brands—new and established, small and large—at various levels.

Mr. MacDonough was recruited to Anheuser-Busch by an executive recruiter. A succession of positions with increasing responsibilities and challenges, he notes, has kept the work fun and rewarding. And he's still impressed with the company's commitment to quality and a team approach to management, which has, not incidentally, netted Anheuser-Busch increasing market share in the beer market and a six-fold profit increase in the last ten years.

6

"Positioning" Yourself For A Marketing Consulting Career

Steven R. Baldwin, Partner
Touche Ross & Co.

"**W**hat made you decide to pursue a career in marketing consulting?" I asked the attentive, neatly dressed, young business graduate.

"Well," she responded, "my advisor and everybody else at my school told me that if I really wanted to get ahead these days, I needed to go into either management consulting or investment banking."

It was a comment I had often heard.

"Okay," I pressed, "but why are *you* personally interested in this field?"

Shrugging her shoulders slightly, she said, "You know, if you could just tell me what consulting really is, I could give you the honest answer you're looking for."

This brief dialogue, which actually occurred in my office just before I sat down to write this article, underscores several important points (and the obvious need for an article such as this!) First, the field of management consulting is receiving a great deal of interest these days, particularly at the graduate school level. Second, except for a few large schools which have "consulting clubs," students generally have little access to the information they need on the consulting career path. Finally, to be effective in our interviews (or, for that matter, *any* interview), you have to know your topic. In fact, the successful consulting candidate approaches the initial job search like a good "marketer," taking the necessary steps to "position" himself or herself for a career in consulting even while still in school.

The purpose of this article, then, is to help fill the information gap regarding the field of consulting. While it is skewed to those of you hoping to get an entry-level position as a *marketing* consultant, much of the information is equally applicable to other areas within the consulting field. I hope this article will help you to assess your own career goals and put you in a better position to develop your own personal "marketing strategy."

The Consulting Industry

The starting point of any good strategy is defining a target market. The consulting industry is large and diverse—the latest directory I've seen listed several *thousand* consulting organizations, ranging in size from those with half a dozen practitioners to huge organizations with more than a thousand.

The basic process that consulting firms follow to generate new business and deliver services is generally common among all firms, large or small. "Leads" are generated from a wide variety of business contacts and marketing activities. These leads represent an inquiry as to the firm's ability to provide assistance in a particular area (e.g., helping to decide if the company should expand its distribution into the Midwest).

After some preliminary investigation, the consulting firm submits a "proposal" that outlines a problem definition, suggested approach, qualifications and estimated fees. If the consulting company is selected, a team is formed from among the consultants, based on the skills and industry knowledge that will be required to execute the work plan. As the work proceeds, the client is periodically billed for completed work. The assignment is usually concluded with some type of report or presentation.

Despite these similarities, consulting organizations do vary significantly. There are at least four distinct categories of consulting organizations that might be contacted by a prospective candidate:

Large, General Consulting Firms

These firms, most of them well-known, typically range in size from 250 to 750 consultants and have several offices nationally and internationally. Although many of them are known for a particular area of expertise, they all actively practice in a large number of service areas—marketing is just one.

Large Accounting Firms

Many of the larger professional services firms that specialize in accounting and auditing also have separate "management advisory services" departments. These consulting organizations can be fairly diverse in their scope of services.

Some firms focus heavily on systems consulting and have no involvement in marketing consulting. Others are much broader in scope and have strong marketing practices and are, in fact, similar to the general consulting firms.

Small To Medium-Sized Specialty Firms

There are many very good consulting companies that specialize in marketing and related fields, but whose practices are typically local or regional in scope. These firms have 10 to 50 consultants on staff and tend to serve the many medium-size businesses not usually targeted by the large national consulting firms.

Individual Practitioners

There are many sole practitioners in the field of marketing consulting. This category of firm tends to be the most volatile one—these organizations tend to come and go, depending upon the career pursuits of the principle. In theory, you should consider this type of firm a possible entry point—it often takes on staff on a project basis to help handle particularly large or complex engagements.

Several sources exist to identify specific consulting companies. Check with your college or university, in your local library, and with the several national consulting industry associations that might provide referrals. Also, national marketing associations might help you uncover regional or local firms that provide marketing consulting services. *(These associations are listed in Appendix A—Ed.)*

The Nature Of The Service

Perhaps contrary to their popular image, consultants do much more than smoke a pipe, scratch their chins, and provide well-worn armchair advice. Consulting involves careful research, hard work and the mastery of a set of skills and techniques which, in our office, we call "the consulting process."

Simply stated, consulting is a process of: (1) helping business people add definition and clarity to their specific problems and needs; (2) working to identify the best, practical solution among available alternatives; and (3) helping to build consensus around that solution. Some consulting firms also get involved in helping management carry out the actions and programs which consultants have recommended.

Marketing consultants, in turn, get involved in virtually every area of a company's marketing function. Some typical projects include:

> *Marketing audit*—To help diagnose opportunities for improving the way the company's marketing function plans, organizes and controls its activities (typical duration 3-5 weeks).
>
> *Market feasibility study*—To assess the potential revenues and profits that might be generated through a proposed new product or service, based on an examination of demand, competition and the company's own internal capabilities.
>
> *Strategic marketing plan*—To help define the long-term direction for the goods or services the company wants to provide and the manner in which they will be distributed, promoted and priced.

As the above examples demonstrate, these types of marketing consulting projects can have a profound impact on a business beyond the marketing department staff. Last year, for instance, I was engaged to help a large manufacturer prepare a strategic marketing plan. My initial research, however, indicated that the present plan was quite sound—the real problem was with its execution. More specifically, day-to-day operating methods and even corporate reporting relationships were hindering the company's marketing and sales effectiveness. By the time my assignment was complete, I had helped the company develop a completely new organizational structure and streamlined many routine marketing-related activities to make them more effective.

Current Trends

Like many service industries, the consulting profession is in the middle of a sea of changes, changes that are influencing the career decisions of everyone from the new staff consultant to the senior partner or principal. Some of the most important factors are:

Growth in the industry—Bolstered by a strong economy and relatively high rates of investment, the demand for consultant services appears to be strong and growing. But even in recessionary times, the best firms generally continue to prosper, though the types of services demanded may vary. These conditions have kept the demand high for bright and talented young recruits.

Opportunity where there is change—The demand for consultants with certain types of industry expertise seems to be particularly high. As industries undergo changes (e.g., telecommunications, banking), businessmen seek out consultant expertise to help guide them. The difficulty is that the "window of opportunity" for some of these changes is short-lived, forcing consulting firms to "re-tool" periodically to meet the demands of the marketplace.

Specialization—The time has just about passed when one could be a successful consultant by "knowing a little bit about everything." As demand has grown, numerous, highly-specialized practices have emerged. In addition, the now more-sophisticated user of consulting services is demanding deep functional and industry expertise. The implications upon the training and development of consultants are profound.

Within the marketing consulting field itself, I have observed several important trends which are influencing the types of services we provide and, in turn, the types of staff skills we seek. The three most important trends are:

Greater marketing orientation—As the marketplace has become more segmented and complex, more business people have grown to recognize the importance of the marketing function. They are learning to distinguish between marketing and sales activities and are actively seeking help to make their organizations more "marketing-oriented."

Line management participation—Responsibility for the development of marketing strategy is shifting away from a purely staff function. Nowadays, line management is getting actively involved in studying new product offerings and formulating marketing strategy. This participation has redefined, in part, the identity of the user of marketing consultants and introduced a whole new frame of reference from which the service is delivered.

Implementation orientation—There is more and more emphasis on a consultant's demonstrated ability to help *implement* a marketing program or strategy. This requires a different set of skills than those needed to conduct a market study and write a report.

Getting Into Position

As you might suspect, consulting is a labor-intensive business—the basic raw material that goes into its "product" is people. For this reason, the most successful firms place a high degree of emphasis on recruiting, training and developing their professionals. This includes hundreds of man-hours per year devoted to screening recruits and interviewing candidates. By way of illustration, a consulting partner in another firm told me that he had calculated that for every *1,080* resumes he received, he found *one* candidate who accepted the firm's initial job offer and, eventually, made it all the way to partner.

Some people wonder how a firm can hire anyone with less than 15 years industry expertise to provide informed consulting advice to experienced businessmen. The fact is, consulting companies do *not* routinely hire personnel into senior-level positions. While these people may have excellent industry credentials, they are inexperienced in something equally important—"the consulting process." Most firms hire younger—but *not* inexperienced— individuals with the basic talents and intellect to acquire both technical knowledge and consulting process skills.

There are two key aspects in the educational background of the successful candidate for a marketing consulting position. First, people like me look for academic excellence in the marketing and business disciplines. Courses such as strategic planning, distribution channels, and marketing management are very important. It is also very valuable for the candidate to have adequate financial training, because a lot of consulting work involves translating projects or programs into financial or economic terms.

The other important dimension of academic preparation is that of communications skills. Leading business schools now offer courses in personal salesmanship, presentation skills, and business writing. It is very important in consulting to be able to acquire and present information effectively.

In general, consulting is not the place to *start* your career. Most firms, even smaller ones, require two to six years of general business experience for an entry-level candidate. This basic experience is important because it provides some "real world" balance against the academic theories learned in school. In addition to this experience, most large consulting practices now require an M.B.A. or equivalent postgraduate degree from a leading business school.

A final dimension of the successful consulting candidate involves the personal traits exhibited during the job interview. In our office, we use a checklist for characteristics that are highly correlated with success as a consultant. These personal traits include a strong work ethic, high energy level, ability to work as a team member, and good interpersonal skills (i.e., as a listener and as a speaker).

If you are selected through the interview process, you will be offered a starting salary and a position on staff commensurate with the firm's assessment of your present level of experience and development. As a general rule, the consulting profession has the potential for earnings significantly above average. Pay varies widely among firms, however, and is often a function of the billing rates a firm can charge based on its position and reputation in the marketplace. Another note of caution: Some consulting firms pay their people according to certain formulas, such as an amount per hour of time actually worked on a "chargeable assignment."

Making A Good Start

Your first assignment as a marketing consultant will likely be as a staff member on a project team. An experienced member of the firm will give you a project plan, part of which you will be expected to execute. Your role will be mostly data collection—interviewing mid-level client personnel or conducting outside (e.g., library) research. At this point, most analysis and development of recommendations would be conducted by the more experienced members of the team.

The first year or two as a staff consultant represent an excellent learning experience and are usually filled with variety. However, there are potential negatives. One of these is the possibility of an extended, out-of-town assignment, since new staffers typically work on one assignment at a time. In addition, some people are always disappointed because their entry-level position doesn't offer the glamour and visibility they imagined inherent in a consulting career. All in all, though, I think the vast majority find the first years "in the trenches" to be a valuable and stimulating experience.

After several successful assignments, the new marketing consultant begins to take on new responsibilities and diverse clients. This happens in several ways. For example, as a senior consultant, you may find yourself directing the work of someone else conducting a marketing audit. You might be assigned to help develop a marketing strategy for a particularly large and complex business. Finally, you might get to work in a new industry or deal with an international marketing issue.

Moving Up Through The Ranks

One of the fears young consultants have is whether they will be able to make the transition from a staff consultant to a consultant who also is required to generate new business. When you have obtained about five years' experience in consulting, this transition begins to occur. In most firms, continued success and further promotions are dependent upon an ability to begin to generate new clients and projects.

Experience has shown, however, that the best consultants make the best salespeople. If you have developed good technical expertise in the marketing discipline and have become skilled at diagnosing client problems, there will be a demand for your services. The transition into the selling role is gradual, too. It begins with identifying expanded services with existing clients or assisting a senior member of the firm in developing a proposal. It takes several years of practice before you will become confident at generating leads and closing new business.

Another change which occurs at the five to six year mark is that you begin to get involved in the internal management of the practice. This includes activities such as recruiting, account administration and staff training.

Assessing The Options

After seven to ten years in the consulting firm, the typical individual is an established senior practitioner with a fairly well-defined field of expertise. Although the pay has been very good all along, he or she would now be in a position to share in other financial rewards, such as bonuses or profit incentives.

At this point in your career, a variety of options would be presented. In larger organizations, they could include moving into firm management (which also might mean a transfer). Some people find the idea of moving out of line consulting and into upper management unattractive. These people have stayed in consulting because it is what they like to do; they want to continue working among their clients, out where "the action is." Fortunately, most firms are beginning to give greater recognition to the role of the senior line partner or principal and providing the corresponding financial incentives.

A third career path that some pursue at this point involves leaving the firm for "general industry" and securing a position that involves profit responsibility. One example of such a position would be to become vice president of a division with production and sales responsibility for a particular product line. Those choosing this alternative are often heard to say that they simply grew tired of giving advice to others and wanted to try out their ideas out for themselves.

A marketing consulting career holds excellent potential in terms of personal development, financial rewards, and multiple, continuing career options. The trade-offs sometimes involve lifestyle issues, travel and the pressures of an intense work environment. Those of you thinking about a consulting career should consider carefully your academic preparation and the compatibility of your personal characteristics with those found in most successful consultants.

STEVEN R. BALDWIN is one of Touche Ross's leading practitioners in the field of marketing and strategic planning. He specializes in working with multinational enterprises and has assisted a variety of clients in South America and Europe.

Prior to joining Touche Ross in 1977, he was a consultant with an Atlanta-based inter-national consulting firm.

Mr. Baldwin received his undergraduate degree in industrial management from the Georgia Institute of Technology. He holds a Masters degree in business administration from Georgia State University, where he received the George J. Manolos award for scholastic achievement.

Steve has been actively involved in the American Marketing Association. Since 1983, he has served as an officer and board member of the AMA's Atlanta chapter. He is also presently serving a three-year term on the Global Marketing Council of AMA International.

7

Careers in Services Marketing

James B. Shanahan, Senior Vice President
Payment Systems Div.—Maryland Bank, N.A. (MBNA)

The Service Sector is arguably the most important part of the United States economy today. Services are not only the largest part of our economy and the fastest growing; they have driven most of the economic growth of the past two decades. Consider these startling statistics: Services represent over 75% of the Gross National Product, employ over 65 million people, and are responsible for most of the growth in the economy. In fact, since 1980, employment in the services has increased by 35% from 48 million to 65 million, while employment in goods has remained unchanged at 26 million.

Besides being larger and growing faster, the Service Sector is extremely diverse. Services affect every aspect of our lives, from communications and finance to transportation and health care. Services can be classified as *consumer services*, marketed to individuals, or *business services*, marketed to companies. Other service areas are *professional services*, such as doctors, lawyers, and accountants, and *nonprofit services*, such as museums or philanthropic organizations. Whether they know it or not, all of these organizations are in services marketing, and each can benefit by applying the principles of modern services marketing to their business.

But what, if anything, does all this mean to you? Well, very simply, it means opportunity, *unparalleled* opportunity, especially for people just entering the job market. The opportunities for long-term career growth in services marketing are enormous because of the size and long-term growth prospects of the services sector itself. And service companies will continue to grow faster than manufacturing companies and will, therefore, continue to provide more opportunity for employment.

Add to this the fact that the marketing function is relatively new to service firms and growing even faster than the service economy itself, and you have even *more* opportunity. The diversity of service companies also means more opportunity to be a part of a business that you personally find exciting and meaningful.

You may be thinking to yourself, "This is all well and good, but is a marketing job with a service company really different from a product management job with a 'packaged goods' company or other manufacturing companies?" The answer to this is decidedly *yes*. Service firms are quite different—they require different marketing skills, usually have a different corporate culture or environment, and perhaps most importantly, require different managerial skills for personal success.

Before describing a typical job in service marketing, however, let's briefly highlight some of the key factors that distinguish services from goods. An understanding of the basic definitional differences will help you better understand the practical differences that will affect you later on the job.

Why Services Are Different

While complete textbooks have been written on this subject, there are three basic differences between services and goods.

1. Services Are Intangible

First, and perhaps most important, services are intangible. Unlike packaged goods, they cannot be seen, tasted, smelled or touched. Services are experienced, not consumed. They are a process, occurring over time, not a thing. Some services are more intangible that others, of course. A doctor's diagnosis —extremely intangible—vs. a car rental service, in which the car itself is a most tangible component of the basic *in*tangible service of renting the car. Nonetheless, *intangibility* is the key distinguishing factor of services. It has far-reaching implications for the service marketer.

2. Services Are Produced And Consumed—Simultaneously

Packaged goods are typically produced in a factory, distributed to an intermediary, purchased by the customer, and, finally, consumed. These are all segmented events that occur sequentially at different times and in different places.

The production/consumption process for services, on the other hand, is completely different. A service is produced and consumed simultaneously. It is not manufactured in some distant factory, but, rather, at the same place it is being consumed. Consider the airline industry, in which the basic service is "flying on an airplane." This service does not exist until passengers are on the plane, in flight. Oh, it exists in *latent* form when the airplane is fueled and inspected, the crew in place, and the schedule set. But it is actually produced for the passenger at the same time the passenger "consumes" it—during flight. Like the intangibility factor, the simultaneous production and consumption of services has many implications for the service marketer.

3. People Are Part Of The Service "Product"

The third major distinguishing factor between services and goods is the enormous role of people in services. People are actually part of the product, like the package is part of a packaged good. Employees are part of the product, as they interact with customers to actually deliver the service. Intermediaries are part of the product, as their manner in selling the service greatly effects the customer perception of it. Finally, customers are part of the product, as they often interact with the employees providing the service as they are using it. How these different people involved with the service act will affect greatly the quality of the service and the definition of the service itself.

Now that you understand something about the inherent differences between services and goods, let's take a look at the effect of these differences on your potential career in Services Marketing. Two major areas which will be affected—the *marketing skills* you will need on a daily basis to successfully achieve your marketing objectives, and, perhaps more important, the *management skills* you will need over the long term to perform effectively at a services firm.

Services Marketing Business Skills

Many marketers believe that "marketing is marketing" and that the same basic marketing principles can be equally applied to all business areas. These principles include the importance of identifying a target market and understanding that market segment's need, developing a "bundle of benefits" (the product) that meets those needs better than the competition, developing and implementing a marketing plan to bring customers and products together, and, finally, monitoring results to allow for ongoing product modification and improvement.

Undoubtedly, these basic principles *do* apply on a general level to the marketing of any product—tangible or intangible, for-profit or not-for-profit, consumer or industrial. However, when it comes to the marketing of services, there are many differences on a more specific level, differences which, if not properly understood, can snatch defeat from the jaws of victory. Let's look at some of these specific differences between services and packaged goods in terms of implementing the "4 P's of Marketing"—Product, Place, Price and Promotion.

Product

The intangibility of a service makes it very difficult to describe and define it; it requires a whole new language, called "service blueprinting". Quality control is very difficult, due to both the intangibility factor and the role of people as part of the product. How do you insure that a bank teller is providing a "high quality" service? How can you measure the extent to which he or she is doing so? And isn't the service provided by a bank teller a little bit different each time?

The role of the tangible aspects of a service in affecting consumers' perception of it is also important. This consists of things like the physical environment in which a service is consumed—furnishings, color, room layout, lighting, noise level, etc. The "product" also includes facilitating goods such as tickets, applications and forms, as well as aspects of the people involved—their age, dress, speech, and overall behavior.

Place

Due to the simultaneous production and consumption of services, there is no product to distribute, only a capacity to provide that service. Time is a key aspect of service distribution —time of day, week, and year. Once a plane takes off, the unsold seats are worthless.

Electronic distribution of services is becoming more and more important, since services don't need to be physically seen (there's nothing to see, anyway!) to be purchased. Also, services are usually distributed directly to the consumer, without intermediaries.

Price

Services are more difficult to price correctly than packaged goods, because it is difficult to determine how much they cost and because the "same" service may have very different costs each time it is delivered, depending on such things as the length of interaction between the customer contact employee and the service consumer.

Traditional market research methods do little to help set appropriate price points from a consumer perspective, due to the difficulty of getting consumers to react to something intangible.

Promotion

Advertising a service is difficult due to its intangible nature. Successful service advertisers overcome this obstacle in a number of different ways. They can focus on the tangible aspects of the service (e.g., the airplane) or on the experience of people enjoying the service (e.g., happy children in a fast food restaurant). Sometimes they create a tangible image to symbolize the firm. This tactic is especially popular for that most intangible of services—insurance; consider "The Rock," Fireman's Hat, Helpful Hands, the Key, and the Red Umbrella, to name a few. Service firms often compensate for this by trying to develop a strong overall image for the company as a whole.

Lastly, it is often useful to focus on the higher level, "end-end" benefits that services often provide to a greater extent than packaged goods. Examples include the benefit of security for financial services, self-esteem for lodging services, and safety for transportation services.

Services Marketing Management Skills

The preceding examples illustrate why the specific issues that a service marketer needs to address on a day-to-day basis are different than those confronting packaged goods marketers. There is another set of issues that are more important, however, issues related to managerial skills, the manner and style in which a person deals with business problems and fellow workers.

These differences are more important because they are more difficult to learn. A specific marketing technique can be learned by anyone with the dedication and intelligence to do so. In contrast, the manner in which a marketing executive operates within a firm is more related to the personality, interpersonal skills and basic approach to problem-solving that he brings to his first day on the job. Here are five characteristics of successful service managers:

1. Service Marketers Are Generalists

The service marketer must be a generalist, knowledgeable in all of the functional areas related to service delivery. While this is also true for packaged goods product managers, it is more pertinent for service marketers because the marketing responsibility is distributed throughout the firm. For example, Customer Service is often part of Operations, and customer contact personnel, such as branch tellers, are often located in line management. Yet because these people affect customer perceptions of the service, they should be influenced, if not directed, by the Marketing department, usually on a matrix basis. Finally, it becomes critical for the success of the firm that the service marketer integrates and unites all of the disparate functional areas so the customer receives a clear and consistent message.

2. Service Marketers Are Good People Managers

Because people are such an integral part of services, the service marketer needs to be familiar with the basic "human resource" skills of hiring, training and motivation. More importantly, he must be able to inspire and motivate the customer contact people to provide the service according to predetermined standards and in the manner intended. This leadership and motivational responsibility is critical to successful service marketing.

3. Service Marketers Are Intuitive Managers

Traditional business education emphasizes an analytical, data-based approach to problem-solving. This approach is very effective in most packaged goods industries, where there is a wealth of data to analyze and the necessary time to do it. However, it is not as effective in service companies, where there is a relative shortage of "hard" historical data and little time to apply sophisticated analytical techniques and models.

The service marketer needs to make intuitive, "gut" decisions based on whatever information is available. Paradoxically, service marketers usually need to process *more* information, due to the many macro environmental factors that tend to affect service companies more than manufacturing companies. These include deregulation, rapidly changing competitive strategies, and the impact of technology on service delivery.

4. Service Marketers Are Flexible

Most service companies are currently going through a period of severe and rapid change. Service marketers must be flexible enough to react quickly to these changes and willing to discard ineffective strategies. The service firm needs executives who can manage where there is no precedent and lead where there is no one to follow. The effective service marketer will be one who is not uncomfortable with uncertainty, but, rather, thrives in it.

5. Service Marketers Are Marketing Marketers

Service marketers often are responsible for educating the management and employees of their firm about general marketing concepts and the importance of meeting customer needs. This is especially true in those service firms where marketing is a new function. In these cases, the Marketing department usually has relatively little formal power. The service marketer must be willing to pioneer the marketing concept throughout the firm, spreading the "gospel" to those many people who are involved in marketing the service to the consumer.

Career Paths In Services Marketing

There is *not* one, clear-cut, easy-to-define career path. Not only will paths differ from one industry to another, they will usually differ from one company to another within the same service industry and, often, from one person to another within the same company!

This contrasts greatly with the usually clear-cut career paths in packaged goods marketing that include well-defined job levels and standard times for working at each level. Services are different because the marketing function itself is usually relatively young and because the job responsibilities must change to keep pace with rapidly changing competitors. So people entering service marketing should not require a well-defined career path; rather, they should enjoy the opportunity to develop a unique career path based on their own individual skills and desires.

Career paths for service marketers often lead out of marketing and into other positions within the firm, usually either in line management or support areas like Operations. This is because the marketing responsibility is spread throughout the organization, so service marketers are exposed to and knowledgeable in all aspects of service delivery.

Getting Started

The most obvious way to obtain a marketing position in a service firm is by interviewing with companies on campus. Oftentimes, however, service companies do not actively recruit for marketing positions—either because the Marketing department is not large enough or the company fills its marketing positions internally. So you may have to actively seek out a service marketing position. Ideas for companies to pursue are all around you—those in your home town or where you go to school, companies in articles you read, or even basic services that you use.

No matter how you learn about the company, however, be sure to be prepared for the interview. Find out ahead of time as much as you can about them, and let the interviewer know *you* know something about the company. Consider the points discussed in this article (and the many others in this *Career Directory*) and see if you can apply them to the firm or job for which you are interviewing. Finally, let the interviewer know you are interested in working for the company and why.

Good luck on your new career, whatever and wherever it may be. If you are the kind of person who likes challenges, who enjoys finding his own way, and, above all, enjoys working with and through other people, a career in service marketing may be the place for you.

JAMES B. SHANAHAN is currently senior vice president of the Payment Services Division of Maryland Bank, N.A. (MBNA), where he is responsible for overall management of credit card processing services for 20,000 merchants and medical providers nationwide. Prior to MBNA, Mr. Shanahan was sector vice president of marketing at Mastercard International. Before that, he was vice president of new product development for Chemical Bank. He also spent six years in various marketing capacities with American Express.

Mr. Shanahan is actively interested in services marketing and has written two articles on the subject. He was previously vice president for the service marketing division of the American Marketing Association and served on the AMA's board of directors for two years. He is a graduate of the University of Notre Dame and holds an MBA in marketing and finance from Columbia University.

MBNA is the credit card subsidiary of MNC Financial Corporation, a $20 billion financial institution headquartered in Baltimore, Maryland. MBNA pioneered the development of affinity land credit card and is now the fifth largest credit card issuer in the United States and the world's largest issuer of the Gold Master Card.

8

Retail Marketing— Satisfaction Guaranteed

Thomas E. Morris, Vice President—Marketing Sears Merchandise Group

Kenmore, Craftsman and DieHard have become some of the most trusted brand names in America. But they are not national brand names in the traditional sense. They are private label brands sold only by Sears Merchandise Group, the merchandising arm of Sears, Roebuck and Co. But the *perception* of them as national brand names attests to and demonstrates the power of total marketing, from product development through customer satisfaction.

It is this type of marketing that begins with a concept and continues through service which helps set retail marketing apart from other types of marketing.

Marketing is at the core of retailing—a fast-paced, endlessly diverse business based on people's wants and needs. It is the leading edge of enterprise, where customers from many walks of life seek a wide array of merchandise and services. Retailing offers the excitement of constant change and the challenge of a competitive marketplace. Its demands—and rewards—add up to excellent career opportunities.

The story of Sears, Roebuck and Co. is built on marketing. It began in 1886 when Richard W. Sears, a railway station agent in North Redwood, Minnesota, began selling watches to other agents up and down the line. From this beginning came the R. W. Sears Watch Company. Sears then moved to Chicago, where he hired watchmaker Alvah C. Roebuck. Later, the corporate name Sears, Roebuck and Co. was adopted. Initially the company marketed by mail, through its now-famous catalogs. It opened its first retail store in 1925.

Since my entire retailing career has been spent with Sears, you will find, not surprisingly, that this article is very "Sears-specific." But while some titles and organizational details may be unique to the Sears setup, you'll find that most, if not all, of the points regarding the importance of marketing are pertinent to all major retailers.

Learning The Retail Business

In retailing, while very few jobs contain the word "marketing" in their titles, *every* job is directly involved in marketing on one level or another. No other industry offers all its individuals more opportunity to utilize marketing concepts and techniques on a day-to-day basis.

There are basically two ways to develop a career in marketing at Sears (or any other large retail chain). An individual can begin working face-to-face with the customer on the sales floor, learning about the shopping process firsthand.

Or begin working with the buying organization, which lets you see how the products make it onto the sales floor or into the catalog. An entry-level position in the buying organization might be a *retail or catalog advertising copywriter*. Copywriter trainees at Sears begin at $18,720, with salary reviews at six months and one year.

Even without a college degree, a high school graduate, after experience in a store, can be promoted to a more marketing-related job and eventually achieve an executive position.

Personality is a key to success. You must have self-confidence and the ability to move easily among people. You must also be capable of moving quickly and easily between different types of jobs or situations. It also helps if you are naturally enthusiastic and a good listener. Listening allows you to be "in tune" (in touch) with the customer.

If you want to pursue a career in marketing, you must be able to understand the changing mix and moods of customers, know what the customer is doing today, and anticipate what the customer will want tomorrow. Accurately anticipating customer demands is the difference between a market leader and a market follower.

Other important personality traits are objectivity, tolerance, cooperativeness, firmness combined with the ability to listen to other points of view, a willingness to take risks, and decisiveness.

Retail Management Training

Many enter Sears through our management training program, which is conducted in training centers established in selected major retail stores. The main purpose of the management training program is to prepare you for an entry-level management assignment, with the expectation that you will have the potential to advance within the executive ranks at a later date.

There are two phases of training. The first is designed to familiarize you with the retail operation in general; the second phase is to prepare you for your first sales management assignment. In the initial phase of the Sears management training program, our national retail trainees earn $21,000 a year; salary is then reviewed on an annual basis.

The training program exposes you to the basics of the business and the concepts and skills necessary to deal with customers, employees, merchandise and systems. Assignments can include sales of installed products and services, visual merchandising, catalog sales, customer service, receiving and shipping, credit, operating, accounting, auto center, and personnel.

On a daily basis, you will be dealing with customers, learning to understand and anticipate their wants and needs. The most educated individual at Sears is the person who has sat in enough chairs and touched enough retail components to be able to do the job effectively.

Career Advancement

There isn't just one road to success in retailing; there are many. Sears is a "promote from within" company. We like our executives to be exposed to as many aspects of the company's operations as possible. Practically all of our executives who started from an entry-level position, were successful in their assignments, recognized for their superior performance, and promoted within the executive ranks on that basis.

Individuals with a proven track record of success and an interest in increased responsibility are usually rewarded with a larger range of duties. A successful salesperson might be promoted to a sales manager spot where he or she can direct the selling activities of a group of employees. From there, the individual might move on to a larger group or area of management.

Sales Management

Your first assignment will be determined by the available openings at the time you complete the training program. Sales management provides you with a great deal of responsibility at an early stage in your career. It also gives you an opportunity to prove yourself as a manager and leader of people, as well as a chance to prove how successful you can be in a business situation. Some of the factors for which you will be held accountable as a sales manager are:

- Implementing sales plans and promotions.
- Maintaining good turnover of merchandise.
- Managing merchandising systems (point-of-sale, inventory management, and so on).
- Inventory control.
- Good profit performance.
- Productivity through supervision and training of employees.
- Visual merchandising (display).
- Housekeeping (assuring merchandise availability on the sales floor while maintaining visual presentation).
- Staff responsibilities, including security.

Beyond Sales Management

As you gain experience in sales management and demonstrate increasing competence, your responsibilities will grow. When and where you progress to a new position depends on the availability of openings and the competition for them among your peers.

And there *is* competition—at Sears (or anywhere else, for that matter), you advance by proving you can produce.

Beyond sales management, your future could take many forms; career path possibilities in retail are many and varied. Adding to them, however, is the fact that almost any point in the retail career path can serve as a branching point for a move to a regional or national headquarters assignment...and a completely new career direction.

One advantage of working for a big company like Sears is the variety of available job possibilities. Opportunities in buying, merchandising, advertising, personnel, distribution, market research, packaging, credit, operations, technical services, and customer services are all available and attainable without leaving the company. There is an opportunity to grow in numerous ways, find out what your real interests are, and test yourself in a variety of challenging positions without moving to another company.

Sales managers in the stores report through separate business structures. To use home appliances and electronics as an example, the sales manager in a store for that business works closely with a district business manager who is an expert in the home appliances and electronics field and visits stores within a district.

These district managers work with region business managers to focus on local market needs. The region business manager reports to the home office in Chicago, thus filling out a selling organization that truly has the customer at the top of the chart. There is also a marketing organization and a buying organization in the home office as part of each merchandise business, but it all begins with the customer, and people who know first-hand how to service him or her.

Incidentally, sales managers in the stores help keep customer service high by working closely with the store manager, and his or her staff, who are measured on how their unit takes care of the customer, and how well they keep operating costs to a minimum.

The Umbrella

Marketing opportunities exist throughout Sears and other major retailers—in the stores, the regional offices, and the national offices. Marketing is the umbrella—an ability to bring a product to market at a price the customer is willing to pay. Effective marketing is the combined output of every department. Each activity in its own way is a marketing job.

For instance, packaging is a very important element of marketing. Without an attractive, useful package that presents the merchandise in an effective manner, other aspects of marketing might be useless.

Product distribution is also important. All the selling techniques in the world are worthless if the products don't move from the manufacturer or warehouse to the selling floor when the customer wants them. Having the right products at the right time also means transporting the goods in a cost efficient method that enables the retailer to keep its cost down.

Diehard Sets The Standard

About twenty years ago, customers wanted more in their automobile batteries—more power to start their cars in cold weather and under other trying conditions. The rest of the story is an example of Sears total marketing.

Working with its leading automobile battery manufacturer, Sears automotive merchants and laboratory engineers developed a revolutionary battery that utilized new materials and provided more interior space for the storage cells.

The resulting product was lab and field tested. The results proved the battery to be stronger and more reliable. Quality-stringent production guidelines and schedules were established. The battery had to be produced to standard, but at a cost consumers would be willing to pay in relation to the power and service it would deliver—the value.

An innovative see-through battery case was designed, bearing the product's newly-chosen and distinctive name. Display materials and point-of-sale information were readied for the stores. Publicity kits were prepared to introduce the battery to consumers through news coverage by the media. Training materials were prepared for sales people and automotive center installers. A complete newspaper, magazine, radio and television advertising campaign was developed to introduce the product.

Introduced with a strong coordinated marketing program, and backed by a continuing marketing effort, the private label Sears DieHard battery has become the most recognized battery in the automotive aftermarket.

The Challenge Is Broad

Retail marketing is much broader than other types of marketing. First, it encompasses a whole store of merchandise. Consumer and manufacturing marketing are a lot more single-focused in nature, usually revolving around one type or group of products, like cereals or car models. Their marketing is very narrow and very deep.

At major retail chains like Sears, the challenge is selling the entire store—apparel and paint, laundry detergent and lawnmowers, home fashions and automotive accessories, an array of products related only because they are under one roof.

The Buyer Is Key

At Sears Merchandise Group national headquarters, the *buyer* is like a brand manager (and similar to a marketing executive) at a consumer goods or industrial product company. He or she is directly responsible for bringing a product from its inception to the sales floor. Along the way, the buyer is involved with contracting for producing, packaging, pricing and advertising the product.

The buyer is part of a department of merchandise. For instance, the battery buyer is part of the Automotive department. There are other buyers within the department for shock absorbers, mufflers and exhaust systems, and automotive accessories.

Within the Automotive department, marketing determines product position on the retail sales floor and on the catalog and specialty book pages. In reaching these critical decisions, the product buyer works with the retail and marketing managers. They, in turn, rely on information from Sears' Marketing Research department, as well as feedback from the point-of-sale.

Sears is made up of 17 merchandise departments (like the aforementioned Automotive department, with more than 800 different lines of products, of which automotive batteries is just one). Without a larger marketing organization concerned with selling the *entire* store, there would be no cohesion within the departments and across the company.

Starting As A Copywriter

Many of the executives in the national offices of Sears Merchandise Group began their careers as copywriters in Chicago. Starting your career as a copywriter means you'll train on-the-job with some of the best and most experienced copywriters in the catalog and retail business in the 110-story Sears Tower.

You'll work with other highly skilled communications specialists—artists, typographers, etc.—have direct contact with a number of different people involved in the buying and merchandising functions, and learn to work with them as part of a total marketing team with a common objective—increasing sales. In the process, you'll get a solid grounding in catalog and retail selling as you learn their marketing objectives and the bases on which they make their decisions.

Working within the established objectives, you'll learn which items to feature and decide how to emphasize them. You'll also gather the necessary product information and design rough layouts for each ad. You will approve each stage of production to ensure accuracy of layout, copy and photography.

Copywriters must be able to contribute original ways of presenting merchandise, but they also need a ready knowledge of the editorial guidelines, advertising policies, and media formats established by the company. They must be aggressive enough to get all of the necessary product information from busy marketing managers and buyers, yet be able to maintain their composure when pressed by deadlines, delays in getting needed information, and the seemingly inevitable last-minute changes.

To help you get the broad range of experience a seasoned copywriter requires, you'll be reassigned periodically to work with different merchandise departments having varying needs and problems.

Beyond Copywriting

Because of the size of the Sears Merchandise Group, and the unusual amount of experience Sears copywriters get in marketing and merchandising, there is an exceptionally wide range of career paths open to them that are marketing oriented.

The most obvious is, of course, to advance directly within advertising departments to *copy chief* or *art buyer.* Even if you choose to move into advertising management, you may work for a time on the merchandising side as an *assistant catalog marketing manager* or *merchandising assistant.* From there, you could move up the merchandising career ladder into catalog or retail marketing or return to advertising management.

Other copywriters move into the buying area by beginning as *assistant buyers* for a small-volume line of merchandise.

In addition, there are career possibilities outside of buying and merchandising. Some of our people go to work on promotional or display materials, advertising production, circulation, catalog market development, marketing research, or public affairs.

The Challenge Of Change

Sears, Roebuck and Co. has changed a great deal since Sears and Roebuck began marketing by catalog to rural America. The company has grown dramatically and we've adapted out operations all along the way—from a mail order catalog to a national retail chain, our base of operations has always concentrated on the products we sell. We want to be the premier provider of products and services to our customers.

The key to achieving that objective will be marketing. At Sears we've always tried to market with anticipation, making changes ahead of customer demand. A career in marketing at Sears can enable you to grow with us into our second century of serving consumers.

THOMAS E. MORRIS was elected Vice President - Marketing for Sears Merchandise Group in May, 1986; he is responsible for all retail and catalog marketing and advertising.

Mr. Morris joined Sears as manager of a catalog sales office in Aiken, S.C. in 1969, after previously serving with the company for one year. Four years later, he was transferred to Sears headquarters in Chicago, where he served in a number of management positions, including assistant retail sales manager, sales promotion manager, and buyer in the automotive department. He became retail marketing manager of the automotive - recreation group in 1981 and, a year later, was named national merchandise manager of the sporting goods buying department.

From 1984 to 1986, Mr. Morris served as vice president - merchandising for Sears Canada Inc., the Canadian subsidiary of Sears, Roebuck and Co. headquartered in Toronto.

A native of Georgia, he is a business administration graduate of Georgia Southern College.

9

Opportunities And Challenges For The Transportation Marketer

Craig Cina, Director of Market Planning
Yellow Freight System, Inc.

Over the last decade, the transportation industry has undergone dramatic change. The era of government regulation has given way to a new era of deregulation, bringing with it a business environment unfamiliar to most transportation professionals. Competition has intensified and bankruptcies become commonplace, as carriers now seek to control costs, price competitively, and gain market share. On the other hand, transportation companies have a unique opportunity to establish a competitive advantage, not just settle for parity, as they had to in yesterday's regulated environment. The only constant in today's dynamic transportation environment is change.

Why is this state of transition important to the prospective transportation marketers? Quite simply, deregulation is forcing transportation companies to become more customer-driven. It's a matter of survival. Transportation companies are increasingly treating their customers as a valued asset rather than a captive commodity.

Not surprisingly, as a result of this shift from an operations/sales orientation to a customer-driven focus, the demand for marketing professionals is increasing markedly. A transportation background is not as important as understanding how to get and keep customers. There is no more challenging and exciting time to work for a transportation company than now.

The Evolution Of The Marketing Function

Before you accept a position with a company, you should understand its organizational structure and how the marketing department fits in. Dr. Philip Kotler, a renowned professor of marketing, states in his text, <u>Marketing Management</u>, that a marketing department evolves through five stages of development—from stage one, where marketing is synonymous with sales, to stage five, where the sales and marketing functions report to a vice president of marketing. Most transportation companies have separated the marketing and sales functions, but the delineation is not always clear.

The importance of knowing the organizational structure before accepting employment cannot be overstressed. If you accept a position that ultimately reports to a vice president of sales (sometimes disguised as a vice president of marketing), the firm's sales orientation may force you to continually face short-term, "brush fire" issues, at the expense of necessary longer term marketing issues. A much better situation is where the transportation company is truly customer-driven and supports this philosophy by setting up a separate, distinctive marketing function that reports up through the president. You can then be assured that all of your talents will be fully employed.

As a key result of deregulation, transportation companies have begun to realize that their existing organizational structure is out-of-date. The marketing departments of many existing airlines, motor carriers and railroads have been reorganized to reflect this reality. The department's role has been expanded and strengthened—common functions include marketing research, marketing communications, customer service, product development and pricing.

In the next decade, you should probably expect to see your department continue to change—until it more closely resembles those of the most advanced consumer products organizations—as transportation companies develop functions in marketing research, product development and management, and advertising. The differences between the marketing departments of transportation and consumer products companies will continue to narrow rapidly as highly qualified marketers become increasingly attracted to the unique challenges offered only by transportation companies.

Preparing For A Career In Transportation Marketing

The requirements for an entry-level position in transportation marketing vary from company to company, from marketing department to marketing department. However, more and more companies are seeking candidates with at least a college degree in business (with a marketing emphasis). Due to the abundance of candidates with advanced degrees in the marketplace, many firms now consider an M.B.A. (or a bachelor's degree in business plus one to two years of experience) the minimal requirement for entry-level positions. Opportunities are becoming scarce for candidates without a college degree.

However, as the role of the marketing department continues to expand and broaden, it is difficult to limit entry-level jobs to those candidates who can boast an M.B.A. Many professionals in product development hold degrees as varied as marketing, journalism and engineering. The business analysis and forecasting function is frequently the domain of economists. Furthermore, marketing communications professionals will commonly have educational backgrounds in advertising, public relations and/or journalism. So marketing positions in transportation companies are *not* restricted to candidates with M.B.A.s in marketing (though the opportunities are greatest if you have one).

A transportation marketer needs to be an excellent communicator. Since the marketing function is still new to most transportation companies, the transportation marketer must be very persuasive in selling his or her ideas. A marketers' way of thinking may, at times, differ rather radically from that of an operations or financial manager. Moreover, transportation companies that have survived the initial wave of deregulation may fall into the "we've done it this way for the last decade, why should we change?" syndrome. It's incumbent on transportation marketers to educate their counterparts in the benefits of a customer-driven philosophy. Obviously, good communication skills are essential.

The best way to learn about the transportation industry is through direct experience. Many transportation companies offer college students internships that provide the student with insight into the workings of a real company. Internship experience can be very helpful in acquiring an entry-level position.

What To Expect In An Entry-Level Job

The transportation industry is complex, due, in part, to its operational nature. It generally takes new marketing employees anywhere from six months to a year before they become productive workers. However, your skills will be applied immediately. To be truly effective, you must first become very familiar with the operational, sales, and customer aspects of the business. The transportation marketer is ultimately responsible for pulling all these aspects together into an integrated set of actions that can provide the company with a sustainable, competitive advantage. Thus, the more rapidly you can learn the business, the more rapidly you will move on to more challenging assignments.

You can expect to spend a great deal of your time talking with customers and the sales force. Transportation people are very down-to-earth and practical, so this is not the place for "ivory tower" thinking. To be successful, transportation marketers must speak knowledgeably from a customer's point of view and, at the same time, provide very actionable, meaningful insight into business decision-making. This can only take place when the transportation marketer has spent ample time with the "outside world." Not surprisingly, transportation marketers generally spend 10 to 20% of their time traveling.

Transportation marketers work in a very challenging environment where the stakes are high. It is not a 9:00 a.m. to 5:00 p.m. job for individuals who want to progress. Due to heavy workloads, you must use your time very efficiently and prioritize each day's activities. A typical day would include one or two meetings with individuals outside the marketing area, handling several phone calls, with the remaining time spent working on high priority projects. Since marketing departments in transportation companies are a recent phenomenon, most projects break new ground, giving the marketer great latitude in his or her approach.

Your Career Path

The typical candidate—with an M.B.A. in marketing and no experience—will begin as a *marketing analyst,* with a beginning salary the low to mid-20s range, depending upon qualifications. The marketing analyst can expect to be promoted in about two to three years to a *senior marketing analyst,* contingent upon successful performance. A manager's position is more difficult to obtain and may take anywhere from two to four additional years. Keys to a successful career path can be summed up as follows:

- Grow beyond the demands of the existing position
- Know your business and your customers well
- Get along with your boss and associates
- Be enthusiastic and enjoyable to work with

Although there is no magical formula for success, these personal attributes are desired by most employers.

Top transportation marketing executives at the vice president level and above earn anywhere from $80,000 to $200,000, depending upon the size of the firm. Generally, these executives have accumulated at least ten years of experience and have demonstrated ability to handle increased responsibilities. Due to an increasing marketing orientation of transportation companies, a few marketing executives are working their way to the top of the organization. However, the majority of presidents of transportation companies have backgrounds in finance or operations. This should slowly change over the next decade, as marketing professionals assume a greater role in their organizations.

The transportation marketer is not locked into the transportation industry. The rich experience gained from working in transportation is easily transferable to other service and business-to-business related industries. In fact, many existing transportation marketers have experience in industries outside the transportation arena.

A Final Word

With the coming of deregulation, transportation companies face a new marketplace with new challenges. Competition has intensified, and, as a result, many companies have suffered bankruptcy. Transportation companies are turning to marketing professionals to help address these challenges by developing a stronger customer orientation. These marketing professionals are expected to possess the analytical skills to determine customer needs and the necessary interpersonal and organizational skills to design actionable programs.

The transportation marketer must be able to develop strategies and an integrated set of actions that help differentiate the company from the competition. The goal of these strategies and actions is to provide the company with a sustainable competitive advantage in the marketplace. Marketers that can either drive or support this type of effort will be in high demand for years to come.

CRAIG CINA's major responsibilities include directing the company's strategic planning, marketing research, product development, business analysis and forecasting, and service analysis efforts. He began his marketing career at Federated Department Stores in 1976 as a research analyst and was promoted to a senior research analyst in 1978. Mr. Cina joined Midland Affiliated Company in 1981 as marketing manager and was later recruited to the Zale Corporation as the director of marketing research and planning in 1983. He has been employed with Yellow Freight since June, 1985.

Mr. Cina is an active member of the American Marketing Association and sits on the board of directors of the Johnson County United Way. He also has contributed several marketing articles to the AMA's Marketing News as well as other periodicals.

He holds a B.S. degree from the University of Utah and an MRCP degree from Kansas State University. He is based at Yellow Freight's Overland Park, Kansas headquarters and resides with his wife and two children in Leawood, Kansas.

10

Career Opportunities In Health Services Marketing

Dr. Bruce Allen, Professor of Marketing
School of Business, San Francisco State University

A job opportunity listing for a top-level health care marketing executive might read as follows:

"A 400+ bed hospital in a Chicago suburb is seeking a Vice-President, Marketing and Planning. This individual will be responsible for the following major areas: strategic and business planning; development and analysis of auxiliary enterprises; marketing communications; sales and product management.

"Position requires an advanced degree in health or business administration, plus 3-5 years successful marketing management experience. Candidate must have demonstrated skills in strategic planning and product development, plus experience in managing comprehensive marketing communications programs. Related consulting experience is helpful. SALARY: $60,000 to $90,000, depending on qualifications."

Just ten years ago, there were few such high-level marketing executive positions available in hospitals. This is surprising, given that health services is the nation's second largest industry (after agriculture). There were also very few marketing departments in health services organizations. In fact, only very recently have many physicians become aware of marketing and its capabilities. Thus, health services marketing has only become a growing career field within the past decade.

A key reason for this change is that federal and state governments, as well as private employers, have worked to move health care from a cost-driven to a competition-driven industry. There is great pressure from these groups to drive down the cost of health care by placing controls on the types and amounts of health services that are available to consumers. Along with this trend, health care consumers are becoming more interested and actively involved in selecting their health services and providers. Thus, hospitals, physicians, health insurance companies and other health services organizations find themselves competing to maintain their revenue bases and market shares in a declining market for their traditional services.

What And Where Are The Entry-Level Jobs?

These health care industry trends have led to great opportunities—and pressure-packed challenges—for those of you just starting out in the health marketing field (who eventually want to attain, of course, the executive position described above). From a supply and demand viewpoint, the largest number of entry-level jobs are found in hospitals, but there are growing opportunities at physician group practices, health insurance companies, and health maintenance organizations (HMOs).

Three "typical" entry-level jobs are described below:

Sales/Outreach Representative

EDUCATION/BACKGROUND: Bachelors degree (in marketing and/or business preferred, but not required) and sales experience.

SKILLS: Strong communications skills (written and verbal); empathy & listening capabilities; mature social presence.

TASKS: Represent a hospital organization or health insurance provider to physicians, employers and other external groups. Sales reps calling on physicians present hospital programs and services to them and attempt to obtain their commitment to and support for the hospital. Reps calling on employers present industrial medicine, wellness programs, or insurance programs that the companies can purchase.

COMPENSATION: $20,000 - $35,000 base salary, plus bonus (which may be as much as 20 to 30% of the base salary).

Public Relations Or Communications Specialist

EDUCATION/BACKGROUND: Bachelors degree (journalism preferred), with publications/media experience (or internship).

SKILLS: Written communication, creativity and organization skills (working on multiple projects at the same time).

TASKS: To prepare internal and external communications in support of organizational marketing programs—e.g., internal newsletters, a health care magazine, brochures for medical services, news releases, etc. PR specialists are also frequently required to organize and implement special events, such as open-houses for new facilities or newly-acquired medical technologies.

COMPENSATION: $25,000 - $35,000.

Planning/Marketing Analyst

EDUCATION/BACKGROUND: Bachelors degree and Masters in hospital or business administration. Planning experience (or internship) helpful.

SKILLS: Analytical abilities, written presentation skills, social presence, and maturity to make presentations to management.

TASKS: Perform feasibility studies and market analysis for new/existing products and services. This position would become involved in marketing research, product planning, and strategic/business planning.

COMPENSATION: $30,000 - $40,000.

These are three examples of entry-level jobs. The titles are *not* generic across the industry, but beginning jobs *are* inevitably in sales, communications or analysis. In fact, marketing jobs in health care can be found reporting all over the organization, not just to a marketing department. These jobs can be in clinical departments, community health education departments, and in subsidiaries operating health insurance plans, industrial medicine programs, or other services.

The next level up from such a starting position is usually a managerial position: *communications manager, product manager, market research manager, sales manager* or *manager of planning.* From there, career paths will vary greatly according to the size and scope of the organization. In smaller organizations, the next level might report to the CEO. In large, multi-hospital systems, there may be another two levels of management before you reach vice president status.

Most of the entry-level jobs described above pay from $20,000 to $35,000. Larger organizations in urban areas typically pay the higher salaries. Generally speaking, the greater the requirement for specific technical skills, and the more extensive the applicant's experience, the higher the salary. Fringe benefits in health care are usually quite good. Typically, health and life insurance, retirement plans and generous vacation policies are available.

One key characteristic of health services marketing departments is that they are usually badly understaffed. Because marketing is so new to most hospitals and budgets so tightly managed, the number of projects to be accomplished is far beyond the ability of most departments to complete them. So health services marketing can be a "burn out" situation. Thus, the *negative* side of this specialized field is that a new employee will typically be expected to work 50 or more hours a week to achieve nearly impossible tasks. The *positive* aspect is that a new employee's learning curve will be very rapid, indeed—there are few industries where an entry-level employee can gain as much practical, "hands on" experience in such a short period of time.

To achieve rapid advancement, it may be necessary for a high achiever to move *out* to move *up*. For example, a young lady began working for me in late 1983 at a West Coast, multi-hospital system (I was VP) as a marketing analyst. Two years later, she moved up (and out) as the director of marketing at a small hospital. Another example is my former director of sales, who has since moved up and out as director of marketing at a sizable hospital on the East Coast. It appears that the fast track in health services marketing is not directly up, but up and *out*.

Some Helpful Hints On Door-Breaking

If you are in the process of obtaining an bachelors or masters in marketing or health administration and want to specialize in health services, GET YOURSELF A GOOD INTERNSHIP. Whether it is paid or unpaid, get summer or part-time experience in a hospital, group practice or health insurance company. This will put you well-ahead of everybody else out there who only has a degree. Also, you should get a good reference from the internship.

Join the national and regional professional health marketing associations. The American Marketing Association (in Chicago) sponsors the Academy For Health Services Marketing. The American Hospital Association (also in Chicago) has the Society for Hospital Planning and

Marketing and the Society For Hospital Marketing and Public Relations. In addition, there are local professional organizations, such as the Northern California Health Care Marketing Association, that will accept student members.

Begin reading the key health industry publications so that you understand the industry environment. These publications include: *Modern Health Care, Hospitals, American Medical News, Health Care Competition Week,* and the *Health Care Marketing Report.* Your college or university library should have most of these publications.

A final point: A career in health care marketing can be exciting and stimulating, but it will be demanding and very stressful at times. An industry in which very bureaucratic organizations (hospitals) and professionals who haven't had to compete (physicians) are suddenly facing a competitive environment tends to place great expectations on marketing. In fact, within the past five years, a large number of health care marketing executives have fallen short of pre-established expectations and left their organizations. The pressure from boards of directors, physicians, clinical professionals, and managerial colleagues can be very difficult to manage.

The managerial challenge is certainly daunting, but for the professional who is knowledgeable, organized, mature, and can communicate well, the sky is the limit!

In addition to his responsibilities at San Francisco State, **DR. BRUCE ALLEN** is also an active consultant with health care organizations. He has B.A., M.B.A. and Ph.D. degrees, all in marketing.

His prior position was as vice president/marketing strategy at Community Hospitals of California, a 950-bed, multi-hospital system based in Fresno. During Dr. Allen's years in Fresno, the hospital system achieved a 27% increase in revenues and a 150% increase in profits. As VP, he had responsibility for corporate planning, product-line management, marketing communications, physician relations and employee relations.

Dr. Allen has also taught in the business schools at Depaul and Kent State Universities, and has worked in marketing positions at B.F. Goodrich and Sears. He is the author of over 40 articles and one book.

11

Telemarketing: The Fast-Track Medium

Fred B. Tregaskis, Former President
CCI Telemarketing Inc.

Direct response marketing has grown and progressed from its early days of generating business by mail order and door-to-door selling. Today, direct marketing uses mail, catalogs, print, broadcast, and videotex. But the fastest growth is occurring in the use of telephone as an integrated component of the direct marketing media mix.

Telemarketing certainly includes making sales by telephone to consumers and businesses, but there are many other activities in which the telephone is used as a marketing tool. Later in this chapter is a matrix of telemarketing applications that include outbound and inbound calls to and from consumers, businesses, and institutions.

Inbound and outbound telemarketing is done by agencies or companies that have their own "in-house" telemarketing operations. Due to the increased use of telemarketing, there is a high demand for experienced managers, supervisors, trainers, script writers, and account executives. This demand also creates, of course, a need for trainees in all of these job descriptions.

Telemarketing agencies usually are more apt to have training programs than in-house telemarketing departments. This is because agencies, by their very nature, have large telemarketing centers, with fifty to several hundred telemarketing representatives or communicators. Concentrations of this size require echelons of management and support personnel.

The Setup & Job Titles At Telemarketing Agencies

Telemarketing agencies are structured like advertising agencies, except that they are in business to use the *telephone* as a medium, rather than print, mail, or broadcast. Let's follow the process of business development in a telemarketing agency. Obviously, not all agencies are alike, but this examination will enable us to review the job opportunities.

Clients hire telemarketing agencies to make or receive calls. These clients are acquired by a *marketing representative*, who develops leads and makes sales presentations. He or she is often required to formulate written proposals.

After the contract is signed, the marketing representative usually maintains responsibility for client communication and client relations. Marketing representatives should have experience or training in telemarketing operations and "basic" sales ability. Students who major in marketing have good academic backgrounds for this position. Earnings vary from $35,000 to $75,000 and usually consist of a combination of salary and commissions. The normal job progression is to vice president of marketing and executive management.

After a client has been contracted for a program, an *account executive* is needed to organize and manage the program internally—coordinating script writing, script testing, list preparation, forms design (to record sales and customer data), and client reports. Once the program has been launched, the account executive monitors the project and provides regular reports for the client.

The account executive (or "AE") needs to understand the workings and capabilities of the telemarketing operation, preferably from experience, and be multi-task oriented, organized, and analytical. Good written and oral communication skills are required. Some agencies have *junior or assistant account executive* positions that are considered entry-level opportunities. Account executives earn from $25,000 to $40,000. This career path leads to marketing or executive administration.

Script writers provide the creative support in a telemarketing agency. Script writing is different than writing advertising or direct mail copy in that a script must be written to be *heard*. This requires the ability to anticipate the impression and reaction to the sound of the copy; material written to be *read* will sound stilted when presented over the phone.

Scripts can vary from verbatim presentations and rebuttals, to structured dialogues that allow for more "personalized" presentations. Script writers are required to learn about many different products and services and to "speak" appealingly to diverse audiences. One project might be targeted to high-level executives, another to homemakers, doctors, or participants in a certain sport.

Journalism and creative writing are good academic backgrounds for script writers, who typically earn from $20,000 to $40,000. Advancement leads to the position of *creative director.*

After the program components have been assembled, and the script written, the *telemarketing center manager* has the responsibility for executing the program. This means either making or receiving the calls in a way that achieves each client's objective.

This position requires the talent and experience to recruit, train, schedule, manage, and motivate large numbers of people. Of course, the number of staff assisting with these responsibilities will be a product of the size of the operation.

The center manager must have extensive experience in telemarketing operations, strong people-management skills, and an aptitude for logistics and scheduling. A business administration background is recommended, including human resource management. Courses in computer science would be helpful, due to the increasing use of automation in telemarketing. Telemarketing center managers earn from $35,000 to $75,000; their jobs lead to executive management positions.

Supervisors manage groups of telemarketing communicators and are directly responsible for their performance. Their job may also include training and scheduling.

Business administration provides a helpful background, though experience as a communicator is required. Salaries range from $20,000 to $40,000. Supervisors normally progress to become telemarketing center managers.

Telemarketing trainers instruct communicators about the products or services and how to use the scripts. Trainers also teach telemarketing efficiency, listening skills, and sales techniques. The instruction is done with groups and by personal coaching, often using audio and video media. In some agency configurations, training and supervision are combined.

Telemarketing Applications

Program	Consumer	Business	In	Out
Refine lists	◊	△		△
Update lists	◊	△	◊	△
Assign names to titles		△		△
Identify decision-makers	◊	△		△
Collect research data	◊	△		△
Profile customers	◊	△	◊	△
Announce new products	◊	△		△
Renewals	◊	△		△
Schedule appointments	◊	△		△
Service accounts	◊	△		△
Check inventories		△		△
Precede mail	◊	△		△
Follow mail/broadcast	◊	△	◊	△
Upsell	◊	△	◊	△
Cross sell	◊	△	◊	△
Verify orders	◊	△		△
Political	◊			△
Fund raising	◊	△	◊	△
Target specific markets	◊	△		△
Reinforce advertising	◊	△	◊	△
Response advertising	◊	△	◊	△
Identify repeat customers	◊	△	◊	△
Build data base	◊	△	◊	△
Maintain communication	◊	△		△
Reactivate past customers	◊	△		△
Convert dissatisfied customers	◊	△	◊	△
Increase attendance	◊	△		△
Maximize sales rep time	◊	△	◊	△
React to market change	◊	△		△
Generate leads	◊	△	◊	△
Generate sales	◊	△	◊	△

(Note: There is no difference between the marks "◊" and "△")

Telemarketing experience is required; education and communication studies are helpful. Trainers earn from $20,000 to $40,000 and usually aspire to becoming telemarketing center managers.

The *telemarketing communicator* could be described as the most important person in an agency, in the sense that he or she delivers what everyone else sells, coordinates, or manages. In today's telemarketing industry, communicators come from all walks of life. Part-time employees are college students, homemakers, and second-job office workers. They earn from $5 to $8 per hour in most areas. Full-time communicators can earn $20,000 to $40,000 per year.

The work is usually in an office environment and provides excellent and necessary training for the previously described positions. Many people find telemarketing to be stimulating and financially rewarding.

As telemarketing becomes more sophisticated, more calls are made to and from people who are likely to be interested in the product or service offered. "Cold calling" is the hard way to use the telephone and is fast becoming economically unfeasible. Target marketing enables communicators to enjoy a higher degree of success and job satisfaction.

Some large, in-house telemarketing centers also offer opportunities for trainees. Although companies who have their own centers do not have marketing representatives and account executives, they often provide career path opportunities in other divisions of the firm. A company with 100 inbound or outbound telemarketing employees is more likely to develop the staff from within than a company with four or five telemarketers.

Predictions about the future of telemarketing vary only quantitatively. The consensus is that the interaction which telemarketing provides, technological advances in telecommunications, and the forces of competition all point to continued growth and demand for new employees with management potential. Add to this the spiraling cost of face-to-face selling— now estimated by McGraw-Hill to be an average of $227 per industrial sales call—and one can understand the impetus behind telemarketing's explosive expansion.

Resources To Use If You Want
To Join Us On The Phone!

Organizations: Telemarketing Recruiters, Inc.   Telemarketing Council
114 East 32nd Street,   Direct Marketing Association
New York, NY 10016   6 East 43rd Street,
    New York, NY 10017

American Telemarketing Association
104 Wilmot Street,
Deerfield, IL 60615

Publications: *Telemarketing* Magazine   *Teleprofessional* Magazine
17 Park Street,   Box 123,
Norwalk, CT 06854   Del Mar, CA 92014

Telemarketing Insiders Report   Directory of Telephone Marketing
470 Main Street, Suite 108,   Services Bureau
Keyport, NJ 07735   Direct Marketing Association
                                     6 East 43rd Street,
                                     New York, NY 10017

CCI Telemarketing, Inc. was a telemarketing and consulting agency in New York which went out of business in 1989. **FRED B. TREGASKIS** joined CCI after 35 years of telemarketing and management at Olan Mills Inc., an international chain of portrait studios.

Mr. Tregaskis is active in the Direct Marketing Association, serving on the board of directors, the Telephone Marketing Council, and as chairman of the Government Affairs Telephone Legislation Committee. He has been a leader in the effort to deter telephone legislation by chairing committees which established DMA's Telephone Preference Service and the Guidelines for Telephone Marketing, testifying before legislative committees, and speaking at conferences in the U.S. and other countries.

12

New Opportunities In Direct Marketing And Direct Response Advertising

Jonah Gitlitz, President
Direct Marketing Association, Inc.

Direct marketing and direct response advertising, both rapidly growing fields, offer career opportunities similar to those in general marketing and advertising, but with some unique attractions. Before we discuss these opportunities, let's look at the differences between these two interrelated fields—traditional vs. direct marketing and advertising.

"Traditional" marketing and advertising has typically:

(1) Supported the marketing of products or services of interest to large numbers of people, often millions of them;

(2) Used broadly-directed advertising media, like network television, to reach as many potential prospects as possible; and

(3) Sought to generate sales through geographical outlets (e.g., retail stores, banks, service centers, etc.).

In a typical general advertising program, the sponsoring firm runs extensive media schedules so that potential customers, whoever they may be, will recognize the product, have a positive perception of it, and take action to buy it when they are shopping.

In contrast, *direct marketing and direct response advertising:*

(1) Identifies those people most likely to be interested in the product or service;

(2) Advertises only to them, usually through selective media like direct mail; and

(3) Makes an offer (e.g., a trial period, premium, reduced price, etc.) that will move them to inquire or order.

Very likely, the product is then delivered or arrangements for the service completed through the mail or via the telephone.

While the overall concept of direct marketing is not new—it goes back at least to the 1870s when mail order catalogs came into vogue—it has been expanding very rapidly in recent years. That has been caused by a combination of social, economic and technological developments. New technologies—notably the computer, the availability of toll-free 800 numbers (as a way to place orders), and the credit card (which makes it easier to arrange payment at a distance)—have combined as strong forces in the growth of the direct marketing field. However, they have also coincided with lifestyle changes that make direct marketing increasingly attractive to many people—women whose careers give them far less time for shopping, senior citizens who find it convenient to shop without leaving home, people who travel frequently, and many others—all of whom find direct shopping ideal for their needs.

As a result of this convergence of technological capability and lifestyle market opportunities, direct marketing has enjoyed substantial expansion. Although precise figures are difficult to pinpoint, observers seem to agree that direct marketing has grown at a rate of at least 10% annually in recent years.

The growth of direct marketing has led to a corresponding growth in career opportunities in the field. First, many organizations previously involved in direct marketing are expanding their direct marketing and direct response functions. Publishers, mail order catalogs, financial services organizations (e.g., insurance companies), fund raising groups, and business-to-business marketers are typical examples.

In addition to the organizations that have emphasized direct marketing for many years, there are many others that are making it an increasingly important and integral part of their overall marketing effort. In particular, financial service organizations and business-to-business marketers are recognizing the benefits direct marketing holds for them.

And there are other industry segments, some of them traditionally thought of as "mass marketers," that are exploring direct marketing or expanding their direct marketing activities. Among these are travel-related organizations (airlines, hotels, etc.), automotive manufacturers, and packaged goods firms.

Career Tracks In Direct Marketing

Because direct marketing functions are found in so many different kinds of organizations, it is difficult to generalize about potential career paths. However, in broad terms, there are two functional areas that entry-level people might want to consider. One involves positions in marketing planning, research and analysis; the other, positions in communications.

Marketing

Marketing positions in a direct marketing department are similar to those in a general marketing function, but with at least one, very significant difference. One of the unique characteristics of direct marketing and direct response advertising is its ability to measure results rather precisely. For the direct marketer, prospects and customers are *individually* identified either before they order (e.g., their name and address on the marketer's mailing list) or when they respond (e.g., by calling a toll-free, 800 telephone number to place an order). As a result, the direct marketer has access to a great deal of useful marketing information. It is possible, for example, to tell whether people in a certain geographic area are responding more frequently, placing orders of higher average value, selecting certain products more often than the average, and a host of other things.

In a similar way, comparisons can be made in the results of direct response advertising. Did one advertising medium "pull" better (i.e., get a better response) than another? Is there a certain time of day, day of the week, or season of the year during which response was higher? Through testing and analysis, the direct marketer can answer questions like these with relative ease. This ability—to almost *immediately* determine results—stands in marked contrast to general marketing and advertising, where the measurement of results may be based on slower and usually less-precise opinion studies, audits of product purchases in stores, etc.

The marketing function is likely to involve three facets (though they may be combined, particularly in smaller organizations). The first is the *planning of marketing activities*—identifying market segments that are currently productive and searching out new ones, evaluating the comparative sales of various products or services and the potential for new or improved ones, and studying competition in the marketplace.

Closely related to the planning function is *marketing research,* which may involve gathering information either from sources outside the marketers' own organization (e.g. from the Census or other government data, from associations, etc.) Many marketers also do original research such as opinion studies, focus groups, etc.

The third area of marketing involves *analysis.* This can include detailed studies of results and responses, cost analyses, etc.

Underlying most direct marketing programs is the use of a computerized database that contains customer/prospect information, transaction records, media tracking information, etc. Graduating students with skills and interest in both marketing and data processing are likely to find excellent career opportunities in positions involved with designing, maintaining, and operating these important data resources.

A typical entry-level position in the marketing area is *assistant product manager,* who is responsible for assisting a product manager in monitoring and recommending product marketing strategies to meet sales and profit goals for a particular marketing product(s) or profit center. Assignments may include the development of media plans, market analyses, list analyses and segmentation, results tracking, etc. This person would also assist the product manager in dealing with creative services to ensure that the product quality remains high and that production schedules are met.

Communications

The second general career path in organizations with direct marketing programs is in what might be called "communications." Positions in this area are concerned primarily with creating print, broadcast or other communications that will generate response from customers and prospects (who may be consumers, potential contributors to fund raising programs, or business-to-business buyers).

Positions in direct response advertising departments and related functions are similar to those in general advertising, but with two broad exceptions, one of which is the measurability of direct response advertising, as explained above. The *advertising manager* in a direct response firm develops campaigns that are likely to be tested and compared to previous efforts. The *direct response copywriter* often creates copy that will literally "compete" with previous "packages" to generate results. The result is both challenging and rewarding, an opportunity to know rather specifically just how successful the effort has been.

The second difference between direct response and general advertising departments is that the direct response units are more likely to have "in-house" creative and media capability, with somewhat less reliance on "outside" agencies. This is particularly true if direct mail is an important element of the organization's media plan. In such an operation, it is not unusual to find *copywriters, artists, list buyers* and other specialists on staff.

In a similar way, many catalog organizations have full in-house creative and related capability. The reason is simple: The process of preparing a catalog, working with buyers to select merchandise and evaluate its prominence in the catalog, and, in particular, the logistics of photographing hundreds of items, are often more easily and efficiently accomplished by an in-house staff. Even in those situations, however, catalog consultants or other specialized organizations may have at least an advisory or supportive function.

A typical entry-level position in an organization with a direct marketing department is *junior copywriter,* who would be responsible for generating simple copy (e.g. headlines) for a variety of products, services and/or markets. This person learns to adapt to creative strategies, formats and/or media. Essentially, he or she is a copywriter in training.

Some Hints On Where To Look

Since virtually any organization can have a direct marketing department, positions in the field can be found in nearly all parts of the country. There are, however, concentrations in certain areas, for the most part paralleling the overall patterns of industry. Openings in publishing firms, which use direct response to promote circulation, for example, are most likely to be found in New York. Several of the large merchandise catalogs are in Chicago, and there are a substantial number of specialty catalogs in the New England states.

The Advantages Of The "Client Side"

College graduates embarking on careers in the direct marketing field may wonder whether they are best advised to start with a "client" organization (corporation, association, etc.) or working for a direct response advertising agency. While there are advantages to either course, the most obvious ones in favor of the former are the opportunities to learn how marketing fits into the organization's overall activities and gain an in-depth, basic knowledge about the whole marketing process, not just the advertising side.

Long-Term Potential

The rapid growth of the direct marketing field over the past decade or so has created a rather severe shortage of experienced people. As a result, capable and well-motivated new people coming into the field have tended to make relatively quick progress in moving from entry-level positions to those with substantial responsibility. There are numerous examples in the direct marketing field of men and women who have, within five years of graduation, found themselves in middle-management spots in "client" organizations, as list managers, direct marketing managers of departments or product areas, or other challenging and rewarding career situations.

I encourage you to explore direct marketing as a career path. For additional information, please contact the Direct Marketing Educational Foundation (6 East 43rd Street, New York, NY 10017).

JONAH GITLITZ has been president and ceo of the Direct Marketing Association since February, 1985. He joined DMA in 1981 as senior vice president-public affairs, responsible for the association's extensive government relations programs and public affairs activities. As president, he has continued his deep involvement with government affairs and broad-based public relations efforts to strengthen the field.

Prior to joining DMA, Mr. Gitlitz was executive vice president of the American Advertising Federation for 12 years. While there, he contributed to the development of the National Advertising Review Board, the highly respected, self-regulatory mechanism that deals with national advertising complaints. He was also responsible for the development of the AAF college chapter program and served as president of the Advertising Educational Foundation.

Mr. Gitlitz currently serves as chairman of the American Advertising Federation's Inter-Association Council and on the board of directors of the Council of Better Business Bureaus, the Advertising Council and the American Advertising Federation. He has also served on numerous industry and business committees.

A native New Yorker, he is a graduate of the American University, Washington, D.C.

13

Direct Mail: The Personal Medium

C. Rose Harper, Chairman & CEO
The Kleid Company, Inc.

That people buy by mail is beyond dispute. The explosive growth (U.S. and abroad) of direct mail supports this premise. The reasons are as varied as the products sold, though "convenience" appears to be the most common.

The most critical factor affecting receptivity is the type of product or service being offered: It is a combination of the right product with the right message to the *target* prospect that counts. This suggests that mail campaigns must be designed to achieve the required results with the smallest total mailing quantity. The ability to *target market* is a plus for direct mail.

Lists: The "Medium" In Direct Mail

A mailing list consists of the names and addresses of people or companies that have one or more things in common. Such a list is said to represent a *meaningful grouping.*

By selecting the proper list, a direct marketer can mail an offer to prospects who have already demonstrated an interest in a particular type of product or service or have demographic and lifestyle characteristics implying a high probability of interest. For example, someone selling toys would select lists of families with at least one child who had previously bought juvenile items (books, records, magazines, clothing, etc.) or "parenting" products. Lacking demonstrated evidence of children in the home, you might luck out once in every 15 to 20 list tests, but that's very expensive research.

Two Broad Categories Of Lists

Internal lists are a company's files, which may include customers, former customers, prospects, inquiries, sales contacts, warranty cards, etc.

External lists include direct response lists (internal files) and compiled lists.

Review Of Lists By Market Categories

Within these broad categories are a number of defined list markets. And within each of *these* categories, even more well-defined sub-categories:

Category	Number of Lists	Universe (in thousands)
Business & Finance	1,195	338,800
New Technology	374	50,338
Educational/Scientific/Professional	171	15,444
Fund Raising	180	75,755
Hobbies & Special Interests	1,101	299,047
Entertainment	457	144,742
Reading	462	109,193
Self-Improvement/Health/Religious	613	252,774
Women/Home Interest/Family/Gen. Merch.	908	607,031
SUB TOTAL	**5,461**	**1,893,124**
Mixed Media	257	309,350
Telephone Marketing	477	957,939
Compiled	170	265,178
Canadian	394	111,979
Foreign	54	6,191
TOTAL	**6,813**	**3,543,761**

List availability, as you can see, is substantial...which is why mailers need the services of list brokers.

The Players In Direct Mail

Companies that serve both the mailer and the owner are known as *list brokers—list marketing consultants*. They identify the list markets that appear to have an affinity for the products or services of the users (mailers).

Some brokers may also prepare mail plans for clients and project response through cost-per-order. Projecting a direct mail campaign means anticipating what is likely to happen by determining which elements will most likely influence the outcome. Computer technicians, statisticians and mathematicians have devised an impressive array of techniques to accomplish this task.

A *list manager* represents lists on an exclusive basis and is responsible for all promotions of the lists and record keeping.

List compilers are manufacturers, generating lists from a variety of printed sources—directories, trade show registrants, membership rosters, telephone books, auto registrations, college student directories, etc.

Service bureaus process the lists being used in a mailing through a system that identifies duplicate names. No one wants to mail an expensive package to the same person or place more than one time. They may also supply a variety of sophisticated marketing data.

Letter shops are responsible for getting the mailing to the post office on time and in the mailing sequence the post office requires.

Direct response agencies are primarily responsible for the creative function. They create the mailing package, space ads, TV and radio commercials.

List Testing

TEST is the most frequently-used word in the direct mail lexicon; it's rare that any mailer uses a list in its entirety without testing. The proper sample size is determined by two factors: sampling tolerance (or deviation) and the degree of risk that the user is willing to accept. As long as we have perfectly random samples, we can keep sampling tolerance small by taking large samples. This part of the equation is scientific. The risk factor is much harder to deal with because this involves subjective judgements. Some companies can't tolerate much risk.

List testing, unfortunately, is not conducted under laboratory conditions. For starters, we can't get a true random sampling. The best we can do is an "nth" name sample. The universal practice is to reconfirm the test with a larger sample. Actually, this type of sequential sampling is reliable because you can schedule quantities on each successive usage in an orderly fashion, supported by monitored results, thus controlling and minimizing the risk.

Response Analysis

The attractiveness of direct mail is measurability—the moment of truth comes when the results are in. Here is a summary of a magazine publisher's new subscription offer and the various data that is obtained and analyzed:

Actual Mail Quantity	150,040
Number of Orders	3,256
Percent Response	2.17
Package Cost per thousand mailed (M)	$180.00
List Cost per M	$45.56
Total Cost per M	$225.56
Total Cost	$33,843
Gross Cost per Subscriber	$10.39
Percent Credit	90.4
Percent Bad Pay	28.1
Net Subscribers	2,428
Net Percent Response	1.61

Net Cost per Subscriber	$13.93
Total Revenue (on Net)	$43,702
Net Revenue (Total Revenue minus Cost)	$9,859
Net Revenue per Subscriber	$4.06

These discriminants (and more, depending on the product being offered) are calculated on a list-by-list basis.

The big players in direct marketing are: publishers (books, magazines and newsletters); book & record clubs; financial services; insurance companies; catalogs; retailers; business-to-business marketers; and fund-raising organizations. These players are both the "users" and, in most instances, are also list owners. Almost *every* company now uses direct mail.

Opportunities For You In Direct Marketing

Direct mail offers an interesting and diversified choice of career paths. In most instances, entry-level positions are relatively clerical, but afford the opportunity to learn the business. Salary levels range from $18,000 to $23,000, though someone with technical training who could move right into a technical position and earn more.

Where do such entry-level positions lead? At list agencies, list managers, compilers and direct response agencies, job titles would include *account executive, sales representative, data processing manager, manager-information systems* and *copywriter* (particularly in direct response agencies).

At book, magazine and newsletter publishers, insurance and financial services, fund raisers and catalogers, representative jobs are *circulation manager, marketing director, product manager, analyst* and *direct mail manager.*

At a service bureau, you may become an *analyst, manager-information systems* or *data processing manager.*

At most such companies, it would take from three to five years to reach the titles shown above. Salary range: $35,000 to $50,000 or more depending on the ability of the individual.

Recommended College Courses include: Direct Marketing, Marketing, Advertising, Finance, Research, Statistics, Computer Science, Mathematics and Liberal Arts (particularly for creative positions).

For Additional Information:

Direct Marketing Association, Inc.
6 East 43rd Street—12th Floor
New York, NY 10017

Direct Marketing Educational Foundation, Inc.
6 East 43rd Street—12th Floor
New York, NY 10017

New York University (Center for Direct Marketing)
48 Cooper Square
New York, NY 10003

Note: Some of the material in this article was taken from my book, <u>Mailing List Strategies: A Guide to Direct Mail Success</u>, published by McGraw-Hill in 1986.

C. ROSE HARPER served as chairman of the board of the Direct Marketing Association (DMA) and also four years as treasurer, the first woman to serve in either capacity. She was inducted into the Direct Marketing Hall of Fame in 1985—the first woman so honored. The Kleid Company is considered one of the most professional list marketing consulting firms and is heavily involved in direct mail planning and analysis for many prominent magazines and book publishers.

Mrs. Harper serves on the boards of the Direct Marketing Educational Foundation, Direct Marketing Idea Exchange and the NYU Center for Direct Marketing.

Her book—<u>Mailing List Strategies: A Guide to Direct Mail Success</u>—was published by McGraw-Hill in March, 1986; it is now in its fifth printing. It was selected by *Library Journal* as one of the best business books published in 1986.

14

Career Opportunities In
Database Marketing

**David Shepard, President
David Shepard Associates, Inc.**

Right now, there are probably hundreds of thousands of students who are thinking about a career in business, marketing, advertising or sales. I dare say only a handful of them are considering a career in database marketing.

The reason for this is simple: Database marketing is a relatively new field, one that grew out of the larger but still relatively unheard-of field of direct marketing. If you asked a hundred students if they were familiar with direct marketing, if they knew what people in direct marketing did, I bet the vast majority would look at you with a blank stare.

In fact, nearly everyone *is* familiar with direct marketing—because we're almost all familiar with magazines, book clubs, mail order catalogs and those two-minute television commercials selling unbelievable record collections for only $9.95. All of these businesses and the people who work in them are in the direct marketing business, along with insurance, mutual funds, credit cards, travel, homes, clothing, food, business supplies, computers, copiers, telephone systems. You name the business, and there's a better-than-even chance that direct marketing plays a role in the distribution of that businesses' products and services.

Typical Direct Marketing Problem—
Launching A Catalog

I still haven't explained what database marketing is all about, but before I do, let me go on for a little more about direct marketing, specifically direct *mail* marketing. Let's imagine that you have searched far and wide to develop a collection of hard-to-find sports souvenirs—bubble gum cards, programs, baseballs, bats, helmets, basketballs, equipment, old sporting magazines, tickets, uniforms—you name it, anything a sports fan would treasure and buy by mail. Let's further suppose you displayed all of the items you'd managed to find in an attractive catalog. Who would you mail it to?

Deciding What Lists To Rent

"What lists do I rent?" is probably the most important question anyone in direct mail can ask. In the old days, before database marketing, the answer would be relatively simple—you would sit down with a list broker and together decide on which lists to rent. You would then send your catalog to the names on those rented lists, perhaps *Sports Illustrated* subscribers, high school coaches, persons who had bought running shoes by mail, season ticket holders, etc In each case, you would be assuming that someone who bought other sports-related items would probably be interested in your catalog of sports souvenirs.

Keeping Track Of Who Responded

After you mailed your catalog, you would keep careful track of everyone who responded and slowly start building your own list of buyers. The next time you mailed your catalog, you would certainly mail it again to those that responded to it the first time.

Typical Direct Mail Results

This kind of relatively straightforward method typified the direct mail industry for years. Direct mail sellers would rent lists, mail their catalogs, and, if they were successful, receive a response of somewhere between 1% and 3%. When they mailed to previous customers, they would achieve a higher response rate, somewhere between 5% and 10%.

Fortunately mail order sellers could make a profit at these low levels of response.

A Short History Of Database Marketing

In the late 1960s and early '70s, changes began to take place in the computer industry, changes that would radically alter the way direct mail sellers would run their businesses and transform them into database marketers.

Here's just one example: One of the problems with renting lists and mailing to everyone on them is that many people are on more than one list. Many people, for example, subscribe to two, three, five or even more magazines. If you thought magazine subscribers were good candidates for you product, you may have wound up mailing to the same people many times. The computer and sophisticated computer software helped solve this problem. Instead of just renting lists and mailing them, you could rent lots of lists, merge them together, eliminate names that appeared on more than one list. and save lots of money.

Turning A List Into A Marketing Database

During the '70s and '80s, some direct marketing companies began to build massive lists of people, lists that included nearly every household in the United States. They contained not only name and address information, but other data like birth dates, the car each person drove, how long he or she had lived at a certain address, the census area he or she lived in, government estimates on the average income of people living in that zip code, how many years of school people in that zip code completed, how they earned their living and on and on.

These massive lists were called databases, and they gave direct marketers access to the detailed information they needed to target their customers as never before. If your research, for example, revealed that of all the people you mailed to, men between the ages of 45 and 55 were by far the best respondents, wouldn't it make sense to target such men in any future mailings? Of course it would. That's *database marketing* or, at least, the tip of the database marketing iceberg.

The process I referred to above—matching your database against someone else's database and adding their information to your database—is referred to as *database enhancement.* There's a whole segment of the direct marketing industry working full-time to make more and more such information available to direct marketers.

Using The Information You Obtain

The central idea of database marketing is that the more information you know about your customers or people you would like to have as customers, the smarter you can be about your marketing activities. You can mail your existing products to people who tend to match the profile of your current customers. And even develop new products to meet the needs of those prospects with characteristics that *differ* from your current customer base.

Database Marketing Today

Today there are hundreds, perhaps even thousands, of direct marketing companies with their own databases of customers. The most sophisticated, advanced companies know a great deal about their customers—what products they bought, when, and in response to which particular direct mail offer or advertisement. They know the promotions their customers received in the past and whether they responded or not. They know a lot of other things about their customers from research questionnaires and by matching their databases with other data bases. And they use all of this information in deciding what offers to make in the future, what products to sell and how to present and price them. This entire process is modern database marketing.

How To Enter The Field

If database marketing sounds interesting and challenging to you, then carefully consider the following points about necessary preparation.

Study General Marketing & Advertising

As with most professions a college education is essential; a graduate degree in business always helps. While not all colleges offer separate courses in direct marketing, most basic marketing courses include sections on direct marketing. So it's advisable to take a broad range of marketing and advertising courses in preparation for a career in direct marketing.

I would also recommend taking one or two courses in market research. More and more direct marketers are adding information gathered from market research to their customer data bases, and it's important to understand how this data is collected and to be able to distinguish good research from bad.

Take Statistics And Computer Courses

But direct marketing *does* differ from general marketing in a number of ways, and these differences mean skills in areas other than general marketing and advertising are required.

For one, direct marketing is very "numbers oriented." General advertisers spend their money on some mix of television, radio, magazine and newspaper ads, hoping that their message gets across and that shoppers buy their products as a result. But no matter which medium they use, it's very hard to measure the effect of each ad or even all of them. Direct marketers have it easy. They know how many catalogs they sent out and how many responses they received. Or how much that couponed magazine cost and how many filled-out coupons they received back. Direct marketing generates *lots* of numbers or statistics.

The best direct marketers are *very* comfortable with numbers and technology. So it's advisable you take at least one (and preferably more) statistics course and to be familiar with computers—how they work and what they can do for you.

Where To Start Your Career

The direct marketing industry is basically divided into two parts: 1). those companies that sell products or services (catalog companies, book and record clubs, magazine publishers, insurance companies, financial services companies, fund raisers, etc.) and 2) those that sell services to the these direct marketing companies (advertising agencies, list brokers, list managers, computer service bureaus, printers, etc.).

My personal recommendation would be to start with a large direct marketing company or advertising agency where you could expect to receive wide exposure to a variety of jobs in a relatively short period of time. After you've gained some experience, you may choose to concentrate in some particular specialty within the direct marketing industry. The Direct Marketing Association maintains compete files on all companies in the industry and is very helpful in assisting students that are interested in a career in any area of direct marketing.

DAVID SHEPARD founded DSA, Inc., a direct marketing consulting firm, in 1976. The company counts among its clients a variety of traditional direct marketing firms, advertising agencies and many Fortune 500 firms new to the direct marketing business.

Previously, Mr. Shepard held a number of management positions in the Book Club Division of Doubleday & Co., including business manager, director of product management and vice president, new ventures.

He is a graduate of CCNY and has an M.B.A from Columbia University. Mr. Shepard is a frequent speaker at Direct Marketing Association events, has taught the Direct Marketing Policy course at NYU's School of Continuing Education and is currently conducting seminars on behalf of the DMA. He was chairman of the DMA's Marketing Council and has written numerous articles on the economics of direct marketing.

15

Computer Service Bureaus: Applying Information Tools To Direct Marketing

Jay Bursky, President
NextStep Marketing, Inc.

Computers and information technologies have become the heart of direct marketing. Without this technology there could be no massive direct mail campaigns to reach targeted prospects for products and services, no telemarketing for communicating directly by voice with these same prospects, no credit cards to easily pay for purchases, no shop-at-home networks to provide an easier way to shop and no videotex to access product information from a database service. In essence, direct marketing—both as we know it today and as we anticipate it for the future—could not exist.

As the cost of processing and accessing data continues to drop and more sophisticated technology develops, direct marketing will increasingly rely on further refinements in the development and utilization of databases. As these refinements demand more powerful hardware and software, as well as the people to create and manage these technologies, the cycle of change will begin anew.

Computer service bureaus are critical to the proper functioning of the direct marketing field, providing data processing services such as duplicate elimination, list maintenance and retrieval, telemarketing, personalized printing, fulfillment, response analysis and demographic analysis. By no means is this list complete.

A computer service bureau facility can be one of two types. First, they can be departments or divisions developed by organizations for their own internal use. These facilities are used as internal resources to support the direct marketing needs of the organization. Some facilities, such as those of American Airlines and J.C. Penney's, have leveraged their experience to offer their expertise to outside clients.

The second type of facility generally consists of organizations that supply their expertise and services almost exclusively to outside clients who lack their own internal facility for handling their projects.

In the direct marketing field, the Direct Marketing Computer Council (previously known as the Direct Marketing Computer Association) of the Direct Marketing Association has available a directory of its members and services. A short description of the company is included and can provide you with important information pertaining to the services provided by these companies.

But what opportunities are available within these bureaus? There are four major areas that provide a wide range of opportunities: sales, system analysis, programming and operations.

Opportunities In Sales

Every profit-making business requires salespeople. If you investigate any organization that provides services to clients, you will discover that salespeople are critical and that good sales people are well paid. Many sales representatives receive a base salary figure with the bulk of their annual compensation consisting of commissions and bonuses. Sales personnel are expected to communicate well and understand both the organization's services and the clients' needs, in order to offer the client the proper blend of services for his or her particular needs.

The *computer service sales support representative*—the usual entry-level position— provides technical support for the sales rep. This individual is responsible for both pre- and post-sales support, system studies, feasibility studies, demonstrations and technical presentations. Candidates for this position should possess good oral and written communication skills and the ability to interface with clients and understand their requirements.

As the number of services in certain segments increases, demand for people who can support the sales function is critical, particularly in those areas employing database management systems. If the individual possesses good communication skills and has a rapport with people, this position usually leads to sales and, later, to sales management.

Computer service sales managers are responsible for the management and administration of the sales representatives. They may also have territory or key accounts that require direct sales duties.

There is a high demand for individuals with proven sales management experience. One path to becoming a sales manager is to first assume sales responsibility, especially in new start-up situations.

Computer industry sales representatives sell the services of the computer service bureau. Most companies are going to hire reps who have a proven track record of sales accomplishment. However, some organizations are willing to consider technical professionals with an aptitude for sales. These individuals are trained by the organization and, after a period of time, provided with smaller accounts as the first stage to building their territory.

The career options in sales could be represented as follows:

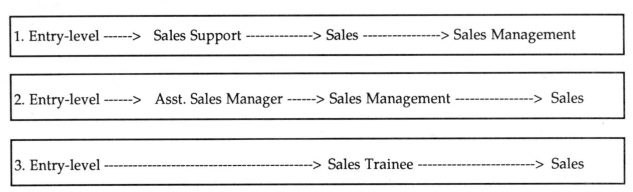

1. Entry-level ------>   Sales Support -------------> Sales ----------------> Sales Management

2. Entry-level ------>   Asst. Sales Manager ------> Sales Management ----------------> Sales

3. Entry-level ---> Sales Trainee ----------------------> Sales

In option 1, the career path passes through each of the positions discussed. Option 2 begins at the sales management function, where the individual will probably work as an *assistant to the sales manager*. Finally, option 3 is based upon an organization that will accept sales trainees.

Opportunities In Systems Analysis And Programming

The *systems analyst* must be able to give logical instructions to a *programmer*. In computer service bureaus, the sales representative will often act as a systems analyst, and systems analysts often sell.

Programmers in direct marketing computer service bureaus are guaranteed a challenging career. Direct marketing files can each contain millions of records and may require special programs to be written to satisfy the requirements of specific projects. As additional developments in direct marketing occur, there will be more demand for programmers to develop the necessary software that will allow the service bureau to offer the new services.

Commercial programmers and *programmer/analysts* (the entry-level positions) perform detailed program design, coding, testing, debugging, documentation and implementation of commercially-oriented information systems. They may also be responsible for overall systems specifications and design

More alternatives appear to be open to commercial programmers and programmer/analysts with on-line database experience than any other group. A continuing trend within user organizations is the combining of programming and systems functions into a single group. This can provide an excellent learning environment. Most opportunities exist for those with a background in COBOL programming. In greatest demand are those with experience in large operating systems, job control languages, on-line database management and direct access techniques, remote accessing, virtual systems, 4th generation languages and database handlers. Structured systems design, programming and database techniques are becoming more important. Conversational programming and remote interconnect experience are also valuable.

Systems (software) programmers create and/or maintain operating systems, communications software, database packages, compilers, assemblers and utility programs. There is a great demand for systems programmers knowledgeable in data communications, network planning and analysis, database concepts, graphics, terminal systems and vendor evaluation.

Database analysts/data management specialists are responsible for designing and controlling the use of an organization's data resources. These individuals analyze the interrelationships of data usage and define physical data structures and logical views of data elements. They utilize the facilities of database management systems and data dictionary software packages to control the data usage. Their responsibilities can range from the design and creation of data structures to the procedures required to insure data security, database backup/recovery and the elimination of data redundancy.

Demand is increasing due to the projected growth in the number of database management systems installations. Computer service bureaus are in need of people with knowledge of programming and systems methodologies to design database-oriented application systems. Background in systems software is valuable for persons moving into the planning of physical database structures and implementation of security and recovery tactics.

Other career opportunities include: *mini- and micro-computer programmers and analysts, software engineers, communication analysts* and *technical specialists, information center specialists* and *senior analysts*.

1990 Professional Compensation Data

Compiled by Source EDP, a personnel services firm, and reprinted with their permission

	20th Percentile	Median	80th Percentile
1. Non-Management Positions (Salary according to length of experience in the profession)			
Computer Operators			
Less than 2 years	19.0	22.0	24.0
2 years—3 years	19.0	23.0	28.0
4 years—6 years	22.0	25.0	31.0
More than 6 years	25.0	30.0	39.0
Commercial Programmers and Programmer/Analysts			
Less than 2 years	22.0	27.0	30.0
2 years—3 years	25.0	30.0	35.0
4 years—6 years	29.0	35.0	400
More than 6 years	35.0	41.0	49.0
Systems/Software/Programmers			
Less than 2 years	N/A	N/A	N/A
2 years—3 years	28.0	33.0	38.0
4 years—6 years	32.0	38.0	43.0
More than 6 years	37.0	43.0	50.0
Microcomputer/Minicomputer Programmers			
Less than 2 years	22.0	26.0	31.0
2 years—3 years	25.0	30.0	35.0
4 years—6 years	29.0	35.0	41.0
More than 6 years	34.0	42.0	50.0
2. Management Positions (Salary according to size of computer system or staff managed)			
Technical Services Manager			
Small	31.0	37.8	52.0
Medium	40.0	46.0	53.0
Large	45.1	52.5	61.0
Data Center Operations Managers			
Small	24.2	28.0	36.5
Medium	29.5	36.0	45.0
Large	35.0	43.5	58.5
Computer Systems Directors			
Small	35.0	42.0	53.8
Medium	43.0	54.5	67.8
Large	55.0	66.0	87.3
3. Sales Positions—Computer Industry Sales Representatives			
Services	38.0	48.0	65.0
Hardware Products	32.0	45.0	65.0
Software Products	32.0	45.0	65.0
Computer Industry Sales Mgrs	49.0	70.0	92.0
Computer Industry Technical Support			
Less than 2 years	23.0	27.0	38.0
2 years—3 years	26.0	31.0	36.0
4 years—6 years	30.0	36.0	43.0
More than 6 years	38.0	45.0	56.0

Opportunities In Operations

Operations covers the range of opportunities from *computer operators* to *customer service representatives*. We already discussed one of those functions: sales support. There are good entry-level jobs for beginners. The small companies in the field don't hesitate to promote people out of operations and into programming, systems analysis or sales.

One entry-level title in the operations area is *assistant production executive*. These individuals are responsible for supporting the day-to-day activities of account management. Duties often include budget control, schedule administration, report writing and trafficking. This is essentially an account executive in-training position.

Account executives are responsible for the day-to-day management of assigned accounts. They coordinate the agency services for the effective execution of clients' direct marketing strategies and organize and present the project for input sessions with the client.

In the computer area, one entry-level position is *computer operator*. Computer operators monitor and support computer processing and coordinate utilization of input, output and interchangeable file media. In addition, they distribute output, schedule machine utilization and oversee control functions. The operator is responsible for supporting the day-to-day activities of the systems analyst.

Another entry-level position is *input control technician.* They are responsible for the interpretation of the orders and submit appropriate control and option instructions to computer programs after determining which programs to use. These individuals report to the computer systems director on the status of orders and may correct any errors caused by improper computer coding or computer malfunctions.

Technical services managers direct the technical staff responsible for operating system software, telecommunications and database systems support, maintenance of software packages and hardware/software planning and evaluation. They may also have responsibility for computer operations, as well as internal technical education.

Although not an entry-level position, the growth of teleprocessing and database management has greatly increased the sophistication of the technical support group. Opportunities will expand as the level of responsibility increases within medium and large user organizations and as smaller installations grow. Typical experience includes five years of systems programming (cont...) background with demonstrated leadership and an in-depth awareness of current computer technology.

The *data center operations manager* directs all computer and peripheral machine operations, data entry, data control, scheduling and quality control. Responsibility for systems (software) programming, software and applications maintenance programming may also be part of the job description.

Minimum requirements for this position may include supervisory operations experience and good knowledge of installed hardware, software and operating systems. Increased emphasis on distributed processing places a premium on those with exposure in large-scale, database/communications-oriented environments. A degree is usually required.

The top computer-oriented operations position to which one can aspire is *computer systems director*. This individual centers his activities on overall management and the direction of all information systems and/or computer processing or development efforts.

An interesting new position—*chief information officer (CIO)*—has opened up in the past few years; it may offer another career path for computer-oriented individuals. The CIO has executive-level responsibility for all information used, stored, managed and marketed within the organization. This individual's range of responsibility goes beyond the computer service bureau and covers the micro-computer environment, as well as the telecommunications environment. For each organization, the responsibilities may be defined differently; however, the opportunity will be both rewarding and challenging.

There are obviously a full-range of opportunities for individuals interested in working in a computer environment, regardless of their technical proficiency.

Compensation

Compensation is dependent upon a number of factors. For entry-level positions, the major rule to bear in mind is to get your foot in the door—don't be overly concerned about the base salary. You need to establish yourself in order to become known. As you establish yourself and as your abilities and talents are recognized, you will move up the ranks. Your salary will increase accordingly.

The salary levels for each position previously discussed will depend upon a number of factors. It is important to research entry-level salaries. Differences in salary levels in various geographic locations will be based upon the following criteria:

- In what geographic area are you interested in working?
- What is the size and reputation of the company you are targeting?
- What is the size of the computer installation of this company?
- What is the size of the staff managing the bureau?
- Are there unique requirements for the position?
- What is the level of your education and what specific training have you received?
- Do you have any experience?
- What is the nature of your experience?
- What is the length of your experience?
- Do you have specific skills that are in high demand?
- Are you willing to relocate away from family and friends?

Generally, the larger the company, the higher the salary. However, smaller companies often pay premium salaries and offer greater responsibilities, authority and benefits in order to attract top talent in this highly competitive market.

The chart on page 90 is based upon the 1990 EDP Professional Compensation Data prepared by Source EDP. The salary levels listed are based upon length of experience in the profession for non-management positions. For management and sales positions, salary figures are based upon the size of the computer system or staff managed.

It is important to realize that the salary levels listed in the chart provide only a reference point. Source EDP is a personnel agency for the computer industry. Their major emphasis is in placing people with experience in new positions. As a result, salary figures in the chart may not accurately reflect the reality of the marketplace. There is the possibility that your skills might even lead you to an entry-level salary that is higher than that listed in the chart. The underlying point is that each situation is different. If you are interested in the dynamic application of information tools to a growing area of marketing, accept the challenge and prepare yourself for an exciting career with a computer service bureau in the direct marketing industry.

JAY BURSKY is president of NextStep Marketing, a customer loyalty company providing programs and services to the travel, retail, and packaged goods industries. He is responsible for the marketing direction and strategic planning of the company.

Prior to starting NextStep, Jay served as vice president of marketing for Printronic Corporation of America, one of the country's leading direct marketing computer service bureaus. He was promoted to the position of vice president of marketing after successfully serving as director of international marketing.

While with Printronic, Mr. Bursky's accounts included McGraw-Hill, VNU-Hayden, Career Track, American Express, Interference Control Technologies, University Seminar Centers (a division of Inc. Magazine), Billion, and Harvard Business Review. He was responsible for all facets of Printronic's marketing.

Before joining Printronic, Mr. Bursky served as director of information systems for Thompson Communications Companies, a New York-based firm that specialized in the development of frequent flyer and frequent traveler systems. In that capacity, Mr. Bursky was responsible for the creation, implementation or management of several successful programs for numerous companies including Hilton Hotels, Finnair, British Airways, Howard Johnson's, and TWA.

An MBA in industrial marketing from Baruch College, Mr. Bursky actively pursued the study of information based systems through his graduate thesis entitled <u>The Development of a Predatory Marketing Information System</u>. Mr. Bursky is a published author whose works have appeared in a variety of publications including Target Marketing, Circulation Management, Successful Magazine Publishing, The Yearbook of Direct Marketing, and the Marketing and Sales Career Directory. In addition, he serves as Co-Chairman of the Direct Marketing Day in New York Education Committee, is an active member of the membership committee of the Direct Marketing Club of New York, the Direct Marketing Creative Guild, and the World Direct Trade Council. An industry speaker, Jay has made presentations at such industry conferences as the Publishers Multinational Direct Conference, the European Direct Marketing Week in Paris, various national conferences of the Direct Marketing Association, the Circulation Management Conference, the Small Magazine Publishers Conference, the Direct Marketing Day in New York Career Conferences, and the Direct Marketing Education Institute's Internship program.

16

Marketing Research On The Corporate Side

Lawrence D. Gibson, Marketing Consultant and Associate
Eric Marder Associates

"**W**hat is marketing research?" is certainly the first and probably the most important question to ask if you are considering a career in the field. Unfortunately, much of the available material isn't very helpful if you really need an answer to the question.

The Hidden Persuaders, a best-seller some years ago, suggested that researchers were devious manipulators of consumer opinion—so powerful they could get you to act against your own self interest. This was and is complete nonsense. The whole pattern of research findings demonstrates the tremendous effectiveness of finding out what consumers want and then showing them a better way to get it. The record also shows the total impotence of attempts to force consumers to do anything they didn't want to do anyway.

Textbooks used by some leading universities have suggested that researchers simply supply the data required by decision-makers for their computers and Marketing Information Systems. *More* nonsense. Marketing research is not just a supplier of facts—it is the use of more scientific procedures to make the entire marketing process more effective. As one observer noted, "Science is no more facts than a house is bricks!"

Recently the American Marketing Association considered this question and developed an excellent definition of the field. They agreed that marketing research "links the organization to its consumers and its customers through information—information used to:

"A) Identify and define marketing problems and opportunities; (*Are our products satisfying our customers? What is our most serious product weakness? Where are sales weak? What's the outlook for demand in the ____ industry? How are consumers reacting to our competitor's new product? Are there unsatisfied needs on which a new product could be based?*)

"B) Generate, refine, and evaluate alternative marketing actions; (*What different advertising strategies should we consider? Which commercial will be most effective? Should we improve our present service or develop a new one? Should we lower the price? Which channel of distribution should we use? Is this a good location for a new retail outlet?*)

"C) Monitor marketing performance; *(Is consumer volume in line with our sales program? Is the market growing as we anticipated? Is the regional promotion test producing the required volume? Are customer prices holding up?)*

"D) Improve our understanding of marketing as a process. *(Does advertising work in small increments, exposure-by-exposure, or can a single exposure produce major effects? Is there taste tiring in food products? Are there 'early adopters' whose behavior precedes and predicts the total market? What causes negative advertising effects? How should we relate overall consumer choice with consumer perceptions and values?)*"

These are the problems, questions, and issues researchers wrestle with each day. They use a variety of techniques, among which the consumer questionnaire/survey has attracted the most attention. However, the researchers "tool kit" includes a wide variety of other techniques from other disciplines—unstructured depth interviews and group interviews from clinical psychology; formal decision analysis from operations research; complex experimental designs from the physical sciences; idea generation heuristics from the think tanks; forecasting models from economics; and sophisticated analysis procedures requiring the modern computer.

How Does It Really Work?

Of course, all researchers don't face all of these problems, and most researchers don't use every one of the techniques. Actually, the character of research work varies quite a bit from company to company and industry to industry. Industrial researchers, for example, may spend much of their effort on the economic forecasts basic to the sales outlook of their companies. Package product researchers are likely to be concerned with advertising and new product evaluation. In some of the newer service industries, researchers may be so closely involved with actual development of the new service that its hard to tell where the research function starts and the development function ends.

Even within the same research department, different researchers do different things. Some may specialize in the data collection procedures, even though actual development of the data is usually contracted through outside research firms. Other researchers become specialists in certain types of research—advertising research or product testing or test marketing. Larger departments may have specialized "research on research" researchers who are concerned with those "understanding marketing" questions.

However, most researchers are generalists who concentrate on the issues and problems of particular products or services in consumer product companies or particular products or industries in industrial companies. Their assignments tend to mirror those of the marketers who are actually in charge of those products or industries. This makes it possible for the researcher to get personally involved with his or her products, develop expert knowledge of the product's marketing issues, and become an important member of the product's marketing management team.

Developing close working relationships with Marketing is critical to effective marketing research. In most companies, it's Marketing that will be responsible for implementing research findings. Often they must approve the budget for specific projects. Even when there is a separate research budget, the opinion of the marketing "clients" has a powerful effect on the size of that budget.

In some companies, there is a single, centralized Marketing Research department managing research for all of the company's products and divisions. This arrangement places the emphasis on efficiency, professionalism, and unbiased independence. In other companies, Marketing Research is decentralized, with researchers located in each of the major profit centers. Obviously, this structure makes it easier to build the necessary working relationships with Marketing, and it helps ensure that the research is integrated into Marketing. A few, very large research users try to gain the benefits of both organizational structures by keeping such functions as "research on research" centralized, while making other functions, such as product and industry support, decentralized.

What Does It Take To Be Successful?

Marketing researchers must have intelligence, intellectual curiosity, facility with numbers, interpersonal and communication skills, and an ability to work under pressure.

Very *high* intelligence is necessary. The marketing and technical issues are complex and require first-rate analytical thinking. Anything less results in shoddy work, superficial findings, unhappy clients, and frustrated researchers.

Intellectual curiosity is a key attribute of most good researchers. When a researcher first spots an unexpected study finding, he's likely to react by saying, "Now that's interesting! I wonder what it means?" Surprises are part of the fascination of research. Faced with a similar situation, most line managers would probably say, "What happened? What went wrong?" Predictable control of events is *their* concern.

Every researcher needn't be a statistician, but each must be comfortable with numbers. Numbers from sales reports, survey analyses, and sophisticated analytical procedures surround the researcher. Computers have been taught to push these numbers around and execute complex formulas, but the researcher still must interpret the meaning of the numbers.

A researcher must be able to work well with others as a staff advisor to the product management team. He or she (and at least half of all new researchers *are* women) must enjoy this role, though staff advisors are no longer expected to be non-involved, passive experts. They are expected to be deeply involved with their products, contributing marketing ideas *in addition to* their research expertise. More researchers fail because they are not aggressive *enough* than because they push too hard.

Excellent communication skills are vital. Much of a researcher's time is spent in meetings with marketing, development specialists, advertising agency representatives, consultants, and outside researchers. He must listen to and understand a variety of different views of the problem before a research plan can be formulated. He must synthesize, translate, and present the findings after the research has been completed.

Research, like marketing, takes place in a demanding, competitive environment. There's so much to be done, and there's never enough time to do it. You simply can't do everything you want to do the way you really want to do it. This creates a great deal of tension—a situation that some people enjoy and others can't take.

What Academic Preparation Is Necessary?

A postgraduate degree is a prerequisite at most major companies. A few prefer a doctorate; most accept any of a variety of masters degrees. An M.B.A. degree with a marketing major is probably the most popular at this time, because it provides a broad business background. However M.As and M.Ss in economics, sociology, psychology, quantitative methods, and marketing are common. Undergraduate training in mathematics or one of the physical sciences, together with an M.B.A., provides an excellent background. A specific "Master of Marketing Research" degree is offered only at the University of Georgia at the present time.

Marketing students from business schools like Harvard, Stanford, Amos Tuck (Dartmouth), Wharton (the University of Pennsylvania) and some others often command higher starting salaries than their peers from "lesser" schools. There are no such "premium" graduate schools (with the exception of the University of Georgia's program noted above) in marketing research. Top research candidates from any of the major schools will be accepted by most employers. Of course, individual companies have their own recruiting patterns, and these may be worth checking into if you are looking for a particular employer.

Course selection should include psychology, quantitative methods, and marketing information systems, as well as marketing research and marketing. Where available, you should also take advantage of courses in the history and philosophy of science, the scientific method, and experimental design.

Grades are important. Perhaps they demonstrate the necessary intelligence, perhaps they merely show a willingness to "play the game." But employers *do* look at grades, and they *do* take them seriously. The most desirable employers don't really consider anyone whose grades are only average.

Extracurricular activities and work experience are helpful. At many schools, work is available in related areas, such as survey interviewing, data processing, and research analysis. This related work provides good experience, and it shows something "extra" on the resume. Incidentally, there are only a few internships available for researchers.

What To Expect On The Job

The starting salary for a candidate with a Masters degree at the top employers is between $35,000 and $45,000 this year. While a candidate with a Ph.D. will earn more, the difference may be as little as $5,000. Less prestigious employers may offer significantly lower salaries. Don't be surprised to find that directly comparable beginners in marketing receive higher starting salaries.

As a new *marketing research assistant* or *junior project director*—there are as many different titles as there are companies—you will probably spend most of your time simply becoming competent in research project management. Each company's procedures are likely to be a little different from those taught in school. And there are so many ways a project can be "messed up" that Murphy's Law does seem to operate until you have actually managed a few.

After 12-20 months, you should be promoted to *assistant marketing research manager* or *project director,* and the character of your work will gradually shift. From project management, the emphasis will move to problem definition and project design. With additional experience, you will start developing integrated research programs for your products and managing other researchers. Throughout this process, more and more of your time will be spent with more and more senior marketing management.

In principle, marketing research should be excellent training for marketing management or any other area of marketing. In practice, few companies see marketing research in this light. Usually researchers are free to transfer to other functions, but this is probably not the ideal development route. In most companies, you should start in marketing if that's where you really want to work.

Job mobility is quite high in marketing research. Many, if not most, researchers make several job changes during their career. Only in smaller job markets is this unusual. Advertising and commercial research jobs are often filled by client researchers.

At the highest level of research management in major companies, total compensation may range from $100,000 to $150,000 or more. The work is a fascinating combination of research leadership, marketing counsel and advice, as well as management of a significant function. Movement into general management at this level is unusual.

Marketing research can be an extremely rewarding career. Creativity and discipline are needed and valued. There are very difficult political and technical problems to be solved. I believe that the combination of intellectual challenge, opportunity to contribute, and personal payoff is unique in all of business.

For twenty years, **LAWRENCE D. GIBSON** was marketing research director for General Mills Inc., where he built one of the most highly regarded departments in the field and trained many of the field's outstanding researchers. Previously, he was a vice president of Audits & Surveys, Inc., where he set up and directed the General Motors Advertising Effectiveness Program.

Mr. Gibson is a frequent speaker and lecturer at leading universities and professional associations. He is often quoted in the literature and has authored papers for the Journal of Marketing, the Journal of Marketing Research, and the Journal of Advertising Research. He is active in the American Marketing Association, as well as a variety of community service, religious, and arts organizations.

His academic training was at Ohio State University, from which he received a B.S. in marketing summa cum laude and an M.B.A. He resides with his wife in Minneapolis—when they aren't visiting one of their five children and three grandchildren.

17

Marketing Research On The Supplier Side

Philip R. Nielsen, VP/Director of Corporate Planning & Development
A. C. Nielsen Company

The U.S. marketing research business is a large and growing industry—the biggest segment of the information industry. It is made up of hundreds of supplier firms of all sizes (though predominantly small, entrepreneurial companies) that, in aggregate, have annual revenues of several billion dollars. The volume of business is expanding which has resulted in the creation of additional jobs and attractive profits for shareholders over the years. The largest marketing research firm in the world is A. C. Nielsen Company, a subsidiary of The Dun & Bradstreet Corporation.

What Marketing Research Firms Do

Marketing research firms provide information on various aspects of marketing new and existing consumer and industrial products and services. The major areas covered by research include:

- *Product analysis:* the importance of features—size, shape, color, packaging, ease of use, etc.

- *Brand position analysis:* current or periodic study of competitive volumes of different brands in a product field.

- *Consumer surveys:* establishing the profile of product users classified by age, sex, economic status, quantities used, reasons for use, attitudes, experiences, etc.

- *Quantitative market and trend analysis:* determining the amount of a commodity that a given market absorbs, or can be expected to absorb, and how these volumes change over time.

- *Channels of distribution analysis:* determining the selection of channels; appraising dealer coverage, credit policies, dealer stocks, costs, profits, etc.
- *Sales and promotion analysis:* determining results by product line, individual items or promotions, territories, class of trade, sales force, etc.
- *Pricing analysis:* measuring demand at varying price levels.

Sometimes marketing research projects also involve coverage of advertising and the communications media—newspapers, magazines, radio and television, etc.—that are used to reach markets and consumers. (If the thrust of the research is *primarily* on advertising and/or media, the project is generally classed as *media research.)*

Marketing research suppliers tend to specialize in particular services. They typically provide information on one of three bases, depending on the nature of their clients' problems and the research design:

- *One-time (ad hoc) projects:* usually sold to a single client on a one-time, exclusive, customized basis.
- *One-time, multi-client projects:* usually sold to a limited group of clients on a one-time, tailor-made basis.
- *Periodic:* usually sold on a syndicated basis to a number of simultaneous subscribers, each of whom receives a standard report that is then used for tracking purposes.

The primary buyers and users of marketing research are consumer and industrial product manufacturers, service providers, wholesalers, retailers, advertising media, government and public agencies, and trade associations.

Where Marketing Research Fits In

The mission of marketing research suppliers is to provide useful information to people in the marketing and sales functions at client companies. This information is the basis for managing client activities and investments. Accurate, relevant, timely, and cost-effective research furnished by outside suppliers can provide both the quantitative and qualitative input that can help clients narrow the options and lower the risks in their decisions. The impartial views of suppliers on the significance of research findings are highly valued by clients.

Speaking broadly, marketing research activities increase the probabilities of success on the part of marketing and sales executives in at least six ways:

1. They keep a business in touch with its markets: Marketing research interprets markets to the client so that business policies and practices may be aimed in the right direction.

2. They reduce waste in marketing methods: The effectiveness of different methods employed by the business is measured to eliminate those which are inefficient.

3. They develop new sources of profit through discovery of new products, new uses for established products, and new markets.

4. They are insurance against unanticipated changes in the market, changes that have the power to make a product or an industry obsolete.

5. They can be used for sales promotion purposes.

6. They infuse enthusiasm and strength of purpose into the business organization: Employees know their decisions and policies are based on sound research.

The Marketing Research Tracking Business

One example of a tracking service is the Nielsen marketing research business, the largest in the country. It consists of providing tracking information to manufacturers of consumer products, such as foods and drugs. Thus, Nielsen fits into the third category above *(periodic)*, in terms of the basis on which it provides research to its clients. Nielsen furnishes a broad array of standardized information on a regular periodic (weekly, monthly or bimonthly) basis to a large number of companies under long-term subscription contracts. An operation of this kind and size differs sharply from those in the first and second categories (project basis), both with respect to its economics and the particular skills required.

Because of its dominant market position, its close and continuous servicing relationship with clients, and its receipt of subscription payments in advance of work performed, Nielsen's business is more stable and profitable than that of the typical marketing research firm. Moreover, Nielsen employees tend to be more specialized in their job functions than employees working in other types of marketing research supplier firms.

The purpose of Nielsen marketing research tracking services is to provide a motion picture of the flow of products through retail outlets—the final stage in the distribution process where manufacturers' and retailers' marketing and selling efforts are exerted to influence consumers to purchase their products. By auditing a representative sample of stores, Nielsen obtains information on the sales in dollars and units of each product category, brand volumes, brand shares of market, inventories, dealer purchases, in-store promotional and advertising activities, retail selling prices, etc.

This "package" of information is processed on Nielsen's own computers. It is put into database form and then analyzed by Nielsen's Client Service executives, who use graphics and numeric tables to present and interpret the findings to clients. In essence, they use the results to assist clients in understanding the effects of their marketing and sales efforts on their own and competitors' brands, in identifying corrective moves, in spotting opportunities, and in developing actionable solutions to problems.

Major Organizational/Functional Units

Nielsen's marketing research tracking service provides a good example of the organizational units and their functions in typical marketing research firms that provide tracking services:

Statistical Research Department: designs and maintains samples of stores to be audited; develops controls for the projection of sample data to universe estimates; assesses the statistical precision of reported results.

Field Operations Department: recruits and maintains cooperation of sample stores; gathers data in sample stores.

Production and Systems Information Department: processes data gathered by the field auditors and produces reports for clients in appropriate media such as print on paper, magnetic tapes, diskettes, and on-line.

Marketing Department: analyzes, presents and interprets reports to clients; sells services to new and present clients.

General Management: manages the activities of the above areas.

Competitive marketing research tracking organizations are structured in similar fashion, although the titles of the units may be different.

Principal Forces Of Change We Face

The entire business world has been affected in recent years by technology, and the marketing research field has felt a significant impact. The growing presence and use of computers, office automation, and data communications greatly speeds up and renders more accurate and cost-effective the gathering, processing, analysis, delivery and presentation of information at all stages of marketing research activities. Technology enables suppliers to furnish data faster and more accurately to clients. It also dramatically increases the productivity of workers in the industry.

Technological advances will continue. We all will become more comfortable with the new technology, and it will be easier to use. As technology continues to improve, we could be faced with new challenges in hiring and training our future employees—technological skills will become vital to successful job applicants.

Entry-Level Jobs In The Supplier Industry

As companies in the marketing research field differ in size, complexity and types of services provided, so do they differ in the number and types of entry-level positions. A large supplier firm such as Nielsen will hire entry-level people in two primary areas: *statistical research* and *production and systems information management.*

Statisticians play a key role in any research project. Beginning *statisticians* gain experience in sample design and maintenance before becoming more involved in numerous other statistical projects.

The people responsible for putting together all the data collected by field operations are in the *production and systems information management area.* These data processing, data production, and data analysis employees prepare the information for the *marketing department,* whose professionals then present the results to clients.

Because of the size and complexity of Nielsen's business, it hires people for entry-level positions and trains them in one, specific aspect of marketing research. This differs from other firms that may hire individuals and assign them project-type work, in which they have the responsibility for sample design, conducting and analyzing the survey, and then making the final report to the client.

Some marketing research companies have a tradition of "promotion from within." Many members of Nielsen's marketing department and general management areas, for example, started in one of the entry-level positions described above and were then promoted to positions of greater responsibility.

The Education, Background And Skills You Need

A college degree in business, marketing, mathematics, statistics, or computer science is a logical start for anyone desiring an entry-level position in marketing research. However, individuals with degrees in liberal arts or the humanities may also be suited for some positions.

We prefer that a candidate for employment have a college degree, but we recognize that a degree is by no means a guarantee of success. Therefore, in evaluating a candidate for employment, we try to look at the whole person—education is just one of many areas we assess.

Technical, conceptual, communication and interpersonal skills are other criteria by which we judge prospective employees. Why are these skills important?

First, most of our entry-level jobs require an interest in working with numbers or analyzing data. Therefore, *technical skills* are very important.

Second, *conceptual skills* enable one to see the whole picture, to better interpret data and offer creative solutions to problems.

Third, in any field, *communication skills*—oral, written, listening—are necessary for success.

Finally, getting along with people and developing *interpersonal skills* with co-workers and clients are essential in a people-oriented profession like marketing research.

Breaking Into The Supplier Industry

You will have to work at it. While in college, you should be involved in business and marketing-related clubs and organizations (like the student chapters of the American Marketing Association). By being active in this type of organization, you will develop a better under-standing of what the real world is like.

Another important step toward getting a job is to develop yourself both intellectually and personally. We are all products or the sum total of our experiences. Marketing research professionals have dealings with people of varying backgrounds, beliefs, interests and abilities. Whatever attributes or experiences you can bring to these relationships—college courses, extracurricular activities, work experience, personality—will help you adapt successfully to the many different business situations you will need to face.

Since most of you do not have actual experience in or first-hand knowledge of the marketing research industry, a good first step is to identify several top companies in the field. You'll find the Databank information in the back of this *Career Directory* most helpful. These companies should be contacted to obtain information. Ask questions like the following:

What services does the company provide?

What is the company's competitive position within the industry?

How long has the company been in business?

Who are its clients?

How many employees does the company have?

How long have employees been with the company?

What is the financial condition of the company?

What is the trend of the company's revenue and profit growth?

What is the company's commitment to research and development?

What are the entry-level job opportunities?

Does promotion to executive positions take place from within?

What is the company's future outlook?

Once you've analyzed the industry and its top organizations, send resumes to or telephone the companies in which you are most interested to arrange interviews. Remember: Resumes should be short (one-page), complete, and to the point. Let these "target companies" know why *you* are the best person for the job. Personalize your effort and mount it in the manner most comfortable for you.

Good luck!

In addition to his titles of vice president and director of corporate planning and development, the latter of which involves him in merger and acquisitions activity, **PHILIP R. NIELSEN** is also a member of A. C. Nielsen Company's board of directors.

He received a B.A. in economics from Stanford University and an M.B.A. from the University of Michigan. He did graduate work in Berlin, Paris, Geneva and Stockholm and has since played a key role in establishing Nielsen's marketing research business in France, Mexico, Japan and Argentina.

Mr. Nielsen is a member of the Association for Corporate Growth, the Executives Club of Chicago, the Information Industry Association, and the Muenchner Kreis.

18

Internships In Marketing Research: Try the Basics

Robert J. Lavidge, President Emeritus
Elrick and Lavidge, Inc.

There is an unfortunate imbalance between the demand for marketing research internships and the supply of them. Many young people seek such internships, but they are hard to find. Why is this? What can you do about it if you want to work in marketing research?

Given the dearth of available internships, the answer is to gain experience wherever and however you can. In this article, I'll discuss two particular areas of opportunity that will help prepare you for a position in marketing research—working as an interviewer or as an editor and coder.

Some Points On Internships

Consider why you want an internship in marketing research. What's in it for you?

Do you want the money you would be paid as a marketing research intern? If that's your reason, you probably should look for a different type of job. If you are fortunate enough to find a marketing research internship, it probably will not pay as much as many alternatives.

Do you want an internship to provide a foot in the door with a marketing research firm or department? If so, read on.

Do you want an internship for the experience it will provide as a foundation for a career in marketing research? Once again, if that is your objective, read on.

Why would an employer hire an intern? Internship programs provide opportunities for employers to evaluate potential employees, as well as for the employees to evaluate potential employers. Some firms look upon internships as contributions to the marketing research field. Some also may expect interns to contribute useful work. However, they are not likely to expect interns to contribute to the planning or design of marketing research studies, to the construction of questionnaires, to project supervision, to the interpretation of data or to the writing of research reports. On the other hand, they may expect interns to do useful work as interviewers, editors, coders or assistants to those handling project analysis.

One note of interest: The University of Georgia has an unusual program leading to a degree of Master of Marketing Research. It is highly selective—in most years, only 15 or 20 new students are admitted. During the second year of the two-year program, the students spend several months as interns with some of the country's major marketing organizations: manufacturers, service companies and marketing research firms. However, other internships are scarce commodities (*Those few that* are *offered by the top research supplier firms are listed in chapter 33—Ed.*).

Opportunities For Interviewers

In contrast to the small number of internships available, there are plenty of opportunities for *interviewers*. Experience as an interviewer will be a valuable addition to your resume when you are seeking a permanent position in marketing research. Moreover, it will help you do better work when you reach positions that involve planning research projects or interpreting studies involving interviewing by others.

Much of this interviewing is done over the telephone, some involving questionnaires which list the questions to be asked and provide places for the interviewers to record the answers. But an increasing amount of the telephone interviewing is computer-assisted. In this type of interviewing, the questions appear on computer screens and the answers are recorded by the interviewers directly into computer terminals. Experience with both types of interviewing is valuable.

Other interviewing involves talking with survey respondents on a face-to-face basis, mostly in shopping centers. Many of the large centers include facilities designed especially for conducting interviews, including places where respondents may be shown products or television commercials.

Other face-to-face interviewing is done in consumers' homes or in offices, stores or factories where people may be questioned about the products and services used by the organizations for which they work. This latter type of interviewing frequently requires a higher level of skill than is needed when conducting most consumer interviews. It also may pay better.

However, the hourly wages paid to beginning interviewers usually are near the mini-mum permitted by law. If you are interested in working in marketing research, consider interviewing as a way to gain valuable experience— a foot in the door—not as a way to make a great deal of money.

Some firms focus entirely on interviewing work. Others also have staff members who design studies, formulate questionnaires, plan survey samples, tabulate data, analyze information, interpret data and prepare reports. If you do a good job as an interviewer for the latter type of organization, you may be able to move from interviewing into other aspects of marketing research. If that is not possible, a letter of recommendation regarding your work as an interviewer may be helpful to you later.

Opportunities In Editing And Coding

Some marketing research firms also hire inexperienced people as *questionnaire editors and coders*. This work involves checking questionnaires for completeness and obvious errors, plus assigning numerical code categories to verbal answers given by survey respondents. This also is good experience for those of you who aspire to careers in marketing research.

This *Career Directory* includes the names of some of the largest marketing research firms, though not most of the organizations that focus entirely on interviewing. Check the classified section of your local telephone directory for a listing of the companies doing marketing research work in your geographic area. These companies often are listed under the heading "Market Research and Analysis."

In addition to marketing research firms, you may be able to find opportunities for interviewing, editing and coding work with manufacturers or service firms, such as banks and large retailers. Most such work, however, is done by marketing research and interviewing firms.

In addition to gaining experience with the basic, very important functions of inter-viewing, editing and coding, you should consider joining one or more of the associations which serve marketing research people. The largest of these is the American Marketing Association—including students, it has almost 50,000 members. If you are in college, there may be a student chapter of the Association in your school.

As a cornerstone for a career in marketing, you can't beat experience with the basics--that is, with interviewing, editing and coding.

Elrick and Lavidge, Inc., which **ROBERT J. LAVIDGE** founded in 1951, is one of the nation's leading custom research firms, with headquarters in Chicago and more than forty offices throughout the United States.

Mr. Lavidge was president of the American Marketing Association during the 1966-67 year. He also has served AMA in a number of capacities, including vice president in charge of the Marketing Research Division, president of the Chicago chapter, a member of the *Journal of Marketing Research* editorial board and many others.

A frequent conference and seminar speaker, he is the author of numerous articles in a variety of journals. He is co-author of Marketing and Society: The Challenge.

Mr. Lavidge was an adjunct member of the faculty of Northwestern University from 1950 to 1980 and has been involved in a number of other distinguished college and university programs. He earned his BA from DePauw University in 1943 and an MBA from the University of Chicago School of Business in 1947, both with highest honors, including election to Phi Betta Kappa and Beta Gama Sigma. He is listed in Who's Who in America.

19

Quo Vadis, World?

Norman Vale, Director-General
International Advertising Association

Quo vadis, indeed. Where in the world the world is going is a question the international business community has always concerned itself with, but never more so than right now. Global dynamics are shifting dramatically as walls tumble, borders open, dictators "retire." Combine those truly incredible and unexpected events with the impending unification of the European Common Market and the increasing impact of the Pacific Rim countries, and you have a business climate that is fascinating, to say the least.

The dramatic changes in international commerce will have direct and substantial effects on international advertising. Here's a brief look at how international advertising evolved, where it's headed, and what you can do to prepare yourself for participation in what promises to be an exciting, challenging, and rewarding field.

The Marketplace Takes Shape

To better understand what's ahead, a look at how business responded to political and economic changes in the past is helpful.

1950s: Post War Recovery

As the world got back on its feet following World War II, European and Asian countries had to start virtually from scratch to rebuild their infrastructure destroyed by the war and, consequently, lived through a long period of deprivation. In the United States, rather than rebuild what *had been*, we were fortunate enough to be able to build upon what we still *had*. Our post-war boom fueled the U.S. economy and made the U.S. an important consumer market.

1960s: U.S. International Expansion

With such a head start, U.S. companies found openings in which to establish new markets and profit opportunities in the free world. At about the same time, the "brand revolution" began, as corporations began to extend their marketing opportunities by placing importance on individual brand-name products over corporate names. This was the beginning of U.S.-based companies' successful foray into the international arena.

1970s: Focus Shifts to Foreign Companies

The free world became more common, commercial brain power was no longer a U.S. monopoly, businesses matured, and, for the most part, technology began a decade of egalitarianism. Large foreign-based corporations looked outside their countries and saw niche opportunities, wholesale benefits, and openings where competition yielded profitable investments. The non-U.S. marketers began their international move, and their advertising agencies began to follow.

1980s: Enter Globalization

Contrary to what scientists were saying about the universe expanding, the world got smaller. Thanks in part to the accessibility of worldwide media, international borders in the free world became insignificant, as major corporations crossed from one country to another with products and services that met the world's increasingly homogeneous needs and wants. "Global" replaced international, transnational or multinational as the word to describe how corporations should approach their worldwide business.

1990s: Centers of Economic Clout

There are three critical centers of influence that will take us through the next decade:

- *North America,* as a result of the 1989 trade agreement between the U.S. and Canada;
- The *European Community*'s 12 member countries that form the Common Market and, as of January 1, 1993, will become the largest consumer market in the world;
- *Japan and Korea,* through a combination of industrial output and strong financial reserves to support increased products and services and overseas developments.

Developments In Advertising

Let's look at developments that took place in the advertising business during these same decades:

1950s: Export Advertising

U.S. companies created advertising in this country and sent it abroad without too much consideration of its final destination. The international or global mindset was not fully evolved, and neither were most companies international capabilities.

1960s: International Overtures

Marketers began to perceive commonalities in overseas markets that created possibilities for international advertising—which, at that time, meant buying space in papers or magazines that reached consumers in two or more countries.

1970s: Multinational Takes Off

U.S. and foreign-based companies were operating in so many markets around the world that the techniques of common strategy and execution became more cost efficient and, therefore, more attractive. Multinational advertising—advertising in 4-5 countries or more—hit its stride in this decade.

1980s: The Era of Globalization

Megatrends author John Naisbitt and Harvard Business School Professor Ted Levitt began the decade championing the concept that the successful corporation could do and sell the same things in the same way everywhere it operated. The advent of satellites allowed advertisers to think about reaching consumers all over the world at the same time with the same message. In 1985, "Live Aid," for example, simultaneously reached an estimated 1.5 billion people in more than 100 countries. Events such as World Cup Soccer regularly achieve almost the same global reach.

The Growth Of Advertising

The following chart illustrates the scope and growth of advertising volumes in the United States and the balance of the free world. It also graphically demonstrates why global opportunities may be in your future:

Worldwide Advertising Trends

(in billions of U. S. dollars)

(Year)	1960	1970	1980	1990	2000
Worldwide Ad Expenditures	18	36	110	313	780
Non-U. S. Ad Expenditures	6	16	55	163	460
U. S. Ad Expenditures	12	20	55	150	320

As you can see, in the '60s and '70s, advertising outside the United States was developing its own momentum, but still did not come close to the level of advertising dollars invested in the U.S. During the '80s, all media expenditures approached the fifty-fifty mark.

What Will The '90s Bring?

For the '90s, we can expect international advertising expenditures to surpass U.S. volume. Reasons for this include:

- *New media* available, following full satellite deployment.
- *New markets,* such as China and its one billion people.
- *Increased confidence* in doing business away from home countries, achieved through four decades of experience.
- *Rapid technological improvements,* including continuing growth of computer interfacing, electronic mail (which will make it easier to do what we do), and high-definition TV (which will make what we do more attractive to consumers).
- *Strengthened gross national products* in so many countries.
- The *elimination of trade barriers* within the European community, come January 1, 1993.
- A *competition-driven increase in production* from Western Europe and the Pacific Rim, as those countries continue to generate products and services that will be supported by advertising and promotion funds.
- The *recent events in Eastern Europe.* All of us who have dedicated our lives to international business applaud the changes as we attempt to understand how they will affect our economic, political, commercial, and financial strategies. Following the initial chaos, we should expect order and opportunity to arise, creating a far better commercial climate for people considering an international future.

Preliminary forecasts indicate that worldwide expenditures will be nearing one *trillion* dollars by the year 2000. And of that, close to 60 percent will be invested outside the U.S.

So should you consider an international career in advertising? Quo vadis...world!

Creating *Your* International Career

It's clear that the opportunities for well-trained advertising professionals on both the agency and client sides will increase during the next ten years. There are several substantive reasons for choosing to "go international."

- Inevitably, the world will be one large market. The best-prepared people for management positions will have a combination of U.S. and international experience.
- The relatively small scale of operations for agencies outside the U.S. necessarily increases your exposure to all facets of the business. Working within a small management group provides an accelerated advancement track; the chance to be involved in the decision-making process comes more quickly in comparison to a parallel course in the U.S.
- The challenge of working and living in a foreign culture is professionally and personally enriching.

How To Get Ready

Should you decide to invest yourself in the global advertising arena, here are six important steps that you can take to prepare yourself for a career in a foreign country:

1. Acquire solid agency experience in either a large U.S. agency or its counterpart in another country, and plan to stay there for 3 to 5 years—less time may not sufficiently prepare you for that next international step.

2. Attempt to work your way into a multinational account, particularly if it's a feeder operation. Many positions are available within agencies where products and services are similarly introduced and available in foreign markets.

3. Make your management aware of your interest, be diligent in your pursuit, and find an appropriate mentor within your organization.

4. Be open-minded and flexible about the country assignment offered. There is a world beyond London and Paris; besides, the talent pool in both England and France is sufficiently large. You may find similar challenges and satisfaction along with greater opportunity for advancement in other countries.

5. Don't view a career in international advertising as a free ticket to travel. It's hard work, and any other perception will not be appreciated by prospective employers.

6. Above all, have patience, patience, and even more patience.

Witnessing world developments in the coming decade will be fascinating. The prospect of participating in them is even more so. Good luck to those of you who choose a career path that leads you to the international arena.

NORMAN VALE has spent 25 years in agency management, lived and worked in three countries, and was a senior officer for Grey International—a $3.2 billion global advertising and communication agency—for 16 years. Early this year, he was named the first director-general of the International Advertising Association.

Mr. Vale has been an occasional lecturer on international advertising and marketing at St. John's University, Wharton, NYU Graduate School of Business, World Trade Institute and at seminars and congresses in the U.S. and Europe. While those have been delivered principally in English, he also speaks Spanish, some Portuguese, and German. He was the chairman of the 4A's International Committee and is a World Board Director of the IAA.

20

The Advertising Scene
In Canada

Charles Abrams, Vice-Chairman/Executive Creative Director
Backer Spielvogel Bates Canada Inc.

If you *can't* make it in New York, Chicago, Minneapolis, Boston, or any other advertising center in the States, don't assume you can show your driver's license to a customs official, cross the border, and have Canadian advertising agencies anxiously awaiting you with open arms. They won't be.

While it may have been more benevolent a few years ago, the fact is the Canadian advertising industry is evolving to world-class status. The colleges, universities and art schools are filled with people who are determined to get into advertising. The competition, in other words, is fierce.

Add to that the fact that Canadian agencies have not been immune to mergers and acquisitions. Practically every major U. S. and U. K. agency has an office here—Saatchi & Saatchi, Backer Spielvogel Bates, WPP Group (J. Walter Thompson, Ogilvy & Mather), DDB Needham (which recently merged with Canadian agency Carder Grey), Y & R, McLaren Lintas, McCann-Erickson, Scali McCabe Sloves and Chiat Day Mojo, Baker Lovic (BBDO), McKim (NW Ayer with a minority interest). It may be just a matter of time before Canadian-owned agencies such as Vickers & Benson and Cossette Communications align themselves with multinational shops.

What all this means is that job opportunities will diminish. But not if you have the talent and determination to fight your way into this business. And many do just that—and not just from the States, but the U. K., South Africa, Australia, Scotland, Ireland and Hong Kong, as well.

And where exactly are they heading? Toronto!

Why Toronto?

Toronto is the New York of Canada. Virtually every major advertising agency is located here, and practically every major Canadian advertiser spends its advertising dollars here. And when I say major advertisers, I mean just that—McDonalds, Procter & Gamble, Warner Lambert,

GM, Ford, Chrysler, Toyota, Nissan, Honda, General Foods, Campbell's, Ralston Purina—the list goes on. Less familiar, though more important, are the big Canadian advertisers such as Petro Canada, Loblaw's Supermarkets (the first North American company responsible for starting the green marketing revolution), Canadian Airlines, Labatts and Molson breweries (Molson being second only to the Canadian government in ad dollars spent).

Toronto has everything a major advertising centre needs and more. Thousands of people move to greater Toronto every year, adding to the 3.2 million people who already live here.

Dynamic, cosmopolitan, sophisticated and clean are words that best describe Toronto, the capital of Ontario, which lies on the northwest shore of Lake Ontario, just across from Buffalo, New York. A mere one-hour flight from New York City or Chicago. It has become an international centre of business, finance, communications, the arts and medical research.

Toronto offers an abundance of excellent shopping and schools, first-class public transportation, diverse housing options, and a healthy economic base. One of the most exciting features of the city is its ethnic diversity, as is illustrated by the publication of official announcements in the *six* most frequently spoken languages in Toronto—English, French, Italian, Portugese, Chinese and Greek.

The city has become a favorite locale for shooting feature films, TV mini-series and commercials. It has a financial district and a vibrant theatre district. If you want chic and expensive, just head uptown to the Bloor and Bay area. Boutiques, galleries and world-class restaurants abound. Many of the city's advertising firms are located here. Canada's largest university, the University of Toronto, is right in the heart of the city.

Toronto has outgrown its past nicknames ("Hogtown" and "Muddy York"). It's a live, vibrant, growing city designed for people. It's safe, sane and civilized.

But a note of caution: In a recent survey, it was reported that Toronto has become the most expensive city in the Western Hemisphere, outstripping pricey locales like New York, Chicago and Lima, Peru. Calgary and Montreal were both in the Top Twelve. And housing costs, which are astronomical, were not taken into account! The good news is that Toronto ranked 28th worldwide.

Just how big is the advertising scene in Canada?

At last count, there were over 260 advertising agencies in operation *in Toronto alone*. If you add the branch offices coast-to-coast, the one- and two-man shops, the promotion houses, and the retail and direct response agencies from Halifax to Victoria—to say nothing of Winnipeg, Windsor, Waterloo, Whitehorse and Yellowknife!—the list grows to well over 500.

But 15% of these shops do 85% of the business. The major mergers of the last few years have seen a shrinking of the power base down to five or six multinationals, each with two or more off-shoots or commonly-held sister shops. These are followed by a few strong-and-holding-out Canadian agencies, then by a plethora of smallish, regional and special-interest shops.

The Differences You'll Find

Are the American and Canadian advertising industries very different from each other? Well, yes and no. As an American who was raised on the New York ad scene, I've seen the best and the worst of Madison Avenue and had the opportunity to work with some of the most brilliant names in the business. When I was asked to take this post in Canada, I knew there would be some adjustments, but, in truth, found that the differences between the two countries' ad businesses to be more a matter of geography, language, and government than of people or modus operandi. Advertising people are as dedicated, hard-working, professional, caring, creative and crazy in Toronto as they are in Tucson...or New York or Detroit or Dallas or Seattle. Clients are clients regardless of where they're from. And the creative process of thinking, writing, art directing, presenting and producing really doesn't differ much on either side of the border.

So people aside, here are the differences:

1) Canada has essentially one-tenth the population of the U. S. Hence, one-tenth the advertising budgets and one-tenth the purchasing power. We tend to have to work with tighter budgets, and (generally speaking) our campaigns have to last longer. Creative people have to be generalists—the creative director who is overseeing a big car shoot one day can be writing a small print ad for bird seed the next. In the U. S., particularly in New York, you'll find job titles such as "TV copywriter" and "print art director." Not so in Canada, where *everybody* in Creative has to be adept at creating ads for *every* kind of media.

2) We have two official languages: English and French. 27% of the Canadian population lives in the (French-speaking) Province of Quebec. All government documents must be printed in two languages. As must the labels on every can of soup. So our already-smaller budgets must be stretched even further to accommodate the translations and adaptations needed. And speaking of those, merely "switching" an English-language approach won't necessarily satisfy the cultural nuances of the French language. Consequently, American-based advertisers whose message would fly nicely in the rest of Canada could be faced with major overhauls if they wanted to run the same ad in Quebec.

3) We have incredible government intervention into what we can and can't say about our clients' products in the broadcast media, especially TV. Food is governed by a commission in Ottawa which must approve every word and every picture in a TV spot. Proprietary medicines, cough syrups, other non-prescription drugs, and even sugarless gums fall under the Health Protection Branch (protecting the public from us, I assume), and their TV claims are governed accordingly. In the case of beer and wine advertising, there are no less than *five* Federal approval committees, in addition to the individual rules and guidelines from ten separate provinces. Hence lead times in Canada have to be longer so the government bodies can bestow their stamps of approval on our creative. Which, I might add, is challenged to the maximum every time out.

Now For The Good News

Despite the government restrictions, the Canadian advertising industry is turning out work that is excellent...world-class...exemplary.

Despite the two languages, Canadian agencies, through their affiliates in Quebec, can offer their clients consistently national coverage with well-thought-out, appropriate, market-smart communications.

And despite the smaller population and matching budgets, fresh, innovative concepts—where the idea is bigger than the estimate—are developed, presented and sold every day.

Finally, as far as the commercial film industry is concerned, Canadian production values are highly regarded throughout the world.

Which is why I get literally dozens of phone calls and letters and resumes and portfolios every week. From people like you. Who want, more than anything else in the world, to break into advertising.

Getting Into The Creative Department

Creative is more than a part of the agency; it's the heart of the agency. Oh, sure, we all work together—Creative, Media, Account Management. But the scripts, storyboards, ads, and ideas turned out in the Creative department are, in truth, the *product* of the agency. It's what we *do*. It's what we *sell*. So if my biased viewpoint on the importance of Creative comes from the heart, this fact comes from statistics: Creative receives more applications for employment, *more* letters, *more* phone calls, *more* requests, for interviews *than any other department in any other business in any other industry...in the world.*

Now, please read this. I'm going to say it only once, and then I'm going to go on as if I never said it:

> *Only one in 500 applicants will be successful in landing an entry-level Creative position in a Canadian agency.*
>
> *You have to be better than good to get in—you have to be outstanding. You have to make yourself noticed. And you have to have substance behind your approach.*
>
> *Agencies are not waiting with open arms to hire you. Most of them won't even see you. It's simply easier for them to go with someone with experience than to train a newcomer.*
>
> *Knowing this, plan your strategy accordingly.*

That said, here's some specific advice for you would-be copywriters and art directors.

If You Want To Be A Copywriter

It's very important to realize that a copywriter has different talents than a literary writer. The finest prose in the world is useless to a client who needs to move a brand in six short words on a billboard. The most eloquent screenplay styling must be set aside when the client's product must be seen and sold in 15 seconds.

A copywriter is a specialist. A person with the verbal abilities to hone an idea down to its bare bones and present that idea on the silver platter of originality.

If you want to get started in copywriting, you must, first and foremost, prove that you can *write*. Secondly, and just as important, you must prove that you can write *ads*. Prepare more than your resume. Write a letter or brief essay explaining why you want so badly to work in advertising. Write, write, write ads. Make ads for nonexistent products. Prepare TV scripts for current products and for services you admire. Make up a portfolio of ads and scripts that show you understand the communications art of advertising. If you write an ad, prepare a TV commercial to go along with it and a billboard to complete the campaign. Beg an artist friend to sketch up your ideas. Or make a collage of pictures to illustrate your message.

There is no such thing as a "copywriting school." Apart from having a superb command of language, knowing how to spell (please!), and having skill in grammar and sentence structure, a copywriter can come from almost any academic background. Life experience, people skills, salesmanship, and the power of persuasion are the finest talents a beginning copywriter can have.

If You Want To Be An Art Director

Aspiring art directors usually come with formal training from an Art College or University; they will have been trained in layout, typography, illustration, and the graphic arts in general. Unlike copywriters, they will emerge from school with a portfolio of school projects on which they have been graded.

If you have such a portfolio, don't depend on it alone to get you an interview. Add to it. Make ads. Design your own campaigns. Let the potential interviewer see first-hand that you have something to contribute. That you are more than a talented "wrist." That you can think. That you are an ad-*maker*.

Getting started as an art director is only slightly different than the task facing the would-be copywriter. In your case, however, you don't necessarily have to start in an agency proper. A year or two at a design studio, paste-up shop or type house will give you some experience from which to springboard into a "real shop." Like the copywriter, however, make the rounds with your portfolio, write to creative directors, and be persistent. Your talent will be immediately visible the second your portfolio is opened. So make those opening pages as dynamic as possible.

You *Still* Want To Work In Advertising In Canada?

You've absorbed my blunt caveats stated earlier. You *know* that only a handful of applicants make it in the Creative Department in any given year. But you still have the guts and the hopes to try to break into advertising. Here is some closing advice I hope will make it easier for you:

- Arm yourself with all possible information about obtaining work in Canada. Write to Employment & Immigration Canada, Central C.I.C., 443 University Avenue, Toronto, Ontario M5G 2H6, and ask them to send you their pamphlets on obtaining an Employment Authorization. Your prospective employer/agency will have to show just cause why a Canadian could not be hired for the same job for which you're applying. Difficult, but *not* hopeless.

- Do your homework. Learn all you can about the industry, the agency business, and the accounts those agencies service. For each agency in which you're interested, find out exactly what it does. How it operates. What its reputation is. What accounts it handles. What accounts it has recently won. Or lost. Read the industry journals; find out about mergers, acquisitions, and staffing changes.

- Go to the library and read everything you can find on the business of advertising—Bill Bernbach's Book by Bob Levenson, Playing in Traffic on Madison Avenue by David Herzburn, When Advertising Tried Harder by Larry Dubrow, and others of the same ilk.

- Write to MacLean Hunter Publications (777 Bay Street, Toronto, Ontario, M5W 1A7), subscribe to *Marketing* magazine, Canada's premiere weekly "what's going on in advertising" journal, and ask them to send you a copy of their annual Awards Issue.

- You may also want to subscribe to *Playback*, a bi-weekly newspaper tabloid published by Brunico Communications, Inc. (111 Queen Street East, Suite 330, Toronto, Ontario M5C 1S2).

- If you can't afford any subscriptions, many of the above publications should be available in the reading room of your local library.

- Avail yourself of a wonderful little *free* booklet entitled, <u>So You Want To Be In An Advertising Agency</u>, published by the Institute for Canadian Advertising (30 Soudan Avenue, Toronto, Ontario M4S 1V6). This member-council has possibly the best library of advertising-related publications in the country. I drew heavily upon their material when preparing this article!

- Hang in there. Consider your job search as the most important job you have. Be persistent, polite and passionate in your approach to the people who hold the keys to your career. If the top ten agencies you try don't pan out, try the next ten on your list. And the next ten. And the next. Just keep trying.

- Now here's the big one: *Take the first job offered to you.* Regardless of its humble stature. Regardless of its seeming distance from what you *really* want to do.

  Be willing to work in the mailroom.

  Be willing to carry someone's portfolio.

  Be willing to be willing. And wait like a cat for the chance to move up.

Good luck!

CHARLES ABRAMS recently arrived in Canada from New York, where he was executive vice-president and a member of both the executive committee and the board of directors of Backer's sister agency, Saatchi & Saatchi Compton.

His career spans over 20 years, starting with Doyle Dane Bernbach in 1968, the agency responsible for igniting the creative revolution in the 1960s with its work for Volkswagon and AVIS. In 1983, he joined DDB's International Division as vice president/head art director, creating Pan-European campaigns for Polaroid, Atari and Seagram Corp.

Mr. Abrams has won numerous creative awards throughout his career, and while at Saatchi received accolades for his work on British Airways and New York City's first and highly controversial AIDS prevention campaign.

21

Great Is Better Than Good

**Sander A. Flaum, President and Chief Executive Officer
Robert A. Becker, Inc.**

The attributes of a "good" account manager in a "good" advertising agency are well documented. A typical job description might read as follows: strong communication skills, both verbal and written; a better-than-average work ethic; personable, well-groomed, and ambitious; a better-than-average IQ.

And if being "average" and working in an "average" agency is where you see yourself, this article is *not* for you.

However, if you are among the minority of individuals who want to leave the realm of mediocrity and strive to be a truly *great* account manager, then I have some advice for you. After 25 years in the industry (eighteen on the client side and seven in the agency business), I think I've learned something about "what makes great!"—that is, those special attributes that enable the "cream" to rise to the top. Consider these ideas and separate yourself from those who would settle to be just "good."

Sit In Your Client's Chair

All of you who enrolled in undergraduate or graduate advertising or marketing programs should realize just how little they have prepared you for the reality of the advertising world. Frankly, your college major isn't in the least important! What *is* significant is your ability to sell...all the time—externally to your client and internally to your management and creative people.

You must be able to communicate effectively via well-written presentations and exciting face-to-face interactions. If public speaking isn't your "cup of tea" and you struggled to pull "C's" on writing assignments, advertising probably is not your niche.

The consensus in this industry is that the needs of the client would be best served if anyone wanting to be an account executive first had to spend several years as a product manager. We have always held the view that the needs of a product manager can be understood best by an account person who has already sat in that chair.

If a product isn't making quota, who cares whether the background of the magazine ad is blue or green? The manager of that product needs a person on the other side of the desk with an understanding of distribution, pricing, packaging, and, of course, marketing and sales strategy.

Working for a client company gives you the opportunity to work with a variety of account people and adopt the characteristics and methods of the exceptional ones. Of course, becoming a corporate product manager—at least for a package goods company—means an MBA degree in many cases.

A positive attitude, a desire to accept coaching (from any level), and a compulsion for detail and follow-up can compensate somewhat for a deficiency in the skills mentioned above.

Become Conspicuously Proactive

This term is so difficult to define, yet so pointedly essential to the making of the *great* account executive. We train our young people to literally shower their clients, on a continuing basis, with fresh ideas to enhance brand performance. We encourage them to think big, think "out-of-the-box" on their brands, think competitively. To become *proactive*, an account executive must be convinced that the brand competitive to his is taking bread and butter off his table. In other words, we want "hungry" account people.

The concept of proactivity evolved from the notion that if the client is paying a fair hourly rate for marketing counsel and creative thinking, we'd better have account people who stay a half step ahead of their clients. Product managers need another marketing head—an experienced, strategic brain—on the other side of the desk to consult with before "decision time."

Be A "Great" Manager

One of the qualifications of the "great" agency person is his or her ability to lead people, to manage and motivate them. While I've read the great books on effective management and have taken the full complement of management courses during my MBA and post-MBA studies at Columbia University's Arden House, I'm still inclined to believe that great managers are born, not made.

Great managers have that charismatic style of getting the big things done faster and better. They are leaders who know inherently how to get the best out of people—at their agency as well as the client company. They have a presence, a respect, a credibility, an obvious posture that makes people want to follow and listen and do. They radiate a silent benign power that everyone wants to be close to. John Kennedy had it; Iaccoca has it; Donald Trump has it; Jessie Jackson has it. Do you?

Great managers are focused people. They have the rare ability to ignore (for the moment) priorities #2 to #5 when priority #1 has to be accomplished...now! They can instantly focus all their energies—creative and active—on the one big task at hand. Other things that are in need of attention but can be put off for a day or a week or a month are put into less critical priority slots and handled only when they need to be.

It takes great mental discipline to stay on that one big project until it's successfully completed. Moving off a "high pressure" project to finish some other task is always tempting. Great managers fight off the temptation and stay with the top priority job until it is done.

Settle For Nothing Less Than Excellence

Great account people are compulsive people. They have an obsession to do each successive task better than the previous one. They strive for excellence. Our theme at Becker is: "If it's not excellent, don't show it!"

The uniquely qualified account executive will not settle for an ad, commercial spot, promotional plan, media proposal, etc., unless it's the *best* it can be. Ernie Lewis, manager of professional advertising at Procter & Gamble, advised agency people recently: "Do it right the first time."

Mr. Lewis' point is well taken. There's *always* time, it seems, to *re*do the storyboard. But there's *never* enough time to get it done properly the *first* time. Our people are instructed never to bring material to the client until they are totally satisfied with the effort.

Great account people will call the client—despite an approaching deadline—and bravely request additional time to "get it right" before bringing it to them. The agency person who really cares about the interests of the client and about his or her brand will argue for more time to bring art, copy, or design to the point of satisfaction—at least from the account person's perspective.

Learn The Business Of Our Business

Most account people hesitate talking about fee reconciliation, billing, or post-30 day invoices with their clients. They see themselves as the clients' marketing and advertising consultants and maintain that a discussion of billing would impinge on the sacred "client-agency relationship." Nonsense!

Marketing managers discuss quotas, budgets, billing, the full spectrum of financial matters every day. They pay hourly fees to lawyers, plumbers, electricians, and painters every day. So why would anyone think it wrong for a brand manager to review billing with his agency representative?

The *great* account person considers himself a business manager. He is providing a unique service to his client for which he expects to earn a fair hourly rate and a 20% profit (what any moderately successful business should be able to achieve).

The *exceptional* account executive wants to and should be paid for the dedicated hours his agency team spends on the brand. He is fiscally responsible and responsive to his client—doing hard-bill estimates, revised estimates (when necessary), and on-time billing, with documentation for out-of-pocket expenses.

Thus, a good financial background and understanding of agency finances are a must for the talented, growth-motivated agency account executive.

So *That's* What Great Is!

Now let's rewrite that job description we started with to reflect the desperate need in this industry for truly *great* account managers: They must possess excellent communications skills, a proactive attitude, leadership, managerial and motivational skills, a drive for excellence, and a solid background in agency finances.

If you are one of those rare individuals who already possesses three out of five of these qualities and is motivated to acquire the remaining two, then you are well on your way to becoming a *great* account manager.

SANDER A FLAUM joined Robert A. Becker, Advertising Inc. in August 1988. He previously served as executive vice president and director of marketing at Klemtner Advertising.

Prior to entering the advertising business, Sander worked for seventeen years as a senior marketing director with Lederle Laboratories, a division of American Cyanamid Company. During his tenure with this major pharmaceutical manufacturer, he served on the task force to take the ethical vitamin line over-the-counter. He also served as task force chairman to launch the Lederle Generic Products Division. As product group director, Sander was responsible for the introductions of most of the important Lederle ethical and biological products from 1974 through 1982. As an advertising account supervisor, he helped launch Calan SR and Lozol.

Sander is also a member of the editorial advisory board of *Pharmaceutical Executive* and an adjunct professor of marketing at the graduate school of business at Fairleigh Dickinson University. He is the author of four published articles and was a featured speaker at two international marketing symposia—Paris in 1982 and Lugano in 1988. He holds a BA from Ohio State University, an MBA (magna cum laude) from Fairleigh Dickinson University, and attended Columbia University's graduate school of business program in advanced marketing studies.

22

Getting Into A Corporate Advertising Department

Claudia E. Marshall, Vice President-
Marketing & Communication Services
The Travelers Companies

In some ways, it has never been harder to break into the advertising business, but in *most* ways, it has never been a more exciting business to be in. Over the last 10 to 15 years, the role of advertising agencies has been changing.

In the past, many large corporations looked to their external ad agencies to initiate recommendations about where they should be going and what they should be doing. With business needs changing, becoming increasingly complex, seemingly every day, the client/agency relationship is becoming more of a marketing partnership.

Strategic marketing directions must come from the corporation. The agency must play an increasingly important executional role, focusing on the complexity of creative strategies, media buying and production.

More and more agency account service people who see themselves as broad-gauged marketing people are making the transition to corporations. They see this transition as a way of really getting into a business and having more influence in making advertising work.

If you have already decided that you want to work in a corporate advertising department, there are a couple of routes you can take. First, remember that the primary role of the corporate advertising department is to direct the out-of-house agency, and *that* means you have to know something about the advertising business.

The best way to get that knowledge, obviously, is to work in an agency for a few years in a variety of capacities and learn everything you can. You can also take a more circuitous route—working in a corporate sales or product management support capacity and then moving over to its advertising and marketing services area.

Corporate Advertising Department Setup

The structure of an advertising department varies by company size and other factors. The Travelers department operates on two levels—the corporate advertising program and the in-house agency.

The corporate advertising function develops the positioning strategy for the corporate brand which, in turn, supports the culture and identity of the corporation by reinforcing other product advertising done in the company. Its main responsibility is to direct the out-of-house agency in the development and execution of the corporation's advertising.

The in-house ad agency takes many functions of the ad agency and performs them within the corporate boundaries. Their only client is the corporation and its various lines of business, for which the internal shop produces collateral material, sales promotion and advertising.

The attractiveness of using an in-house agency, rather than "farming everything out" is due to the in-house staff's familiarity with the business, the responsiveness that comes from close proximity, and the ability to maintain close control over costs.

The account service jobs in an in-house operation are essentially the same as those at any ad agency. The titles may vary, but a typical entry-level position is *account coordinator* (or *assistant account executive*), who makes sure each job gets done on time by staying in touch with his or her agency counterparts in creative, traffic and production. Next in line is the *account executive*, also an implementer, but one already starting to get involved in the planning process. Above that is the *account supervisor*, who is accountable for strategic planning on specific portions of a client's business. On top is the *management supervisor* (or *account director*), who takes charge of the overall account and works with the account supervisor on planning, administrative issues, staffing, trouble-shooting and problem-solving.

As you rise through the ranks in account service and the pressure of constant deadlines increases, you will see that advertising is not the glamorous and slick profession that some people think. The long hours and (initially) low pay will test your commitment to the business. If you choose to stick it out, the later rewards—in terms of both personal satisfaction and income potential—can be very gratifying.

The Right Preparation

In most cases, it is pretty difficult to break into a corporate advertising department right out of college because, as I already emphasized, the key role of account service people in a corporate advertising department is to supervise the outside agency. This requires both a good, disciplined, general understanding of marketing and specific knowledge about the business to which you are going to apply it, since the legal and technical problems faced by advertisers have become increasingly important. You also need to have a solid understanding of the technical aspects of advertising—production, media planning, traffic procedures, and how to set advertising objectives.

What I look for when hiring account managers is roughly three to seven years of agency experience. These numbers are not written in stone. A college internship in communications and some extra coursework in marketing or advertising might compensate for less agency time. I strongly urge students who want to work in corporate advertising to get into an agency right out of college. Do anything you can to get in the door—from administrative work to media coordination to research assistant—and use whatever skills you can muster to get exposure to an agency relationship. From there, either keep changing jobs within that agency or move to other agencies in an attempt to keep strengthening your marketing and strategic planning skills and gain exposure to a number of different businesses. As you gain experience, shoot for an account management slot.

The Corporate Route

Depending on your drives and personal ambitions, working your way up from a product management role in a company to its advertising department may be the most logical approach for you. By the time you attempt such a move, you will have been fully steeped in the corporate culture and learned the company's business, products, distribution channels and marketing methodologies.

Your company background can enhance your reputation as a subject-matter expert and boost your credibility with product managers. It may also clarify your perspective about what type of marketing/communications support is needed.

Advertising is the final link in the marketing chain, and it is a logical place in the company for you to round out your marketing career. The buck, in a sense, stops here. The product and pricing setup has been established, and your previous experience in the product area gives you added insight in advising clients about choosing markets, media, and creative strategies.

The Traditional Agency Route

If you really want to get a dose of "street smarts" before coming to work for a client company, I strongly advise you to work on the agency side for a few years. The ability to understand both sides of the fence is, I think, invaluable. After all, from a corporate standpoint, you have to be able to guide the agency in terms of what can and can't be done, where the corporation stands on certain issues, and what business opportunities the corporation wants to push and/or avoid. Accountability is a recurring issue, as your credibility is on the line regularly—with clients, the agency, even your own management.

If you're getting ready to graduate, you might get started in a small or mid-sized agency, working as a "jack (or jill) of all trades." This will enable you to do a little bit of everything and be exposed to as many facets of the business as possible—copywriting, media estimating, strategic planning, and client contact. If you have a graduate business degree, you may be able to get right into a training program in one of the larger agencies where you will receive formal training in various agency departments—media, market research, traffic and production.

Getting a broad smattering of agency experience—print and broadcast, packaged goods, etc.— and handling a variety of accounts, from breakfast cereals to liquor to real estate, will make you increasingly "merchandisable." The real-life experience you gain working for different clients and learning about different businesses will serve you well on the corporate side. After all, there is nothing wrong with going to work for a financial services company and applying a communications strategy that worked well for the razor blade account your agency worked on!

Broad and varied agency experience will teach you how to provide solid marketing communications support for any kind of business.

Personal Traits

An equally important skill you acquire from agency life is *flexible people skills*. This comes in handy in a corporate setting where you interact with a large assortment of people, some of whom support your area and some of whom do *not*. Always remember that advertising is a service business—your success depends on your cooperation with and sensitivity to many different kinds of people.

A high level of *adaptability* is also called for. If you are moving to the corporate side in search of a haven of stability and a respite from the high pressure and long hours of agency life, you may be disappointed. Mergers, acquisitions, and extensive new product development are becoming everyday facts of life in corporations, so you must be amenable to change.

You'll need an *even temperament* to manage and give direction to a broad range of people, bring order to frequently chaotic situations, and deal with ambiguity. You must also be adept at selling ideas and translating vague concepts into specific directions for creative people.

Strong *analytical skills,* perhaps honed in an agency's media department, will help you decipher technical product information so you can communicate intelligently with clients about their business.

The ability to *listen* well is also an asset. You must be able to get clients to open up with you about their marketing objectives and strategies in order to design the most effective marketing communications plan for them, one that helps them position their products in the marketplace and distinguish them from competitors'. What do we want people to think about us when they see our advertising?

Whether you are developing the overall corporate advertising campaign or promoting one of the company's product lines, you have to be willing to *take risks.* You must be willing to support the agency's recommendations, even if they seem radical, if it has followed through on your directions. Similarly, you must be able to send the agency back to the drawing board when you think it is off the mark. That means having *confidence* in your own judgment and being *knowledgeable* about what is going on in the company and in the marketplace.

Education

An undergraduate degree with a major in communications or business, especially marketing, is good preparation for an advertising career. If you choose to go the business route— which will set you ahead in terms of basic business knowledge—be sure to include some technical communications courses like advertising, journalism, broadcasting and public relations. Similarly, if you decide to concentrate in the liberal arts, perhaps majoring in English or history, be sure to supplement them with courses in technical communications and marketing.

If you choose to pursue an advanced degree in either business or communications, I strongly urge you to get some "practical" experience first in an ad agency. This will not only expose you to the business and show you what skills you need to develop further, but should help you decide what area of specialization is best for you. It may also convince you to pick another profession!

A Typical Day Is Atypical

It's hard to describe a "typical" day in a corporate advertising department. There are client consultations, "blue sky" sessions with the agency, time spent with associates in creative, production and traffic, and meetings with your management. There is a great deal of time and energy spent on getting approvals, on everything from strategies to final artwork. In some ways, you could look upon the corporate advertising function as the great gatekeeper for the approval process.

In her current position, **CLAUDIA E. MARSHALL** manages over 100 marketing and communications professionals serving the corporation and its products. She joined The Travelers in 1983 as vice president of advertising and marketing services.

Prior to joining Travelers, she was vice president at Chase Manhattan Bank in New York. She was with the bank for 11 years in a number of executive marketing and communications positions. Ms. Marshall also worked as a marketing representative for the IBM Corporation in the New York financial area.

Ms. Marshall is a nationally known speaker in the marketing and communication field. She is a director of the Association of National Advertisers, a trustee of the Marketing Science Institute, and a steering committee director of the American Marketing Association. She has published numerous books and articles, including Developing New Services (1983) and Creativity in Services Marketing (1985).

She holds an M.B.A. in finance from New York University and a B.A. in mathematics and English (cum laude) from Cedar Crest College. She also received an M.A. in communication from Michigan State University, where she was a professor of mass communication and research methods.

23

Sales Promotion: America's Game

Chris Sutherland, Executive Director
Promotion Marketing Association of America, Inc.

QUESTION: What do basketball, Lee Iacocca and sales promotions have in common?

ANSWER: Despite their distant roots, each is dynamic, very successful and, most of all, uniquely American. The difference is that while Iacocca and basketball do not offer open-door employment opportunities (unless you can sell Chrysler junk bonds or scrape your head on the ceiling with your feet flat on the floor, respectively), sales promotion is booming with opportunity.

The Surprising Dominance Of Sales Promotion

The facts speak for themselves: For every dollar spent on advertising by American consumer product companies, more than *two* dollars is spent on sales promotion. Sales promotion expenditures—over $100 billion—represent the largest single portion of the American marketing budget.

One reason for this surprising dominance lies in the proven ability of sales promotion to motivate purchase. Unlike advertising, which is image based, sales promotion approaches consumers in ways that have an immediate and measurable impact on their decision to purchase. Advertising suggests...promotion motivates.

Sales promotion exists because consumers have a choice, because price is not the only consideration and because most major consumer goods are marketed on a national basis. Our system of open competition creates a never-ending need on the part of these manufacturers to get and maintain an edge, and sales promotion is the most powerful single force in this endeavor. And while advertising—*aka* "propaganda"—exists in virtually every modern economic environment, sales promotion can only exist in a free enterprise system. In America, consumers celebrate their choice of products, as the seemingly endless flow of product introductions and failures attest.

Perceived quality and brand loyalty are important, but consumers have overwhelmingly demonstrated that they want to be wooed. In supermarkets, for example, studies have shown that fully three out of four purchase decisions are made *after* consumers enter the store! Savvy marketers know that sales promotion is their most effective weapon in the "battle" of the open market place.

This newfound recognition of the power of sales promotion has also led to new challenges and opportunities. The need to manage the business of promotion marketing has created opportunities on the corporate side (to manage, track, evaluate and even create promotions), on the agency side (to create, execute, measure and analyze) and on the supplier side (everything from "low-tech" fulfillment and point-of purchase services to "high-tech" scanner data and analysis). Even advertising agencies have reluctantly accepted the reality (and overwhelming importance) of promotion marketing by buying or creating their own sales promotion agencies or departments.

Putting Promotion Into Perspective

So what is a consumer promotion? It is simply a consumer product or service that is combined with a special offer to motivate immediate or continued purchase. To be considered successful, its effect—the amount of "incremental sales" (those over and above the expected norm during a given period) that can be attributed to a specific promotion—must be measurable and its impact significant.

Sales promotion creates that "edge" through several recognizable vehicles:

Price Off

This seemingly mundane practice—a temporary reduction in the price of a product or group of products—actually has many applications, depending on the promotion goals:

- *"Sales Price"*—the standard deduction of the regular price, usually communicated through advertising, on the package, or at or near where the product is purchased (known in the trade as "point-of-purchase," e.g., an <u>end aisle</u> display in a supermarket).

- *Modified "Sale Price"*—which usually ties the purchase of several products together to create a sale price. For example, instead of simply saying "25% off any tire purchase," tire dealers might try to encourage multiple purchases by saying "Buy Three, Get One Free". The price-off commitment is the same, but a different, more-focused marketing goal is served.

- *Couponing*—Usually delivered through the mail, magazines or newspapers (e.g. via free-standing inserts—"FSIs"— those glossy inserts that always seem to be the first things that fall out of your Sunday newspaper), coupons are the most common sales promotion tool. They are conceptually identical to a sale price, except that they require a redemption process through the retailer (usually serviced by **fulfillment houses**).

  A variation on this theme are *cash rebate programs*, where the consumer must send in product proof-of-purchase (again, administered through a fulfillment house) to receive a rebate check. Because these offers usually involve either multiple purchases or expensive items (e.g., power tools), rebates are generally worth more to the consumer than coupons.

Value Added

As opposed to a price reduction, *"value added"* promotions offer consumers an extra incentive to motivate purchase, one usually not directly related to the product, These promotions may or may not also contain price reductions:

- *Sweepstakes*—possibly the easiest-understood promotion, sweepstakes are simply chance drawings from entries sent in to (guess what?) a fulfillment house, for generally impressive grand prizes of cash, merchandise or travel.

- *Contests*—essentially sweepstakes, except that the contest requires some level of skill and usually is more complicated. Marketers try to involve consumers quickly through contest devices like" Instant Win" and "Match & Win" formats. Sometimes contests can have secondary benefits, like public relations (e.g., themed essay contests), or cross trial (e.g., "winning" game cards that offer a free coupon for a new product line).

- *Free With Proof-Of-Purchase Offers*—offering a free gift as an incentive to purchase. If a single purchase is all that is required, the gift is usually attached to the packaging in some way. Gifts requiring multiple purchases are usually "fulfilled" like other forms of promotion.

- *"Self Liquidators"*—this intriguing term simply refers to promotions that require a cash outlay on the consumer's part in addition to proofs-of-purchase. Because of this shared responsibility, self-liquidated items are usually more expensive than free gifts. This shared cost is also an attractive consideration to the marketer, because cost liabilities don't become a factor until the item is actually ordered (unless pre-purchase is necessary), hence the term "self liquidator".

There are literally hundreds of variations and combinations of these basic elements, and applications only begin with consumer products. Entries into PMAA's Reggie Awards, symbolic of excellence in promotion marketing, have come from the fields of computers, financial services, airlines, auto parts, even building materials.

In other words, over $100 billion worth of creativity, analysis, management, fulfillment, production, etc. spent by companies that need bright people...people like you!

Finding Your Own Niche In Sales Promotion

Where do you find your start in sales promotion? For starters, there are thousands of consumer products, hundreds of companies that market them, hundreds of agencies that service the companies. Wherever you live or want to work, the opportunities are all around you.

Better still, practically every student starts out equal! That's because there's no MBA in Sales Promotion, no B.A. in Sales Promotion...no degree of any kind in sales promotion. A few universities like Northwestern, Texas and Syracuse offer courses, but marketing's most important new discipline still waits for its first academic department.

Opportunities In Corporate Promotion Departments

In the meantime, the college system's loss can be your gain. Just ask Forest Harwood, former Manager of Sales Promotion for Frito-Lay and Chairman Emeritus of the Promotion Marketing Association of America: "Promotion is the 'fun' part of the marketing mix," explains Harwood. "It's a career where your creative abilities can really shine."

But like many corporate promotion executives, Harwood (president of Harwood Marketing Group) looks for a solid business management background along with versatility in entry-level people: "Be prepared to juggle a variety of project aspects at one time. And remember: They all have to land together. That takes a lot of careful management, advanced planning and flexible perspective. You need to have a 'think fast, think clear, think-on-your-feet' approach to solutions."

Entry-level corporate salaries in promotion departments are about equal to other marketing department positions. Depending on the company, the part of the country and your qualifications, starting salaries can range from about $22,000 to $45,000 per year.

At the top end, new ground gets broken literally every day. At this writing, General Mills was reportedly offering an estimated package of $250,000 for their newly created Vice President of Promotion position.

Opportunities In Marketing Services Agencies

Where corporate promotion departments can provide relative security and control, marketing services agencies typically offer more excitement, more anxiety and more reward. Under the direction and supervision of corporate promotion managers, sales promotion and related agencies design, create, produce, execute, fulfill and measure the kinds of promotion programs mentioned earlier.

Entry-level people in these agencies typically work with the "nuts and bolts" of sales promotion. Don Roux, President of Roux Marketing Services, looks for people who can be both creative and detailed at the same time: "Client confidence and respect is our main goal, and even our entry-level account coordinators are key to this effort."

But Roux feels that being this close to the action requires a special kind of person: "The *account coordinator* position is at the center of a fast-paced, high-pressure environment, requiring an energetic, anxious to learn, personable individual."

Starting salaries may seem low at between $18,000 and $25,000, but commission and profit sharing can often supplement the base salary. More importantly, advancement can be rapid, because it is often closely tied to your personal performance.

In fact, Roux specifically looks for candidates with advancement potential: "In five years, you should be at the account executive level, where average earnings are $58,000 plus. After ten years, good account executives can be in the six figure area."

Like Harwood, Roux looks for people with solid marketing credentials, although he will also consider communication and finance majors. But bottom line is again often a matter of client perception, according to Roux, and everyone shares in that responsibility: "I look for people who can talk well on their feet, have the ability to see the big picture and to converse both 'knee-to-knee' and by telephone."

As Executive Director of the PMAA, a former vice president of a sales promotion firm and a manager at Pepsi-Cola USA, I have witnessed the growth of promotion marketing first hand. Simply put, sales promotion in the 1980s is to marketing what computers are to information management.

And even if you're not the next Lee Iacocca or Larry Bird, there's still plenty of room for you at Chrysler or in the NBA. Because people have the choice to buy their products, and because Lee and Larry alone aren't always enough incentive, each uses promotion marketing extensively.

And that is truly "America's Game!"

CHRIS SUTHERLAND assumed his current position in September, 1987. Previously, he was vice president at Marketing Equities International, a firm specializing in tie-in promotions, where he worked with Sony, Nabisco and Coca-Cola. He also headed up Sports Concepts, his own sports marketing consultancy.

From 1982 to 1985, he managed the national sports programs for Pepsi-Cola USA. In the public sector, he was responsible for managing all corporate-sponsored sports programs for Los Angeles (CA) County.

A graduate of California State University at Los Angeles, he and his wife, Arlene, reside in Ossining, NY. They have two children.

24

Starting Your Career At A Large Public Relations Counseling Firm

Jack Mitchell, Senior VP/Director of Human Relations
Burson Marsteller

Large firms tend to attract large clients who are facing broad-based challenges. This increases opportunities for strategizing, creativity, and for implementing a broad range of communications activities. Another asset of a large firm is the diversity of co-workers' backgrounds. This can mean more experienced role models, as well as exposure to greater variety in styles and approaches to solving business problems.

The large firm, often international and thus globally-oriented, also can afford better opportunity than a small firm can for understanding the complexities of worldwide business. Keeping in mind the industry trend toward globalization, availing yourself early of an international perspective may be tremendously helpful as your career progresses.

Whereas a small firm, often by necessity, is geared towards a certain specialization, the large firm often includes a combination of many specialties. Entire departments can focus on one particular type of client, i.e., the health-care department in which account handlers are specialists in the health-care industry; the consumer department wherein account handlers possess consumer marketing expertise; the hi-tech department comprised of individuals with the specialized technical knowledge needed to aid their clients in this competitive industry. In addition, there are often specialists in communications functions—media, audio-visual, exhibits, communications training, design, internal communications, and on and on.

Also, the large firm often has a broader range of support services available to the account handling staff. In-house libraries, computerized information services, production and printing, word processing departments, secretaries, and well-equipped mailrooms let the account person devote more time to direct client work and give the entry-level person invaluable experience at working with diverse groups.

Another major advantage of a large firm may be formalized training aimed at both the obvious, e.g., writing and editing, and the not-so-obvious, e.g., financial management and supervisory skills. During your interview with a large firm, ask what training is offered.

Other advantages of large firms may not be so apparent. For example, a person interested in working, say, in Hong Kong might ordinarily find it difficult to secure such a position. However, he or she could increase the chances of going to the Far East by joining a firm with offices there. It is important to keep in mind that firms transfer experienced employees more often than junior people. They do this because such experience may be required by the overseas office.

Some individuals who have not worked at a large firm may perceive size as a concern. They might fear they will "get lost." This is not the case if the individual has initiative. People who get involved in their clients' work and in the culture and programs of their firm, inevitably, are highly visible.

And remember, even the largest PR firms are really small or mid-sized companies compared to many U.S. corporations. The leaders in large firms make a concerted effort to know the value of the individuals who work in their company, since these people are so critical to the firm's success.

The Skills You Need

If the large firm appeals to you as a place to start, the next question you must ask yourself is "What must I bring to the job?" Public relations professionals are concerned when college graduates present themselves armed with a broad list of personal attributes, but are unaware of how lacking they are in the basic skills the industry needs. While still in school, you should focus your energies on acquiring the skills necessary to make you a top candidate for a position after graduation. Journalism and communications skills are obvious. No-so-obvious is a basic understanding of how businesses work.

I cannot emphasize too strongly the importance of a solid grasp of the fundamentals of the English language. Numerous studies have concluded that "Little Johnny/Mary can't read." The question facing public relations professionals, however, is: "Can Johnny/Mary write?" Basic writing skills—composition, grammar, spelling, punctuation—must be mastered. Most firms, large and small, make prospective candidates take a writing test. Firms repeatedly face the prospect of hiring from a pool of applicants who cannot pass this basic test. For example, applicants presented with the written text of a client speech too often are unable to identify the actual news in the speech and thus are unable to write the proper lead. You would be well-advised, while still in school, to have your writing critiqued by a journalist to ensure your basic competency in this area. In today's public relations job market, the candidate possessing solid writing skills is far better positioned to get the preferred job.

Another area of strong concern to public relations professionals (in fact, to business professionals at large) is the lack of general business knowledge. If you want "an edge" in the job market, become well-versed in current affairs and major business trends. A top executive, when addressing a gathering of students, has been known to ask "How many of you read the *New York Times* and the *Wall Street Journal* every morning?" It is surprising how few hands go up.

Unfortunately, university guidelines often hinder a student's ability to acquire the broad knowledge base so essential in today's business world. The communications curriculum, for example, usually does not allow for courses in accounting, as accounting is only for business majors. If you are fortunate enough to attend a school that has combined degree programs, such as communications/marketing, you should consider heading in this direction. The student who is well-rounded in both communications and business is far better prepared for facing the day-to-day challenges of the public relations business than the student whose knowledge is so specialized that it severely restricts his or her approach to solving a client's problems.

The Behavior You Need

Your personal goals and how you work are also an essential factor in your success. Large firms are looking for people who are achievement oriented and committed to their jobs, who work well in teams and share information willingly, and who are open to learning new things.

As a young account handler recently remarked, "You have to pay your dues, prove yourself, and show that you are committed. If you want to work in an agency, forget '9 to 5'."

A teamwork spirit is also important since it is a major part of firm life. At a major firm, working on complex, multi-faceted programs, teamwork—dividing that program into well-coordinated, discrete projects—ensures that all projects drive towards the same objective.

Securing A Public Relations Position

In most cases, the human resources professional will be the first person you will deal with at a large public relations firm. What is this individual looking for in your resume and cover letter? Much should be obvious. Your cover letter should be well-written and grammatically correct. A business-type letter, direct and to-the-point, is much more effective than attempts at clever creativity, unusual imagery, and other so-called attention grabbers (which, in fact, usually fall short and accomplish the opposite effect). The well-prepared resume (many guidebooks are available to assist you) is reviewed with an eye towards schools attended, grades obtained, course of study, major/minor, etc.

At a large firm, the ability to work well under pressure and to juggle a myriad of projects is also essential. Participation in a range of extracurricular activities during school while maintaining good academic standing is evidence of these capabilities. Experience with school newspapers, yearbooks, debating clubs and community periodicals are all good learning experiences and will make an excellent impression, too.

If your resume leads to further consideration, be prepared to meet with several different individuals, each of whom will assess your "fit" with their particular client. They will be looking for someone who speaks well, is focused on a career in communications, has a good sense of self, and projects a sense of leadership. Often, emphasis is not only on your ability to do the entry-level job, but also whether you have the potential to grow and be promoted within the organization.

Responsibilities and Expectations

The student entering a large public relations firm will meet people with a diversity of jobs and job titles. These titles reflect the different functions the individuals perform in the firm and the different experiences expected.

As people are promoted in a firm, they are expected to handle a larger number of, and more complex, programs. The expectation, too, is that they will think more and more broadly about the business. And, while the time frame for a project handled by a junior person may be one week or one month, a senior person is expected to work and think in one-year to five-year time frames.

At the entry-level, your job title will probably be *account representative* or *assistant account executive*, a position which primarily entails writing, writing and more writing! Add to this organizational and detail-oriented assignments—coordinating events, compilation of media lists, research, etc.—and you have a good idea of the types of activities the entry-level person handles.

You'll also spend time learning about the firm and its clients—their business, communications needs, marketing plans, competition, the environment in which they work, etc.

For the account representative, there is no such thing as a typical day. By its nature, public relations work is extremely varied in content, though a fast pace is a constant. One day can be a frenzy preparing for a press luncheon; the next can be spent reporting immediate results of that luncheon to a client. At a large firm, the opportunity to learn and develop is enhanced continuously as young account handlers move on to a variety of projects and clients, and even new departments, as new career opportunities and projects arise.

Compensation

There are certainly a number of professions where entry-level compensation is higher than in public relations. However, for the person who gets excited about communications, about the psychology of what makes people react, starting salary may not be of paramount importance. At this level, job satisfaction and potential are extremely important. This is not to imply, however, that your career cannot lead to a six-figure income. Success brings rewards.

Salaries differ, too, depending on locale. More than likely, a student directly out of college with no significant experience should expect to receive a starting salary in the New York City area of around $20,000. In addition to straight salary, you should consider whether the company provides bonuses, good savings plans, and solid medical and dental benefits.

Perhaps the most important element to keep in mind when embarking on your public relations career is *flexibility*. If, after reading this article, you find yourself leaning towards a career at a large firm, keep open to all opportunities that may present themselves. Each firm is unique and exploring all options is profitable. Although industry patterns may reveal that certain characteristics are prevalent in large firms, while still others prevail at smaller ones, the patient career detective will uncover what's best for him or her. A thorough review of opportunities and your own personal preferences should lead you to the firm best suited to your career ambitions.

JACK MITCHELL joined Burson-Marsteller in 1986 as senior vice president/director of human resources. Prior to 1986, Jack served as vice president, human resources at Benton & Bowles and at D'Arcy Masius Benton & Bowles. He has also held positions as director of training and development and director of human resources for Cadence Industries and began his career as a therapist.

25

Chances Are You Will Work For A "Small" PR Firm

Leonard Stein, President
Visibility Public Relations, Inc.

The public relations field may be dominated by several giant, multinational firms, but it is basically an industry populated by a multitude of "Davids," in which entrepreneurial zeal runs high. While it is commendable to set your sights on the stars, chances are you will spend at least part of your PR career in the employ of a "small" public relations agency. I've worked for both large and small firms and find that the small agency experience can provide a valuable training ground for talented, ambitious, young public relations professionals.

Is Bigger Best?

The big agency environment is highly formalized, bureaucratic, and rigidly structured. With its multiple levels of management and approvals for action, it seems to plod along compared to the "sprint" of a smaller shop. Entry-level professionals will generally be assigned to a single account, often for long periods of time, entrusted with little responsibility, and often saddled with the minutiae of agency life.

Life is not *all* bleak at big agencies. They have tremendous resources, big clients, large budgets, and name recognition. Some people are simply more comfortable in an institutional setting, others in an entrepreneurial environment; sooner or later, you'll have to decide which works for you.

Visibility Public Relations, Inc. is, in many ways, quite typical of the smaller, established agency. We do differ from many PR firms in that we operate a fully computerized office, which significantly enhances our productivity, enabling us to service on average a dozen clients with four PR professionals (president, account supervisor, senior account executive and account executive), two administrative assistants, and a part-time bookkeeper.

Situated in a loft space with an open floor plan, in which each professional has a modular workstation and Macintosh computer, the physical layout mirrors our operating structure—that of a team. We work closely under my supervision, sharing ideas, media contacts, and the day-to-day triumphs, anecdotes, and hassles of the business. In this environment, job titles are largely symbolic of one's professional tenure. In practice, each professional functions as an account executive, myself included, and is responsible for servicing three accounts.

Working on several accounts simultaneously provides excellent training, offers a constant challenge, ample variety, and sharpens one's ability to juggle projects and meet deadlines. It also means *you* are more accountable for the success of the PR program, placing more pressure upon your shoulders on a day-to-day basis. Life in a small agency can be more demanding than in a large firm, but you'll certainly never be bored. As in other professions, if you hope to excel in public relations, don't expect to put in a 9-5 day.

In general, I think you'll find greater opportunities at smaller firms. The economics of profitably operating a small agency virtually requires hiring junior people. This places a certain responsibility on the manager or owner to train the newcomer in exchange for a relatively meager entry-level salary.

One's first PR job should, more than anything else, provide you with paid on-the-job training, the opportunity to observe and participate in the PR process up close, to develop a PR specialty or special interest, and to decide whether small is beautiful or the big agency or corporate route is more appealing.

A Typical Day At A Small Firm

Monday presents a good example of a typical day at Visibility. In the morning, I meet with each PR professional to review their "to do" lists for the coming week. The same procedure holds for all levels, with the more experienced professionals requiring less supervision and support throughout the week. We operate on the Socratic principle: People are urged to think things through on their own, determine a course of action, present their decisions to me, and be ready to defend them. The professional staff is urged to ask questions before making decisions. I never criticize one for asking questions; it is far better to appear unsure than to boldly err, procedurally or strategically.

In the course of a typical day, an account executive might spend the morning writing a news release and photocaption, a company backgrounder, or an executive biography or doing research or interviews toward this end. Drafts of the materials are then faxed to the client for review, and revisions taken over the telephone for immediate document entry via computer. Next, client media lists are reviewed and customized for the specific project, and a work order, describing exactly what is to be mailed to whom, will be completed. The afternoon might be spent telephoning reporters to present a client's story or point of view on a particular issue, preparing a rough layout for an article reprint, or reviewing clippings and writing thank you notes to editors who have printed news of our clients.

The day's progress is not so tidy as this example reflects. Reporters may call at any time, especially near deadline, with questions or to request interviews, photos, or sample products. The account executive must break his routine to order a messenger or prepare an overnight mail package. Or a client may call with news, questions, or a request. This often occurs at lunch or 5 P.M. A successful account person is a juggler who always knows exactly which balls are in play and can keep them in the air, with (seemingly) little effort. Grace under pressure is a valued ability.

Dedicated public relations professionals don't punch the clock. The work day often extends in both directions according to the needs of our clients. One may come in early for a breakfast meeting or meet after the work day. The evening, without telephone interruptions, can be the best time to put in some undisturbed writing or thinking time. And, finally, there is the required reading, the homework of the professional. Account executives must keep up with their clients' industries, which means reading the leading trade journals. The best time to do this is on the train or at home at night.

Who We're All Looking For

An entry-level candidate must be energetic and eager to learn the PR business from the ground up. And, since I'm the boss, they must do things my way (what boss is different?). Candidates are more appealing if they demonstrate related communications job experience, whether in journalism, broadcasting, marketing, advertising, production, etc. Whether one majors in public relations or in journalism, it is still important to obtain a solid grounding in all communications processes, as well as in the liberal arts, sociology, psychology, business, etc.

In my opinion, the days of entering the public relations profession without a college degree are essentially over, especially as the Public Relations Society of America strives to secure the status of "profession" for its members. It is also increasingly rare that small agencies will hire college graduates fresh out of school, unless they have interned or can demonstrate exceptionally strong journalism skills or PR credentials. But many of these potential "rising stars" can hope to land their first job at a medium size or even a large PR firm. The older generation of journalists made the transition to public relations most successfully, followed by a generation of liberal arts graduates (I have a masters degree in history), and, more recently, by public relations and journalism majors. Today, the pendulum appears to again be swinging back in favor of those with a broader liberal arts education.

Classroom success in itself is not enough. Successful job candidates should be able to demonstrate involvement in extracurricular activities, especially those related to their chosen profession. Involvement—especially leadership in the PRSSA chapter or journalism society, editorship or reporting for the college paper, internships with local firms, or volunteer PR work for nonprofit organizations—is what can set you apart from your peers.

In my experience, intensely-curious, self-motivated generalists are better candidates than narrowly-focused, academic specialists or MBAs. However, if one hopes to earn the full respect of one's superiors and clients, especially if one hopes to one day enter the corporate or big agency arena, I cannot stress enough the importance of a solid understanding of basic business principles, the marketing process, and financial markets. In addition, becoming a consummate public relations professional virtually requires a desire to understand how the media works and a curiosity to widely explore its print and electronic offerings, even if they aren't of personal interest, in order to understand the mentality of those to whom they do appeal. So read new magazines, watch new TV programs. And learn.

Internships

Internships, especially at small firms, provide a close-up of the real PR world, which I believe helps students make a smoother transition from academe to the working world. Obtaining an internship may be difficult outside of major cities like New York, Los Angeles, or Chicago, and academic policy differs from school to school. We've hired several interns, and I would heartily recommend it to any aspiring public relations professional. Wherever you live or study, there are public relations internship opportunities, but you may have to create one for yourself. Follow your personal interests. Do you like animals? Visit the zoo or ASPCA. They usually have a public relations department. Volunteer. If you can't get paid, at least you can arrange to get credit and a letter of recommendation.

What You'll Earn

To attract qualified talent in New York, small agencies must offer salaries commensurate with larger firms. Our typical entry-level position is the *junior account executive*, who can expect to earn between $21,000 to $24,000 the first year on the job. The junior AE spot is basically a six-month to one-year training period. I prefer college educated individuals with little direct PR experience, because they are still free of bad habits or preconceived notions of the field. Every agency has its own way of doing things and "untraining" someone is a luxury in which the small agency manager simply cannot afford to indulge.

How Far Is Up?

Cindy joined the firm as a junior AE four years ago. She had a freshly-minted broadcast journalism degree from New York University, six months experience as a copy editor on a weekly newspaper, good people (interpersonal) skills, the ability to listen, the desire to learn, and the motivation to work hard to develop new PR skills.

In less than four years, she progressed through the ranks to account executive and, recently, to senior account executive, a title awarded in recognition of her successful handling of our largest account (Pfizer Pharmaceuticals) for the past two years. Her salary has increased commensurately, and she has become a fully-vested participant in the company's profit sharing plan. Since I am rather strict about handing out titles, her success represents what I expect is close to a best-case scenario for advancement at a small PR agency.

Am I Stuck Here Forever?

To be frank, I do not expect young professionals to be content to remain with a small agency forever. Long term, one's chances for career advancement can be severely limited at a small firm. There are simply less management spots. And small firms often pay less than big agencies or corporations. Because few management positions exist, unless the agency experiences sustained growth, opportunities for promotion remain limited. Realistically, once a young professional has learned all he or she can at a small agency, it's logical to seek new challenges.

If the PR world with its frenetic pace doesn't ultimately satisfy you, there can still be life after public relations. Unfortunately, much of what one learns as an account executive is not directly transferrable outside the realm of public relations. However, there is always a need for individuals with polished written and oral communication skills. There may be opportunities in related fields such as corporate communications, employee training, multi-media, industrial script writing, or executive recruiting.

And because a successful PR professional is, at heart, a good salesman, many doors to sales careers will open. The public relations profession is a lifelong learning experience, and knowledge has ways of opening doors to unexpected opportunities.

LEONARD STEIN has more than 17 years experience in marketing public relations with leading agencies and major corporations. He founded Visibility Public Relations in 1983, directing his practice toward emerging "Information Age" companies, consumer products manufacturers, and marketing services firms.

Prior to founding Visibility, Mr. Stein was director of public relations for Playboy Enterprises in New York City. Mr. Stein's public relations agency experience includes positions at top ten PR agencies, including Harshe, Rotman & Druck, Ketchum Communications and a large independent, the Geltzer Company. Prior to joining the agency side of the business, Mr. Stein was an assistant vice president and public relations manager for Home Savings of America, the nation's leading thrift institution.

A native of Los Angeles, he holds masters degrees in history and mass communications from California State University, Northridge, where he held California State Scholarships and a California State Graduate Fellowship. He is a member of the Public Relations Society of America and serves on its Technology Committee.

26

Breaking Into Public Relations In Canada

Brian Hemming, President & CEO
Hill and Knowlton Communications

One of the great things about the public relations profession is that many of its skills are transferable from one country to another. And as economies and media become ever more global in focus, the opportunities for international experience become increasingly exciting—and more in demand.

Part of the reason for this is that the basic skills required to be a good communicator are universal. It's safe to say that, essentially, what you need to enter PR in the United States is what you'll need to join the profession in Canada.

With few exceptions, the recommendations of other contributors to this *Career Directory* with regard to education, internships and involvement in industry associations are every bit as true for Canada as for the U.S.

Every employer in Canada will stress the importance of having a university degree with emphasis on the liberal arts and communications. Like employers in the States, they will be looking for evidence that along with your degree you've picked up some work experience through internships or summer employment. And, without fail, they'll be looking for strong writing skills and creativity. No matter what part of the business you may want to specialize in, the ability to think clearly, strategically and creatively—and to put your thoughts in writing—will be among the strongest attributes you will have.

There Are Differences

Now, having said that the basic skills are the same for entering the business in Canada and the U.S., there are some differences to be taken into account.

Size Of The Market

A convenient rule of thumb for comparing the size of Canadian markets with those of the U.S. is to divide the U.S. market by ten.

For the public relations business this often translates into smaller scale projects and correspondingly smaller budgets. However, many of the elements of a communications program are, in my experience, very similar, and practitioners in Canada can achieve the same level of professional satisfaction as their U.S. colleagues.

Canadian PR agencies vary in size just as much as U.S. firms, though the biggest ones in Canada are definitely smaller than their American counterparts. For example, Hill and Knowlton in Canada, which incorporates a public opinion research firm and a specialist government relations practice in addition to its other public relations practices, has a total of some 150 employees; in the U.S., Hill and Knowlton employs over 1,000.

Regional Differences

The majority of Canada's population is concentrated in Ontario and Quebec, and this is where the major PR agencies are located. However, well-established, small to medium-sized firms thrive in other provinces, serving the needs both of local clients and of clients in central Canada with markets and operations across the country.

The need to know two languages is, generally speaking, far more pressing in Canadian agencies than in American firms. In the province of Quebec, for example, it really isn't possible to work if you cannot speak French. In Ottawa, the national capital, there is a strong preference for bilingual staff. Even though the business language outside Quebec and Ottawa is predominantly English, bilingual candidates will have an edge over those with only one language. In fact, at Hill and Knowlton Toronto, we find ourselves continually executing dual-language campaigns to serve the needs of clients with interests in both the English-speaking and French-speaking markets.

Generalist Or Specialist?

As the public relations profession matures and expands, the trend towards specialization continues to grow. This tendency is certainly part of Canadian PR, although, again, the size of the market to some extent lessens the impact. While there are increasing opportunities for career development in areas such as government relations and public affairs, financial relations, environmental communications and so on, these specializations often come after some years in the business.

My recommendation is that new entrants into the field try to gain some experience in a variety of areas. An understanding of what's involved in various aspects of the business will give you an opportunity to decide where you want to direct your career. As well, broad experience increases your professional value because you have seen business from varying perspectives. Knowing how different parts of a company's operations interrelate enables you to provide the most realistic and effective counsel.

An environmental problem or some proposed legislation could have a marked impact on a company's marketing strategies. If you know about marketing communications as well as these other areas, you'll be in a much stronger position to develop strategies and plans that are sensitive to all aspects of the business.

So What's A Typical First Year?

What you do in your first year in a Canadian agency is probably not too much different from what you'd do in the U.S. But no matter where you practice, your job description depends on a number of things. It depends on the size of the agency, its client list, its specializations. But most important of all, it depends on you.

I don't know of any agency that isn't looking for good young people who are going to make a difference to the future prosperity of the business. If you are keen and show a willingness to do anything to learn more about the public relations business, you will create opportunities for yourself that will propel you ahead of someone just putting in time.

Despite everything we say about academic qualifications, there is simply no substitute for experience. You have to have faced certain situations to know how to deal with them. To a large extent this is a function of time, and time moves at its own pace no matter how quickly we try to gain experience. But you can squeeze more into your learning years by being a team member, learning by observation and by participation.

To double-check this idea, I asked some of our staff who had joined us last year to give me a summary of the kind of work they had been doing in their first year with us. I'm pleased to say their work was wide-ranging. It involved, of course, the usual media list preparation and researching of background material for proposals and events. It also included a good deal of direct media relations and writing, including first drafts of program ideas.

And most importantly, it included exposure to clients. No one in their first year is managing a client relationship, but nor are they kept out of sight. Our philosophy is that our junior people learn by being part of the process and taking an appropriate part in client meetings and dealing directly with clients on some aspects of an assignment. All this is part of the learning experience, and, in some ways, the most exciting education is found not in the classroom, but in the boardroom.

BRIAN HEMMING joined Hill and Knowlton (Canada) Limited in July 1984 as deputy manager and was appointed head of the Canadian operation in early 1985. He was named to his current position following the merger of Hill and Knowlton Canada and the Public Affairs Resource Group of Companies in February, 1989.

Mr Hemming was previously assistant general manager of Hill and Knowlton Australia Pty. Ltd., the Australian subsidiary of Hill and Knowlton, Inc., where he worked for eight years. During his seventeen years in the public relations business, Mr. Hemming has counselled many leading companies and organizations on all aspects of corporate, financial, and marketing communications. His clients have included major financial institutions, international mining companies, breweries, insurance companies and industrial products manufacturers. He has counselled these clients on a wide range of communications issues, from environmental crises, to corporate positioning, to takeovers and mergers, to general corporate communications strategy and planning.

Born in Australia, Mr. Hemming studied commerce at the University of Queensland. His earlier career included positions in investment sales, marketing, and marketing research.

Section 2

The Job
Search Process

27

Getting Started: Self Evaluation And Career Objectives

Getting a job may be a relatively simple one-step or couple-of weeks-process or a complex, months-long operation.

Starting, nurturing and developing a career (or even a series of careers) is a lifelong process.

What we'll be talking about in the five chapters that together form our Job Search Process are those basic steps to take, assumptions to make, things to think about if you want a job—especially a first job in some area of marketing and sales. But when these steps—this process—are applied and expanded over a lifetime, most if not all of them are the same procedures, carried out over and over again, that are necessary to develop a successful, lifelong, professional career.

What does all this have to do with putting together a resume, writing a cover letter, heading off for interviews, and the other "traditional" steps necessary to get a job? Whether your college graduation is just around the corner or a far-distant memory, you will continuously need to focus, evaluate and re-evaluate your response to the ever-changing challenge of your future: Just what do you want to do with the rest of your life? Whether you like it or not, you're all looking for that "entry-level opportunity."

You're already one or two steps ahead of the competition—you're sure (pretty sure?) you want to pursue a career in some area of marketing and sales. By heeding the advice of the many professionals who have written chapters for this *Career Directory*—and utilizing the extensive entry-level job, organization and publication listings we've included—you're well on your way to fulfilling that dream. But there are some key decisions and time-consuming preparations to make if you want to transform that hopeful dream into a real, live job.

The actual process of finding the right company, right career path, and, most importantly, the right first job, begins long before you start mailing out resumes to potential employers. The choices and decisions you make now are not irrevocable, but this first job will have a definite impact on the career options you leave yourself. To help you make some of the right decisions and choices along the way (and avoid the most notable traps and pitfalls), the following chapters will lead you through a series of organized steps. If the entire job search process we are recommending here is properly executed, it will undoubtedly help you land exactly the job you want.

If you're currently in high school and hope, after college, to land a job in some area of marketing or sales, then attending the right college, choosing the right major, and getting the summer work experience many companies look for are all important steps. Read the section of this *Career Directory* that covers the particular job specialty in which you're interested—many of the contributors have recommended colleges or graduate programs they favor.

If you're hoping to jump right into any of these jobs with*out* a college degree or other professional training, our best and only advice is—don't do it. As you'll soon see in the detailed information included in the *Job Opportunities Databank*, there are not *that* many job openings for students without a college degree. And why sales is a career one can often pursue without a degree, your upward mobility and ability to move into management may well be stymied without it.

The Concept Of A Job Search *Process*

These are the key steps in the detailed job search process we will cover in this and the following four chapters:

1. *Evaluating yourself*: Know thyself. What skills and abilities can you offer a prospective employer? What do you enjoy doing? What are your strengths and weaknesses? What do you *want* to do?

2. *Establishing your career objectives*: Where do you want to be next year, three years, five years from now? What do you ultimately want to accomplish in your career and your life?

3. *Creating a company target list*: How to prepare a "Hit List" of potential employers—researching them, matching their needs with your skills, and starting your job search assault. Preparing company information sheets and evaluating your chances.

4. *Networking for success:* Learning how to utilize every contact, every friend, every relative, and anyone else you can think of to break down the barriers facing any would-be marketing professional. How to organize your home office to keep track of your communications and stay on top of your job campaign.

5. *Preparing your resume:* How to encapsulate years of school and little actual work experience into a professional, selling resume. Learning when and how to use it.

6. *Preparing cover letters:* The many ordinary and the all-too-few extraordinary cover letters, the kind that land interviews and jobs.

7. *Interviewing:* How to make the interview process work for you—from the first "hello" to the first day on the job.

We won't try to kid you—it *is* a lot of work. To do it right, you have to get started early, probably quite a bit earlier than you'd planned. Frankly, we recommend beginning this process one full year prior to the day you plan to start work.

So if you're in college, the end of your junior year is the right time to begin your research and preparations. That should give you enough time during summer vacation to set up your files and begin your library research.

Whether you're in college or graduate school, one item may need to be planned even earlier—allowing enough free time in your schedule of classes for interview preparations and appointments. Waiting until your senior year to "make some time" is already too late. Searching for a full-time job is itself a full-time job! Though you're naturally restricted by your schedule, it's not difficult to plan ahead and prepare for your upcoming job search. Try to leave at least a couple of free mornings or afternoons a week. A day or even two without classes is even better.

Otherwise, you'll find yourself, crazed and distracted, trying to prepare for an interview in the ten-minute period between your Product Marketing lecture and your Entrepreneurship seminar. Not the best way to make a first impression and certainly not the way you want to approach an important meeting.

The Self-Evaluation Process

Learning about who you are, what you want to be, what you *can* be, are critical first steps in the job search process and, unfortunately, the ones most often ignored by job seekers everywhere, especially students eager to leave the ivy behind and plunge into the "real world." But avoiding this crucial self evaluation can hinder your progress and even damage some decent prospects.

Why? Because in order to land a job with a company at which you'll actually be happy, you need to be able to identify those firms and/or job descriptions that best match your own skills, likes and strengths. The more you know about yourself, the more you'll bring to this process and the more accurate the "match-ups." You'll be able to structure your presentation (resume, cover letter, interviews) to stress your most marketable skills and talents (and, dare we say it, conveniently avoid your weaknesses?). Later, you'll be able to evaluate potential employers and job offers on the basis of your own needs and desires. This spells the difference between waking up in the morning ready to enthusiastically tackle a new day of challenges and shutting off the alarm in the hopes the day (and your job) will just disappear.

Creating Your Self-Evaluation Form

Take a sheet of lined notebook paper. Set up eight columns across the top—Strengths, Weaknesses, Skills, Hobbies, Courses, Experience, Likes, Dislikes.

Now, fill in each of these columns according to these guidelines:

Strengths: Describe personality traits you consider your strengths (and try to look at them as an employer would)—e.g., persistence, organization, ambition, intelligence, logic, assertiveness, aggression, leadership, etc.

Weaknesses: The traits you consider glaring weaknesses—e.g., impatience, conceit, etc. (And remember: Look at these as a potential employer would. Don't assume that the personal traits you consider weaknesses will necessarily be considered negatives in the business world. You may be "easily bored," a trait that led to lousy grades early on because teachers couldn't keep you interested in the subjects they were teaching. Well, many entrepreneurs need ever-changing challenges. Strength or weakness?)

Skills: Any skill you have, whether you think it's marketable or not. Everything from basic business skills—like typing, word processing and stenography—to computer, accounting or teaching experience and foreign language literacy. Don't forget possibly obscure but marketable skills like "good telephone voice."

Hobbies: The things you enjoy doing that, more than likely, have no overt connection to career objectives. These should be distinct from the skills listed above, and may include activities such as reading, games, travel, sports and the like. While these may not be marketable in any general sense, they may well be useful in specific circumstances. (If you love travel, you may be perfect for that entry-level job working in P&G's International Department. And your "hobbies"— and the knowledge and expertise they've given you—may just get it for you!)

Courses: All the general subject areas (history, literature, etc.) and/or specific courses you've taken which may be marketable, you really enjoyed, or both.

Experience: Just the specific functions you performed at any part-time (school year) or full-time (summer) jobs. Entries may include "General Office" (typing, filing, answering phones, etc.), "Creative Selling," "Marketing 403," "Statistical Analysis," etc.

Likes: List all your "likes"—those important considerations that you haven't listed anywhere else yet. These might include the types of people you like to be with, the kind of environment you prefer (city, country, large places, small places, quiet, loud, fast-paced, slow-paced), and anything else which hasn't shown up somewhere on this form. However, try not to include entries which refer to specific jobs or companies. We'll list those on another form.

Dislikes: All the people, places and things you can easily live without.

Now assess the "marketability" of each item you've listed. In other words, are some of your likes, skills or courses easier to match to a specific job description, or do they have little to do with a specific job or company? Mark highly marketable skills with an "H." Use "M" to characterize those skills which may be marketable in a particular set of circumstances, "L" for those with minimal potential application to any job.

Referring back to the same list, decide if you'd enjoy using your marketable skills or talents as part of your everyday job—"Y" for yes, "N" for no. You may type 80 words a minute but truly despise typing or worry that stressing it too much will land you on the permanent clerical staff. If so, mark typing with an "N." (Keep one thing in mind—just because you dislike typing shouldn't mean you absolutely won't accept a job that requires it. Many do.)

Now, go over the entire form carefully and look for inconsistencies.

The Value Of A Second Opinion

There is a familiar misconception about the self-evaluation process that gets in the way of many new job applicants—the belief that it is a process which must be accomplished in isolation. Nothing could be further from the truth. Just because the family doctor tells you you need an operation doesn't mean you run right off to the hospital. Prudence dictates that you check out the opinion with another physician. Getting such a "second opinion"—someone else's, not just your own—is a valuable practice throughout the job search process, as well.

So after you've completed the various exercises in this chapter, review them with a friend, relative or parent. These second opinions may reveal some aspects of your self description on which you and the rest of the world differ. If so, discuss them, learn from them, and, if necessary, change some conclusions. Should everyone concur with your self evaluation, you will be reassured that your choices are on target.

Establishing Your Career Objectives

For better or worse, you now know something more of who and what you are. But we've yet to establish and evaluate another important area—your overall needs, desires and goals. Where are you going? What do you want to accomplish?

If you're getting ready to graduate from college or graduate school, the next five years are the most critical period of your whole career. You need to make the initial transition from college to the workplace, establish yourself in a new and completely unfamiliar company environment, and begin to build the professional credentials necessary to achieve your career goals.

If that strikes you as a pretty tall order, well, it *is*. Unless you've narrowly prepared yourself for a specific profession, you're probably most *ill*-prepared for any real job. Instead, you've (hopefully) learned some basic principles—research and analytical skills that are necessary for success at almost any level—and, more or less, how to think. Maybe how to write...a little. Or develop a marketing plan...a little less. Or type.

It's tough to face, but face it you must: No matter what your college, major or degree, all you represent right now is potential. How you package that potential and what you eventually make of it is completely up to you. And it's an unfortunate fact that many companies will take a professional with barely a year or two experience over *any* newcomer, no matter how promising. Smaller companies, especially, can rarely afford to hire someone who can't begin contributing immediately.

So you have to be prepared to take your comparatively modest skills and experience and package them in a way that will get you interviewed and hired. Quite a challenge.

But Is Marketing Right For *You?*

Presuming you now have a much better idea of yourself and where you'd like to be—job-, career- and life-wise in the foreseeable future—let's make sure some of your basic assumptions are right. We presume you purchased this **Career Directory** because you're considering a career in some area of marketing and sales. Are you sure? Do you know enough about the particular specialization you're heading for to decide whether it's right for you? Probably not. So start your research *now*—learn as much about your potential career field as you now know about

In Appendix A, we've listed all the trade organizations associated in some way with the marketing or sales functions. Where possible, we've included details on educational information available from these associations, but you should certainly consider writing each of the pertinent ones, letting them know you're interested in a career in their area of specialization, and that you would appreciate whatever help and advice they're willing to impart. You'll find many sponsor seminars and conferences throughout the country, some of which you may be able to attend.

In Appendix B, we've listed the trade publications dedicated to the highly specific interests of marketing and sales professionals. These magazines are generally not available at newsstands (unless you live in or near New York City), but you may be able to obtain back issues at your local library (most major libraries have extensive collections of such journals) or by writing to the magazines' circulation/subscription departments.

You may also try writing to the publishers and/or editors of these publications. State in your cover letter what career track you're considering and ask them for whatever help and advice they can offer. But be specific. These are busy professionals and they do not have the time or the inclination to simply "tell me everything you can about business-to-business marketing."

If you can afford it now, we strongly suggest subscribing to whichever trade magazines are applicable to the specialty you're considering. If you can't subscribe to all of them, make it a point to regularly read the copies that arrive at your local public or college library.

These publications may well provide the most imaginative and far-reaching information for your job search. Even a quick perusal of an issue or two will give you an excellent "feel" for the particular industry and job you're heading for. After reading only a few articles, you'll already get a handle on what's happening in the field and some of the peculiar and particular jargon. Later, more detailed study will aid you in your search for a specific job.

Authors of the articles themselves may well turn out to be important resources. If an article is directly related to your chosen specialty, why not call the author and ask some questions? You'd be amazed how willing many of these professionals will be to talk to you and answer your questions. They may even tell you about job openings at their companies! (But *do* use common sense—authors will not *always* respond graciously to your invitation to "chat about the business." And don't be *too* aggressive here.)

You'll find such research to be a double-edged sword. In addition to helping you get a handle on whether the area you've chosen is really right for you, you'll slowly learn enough about particular specialties, companies, products, etc., to actually sound like you know what you're talking about when you hit the pavement looking for your first job. And nothing is better than sounding like a pro...except being one.

Marketing Is It. Now What?

After all this research, we're going to assume you've reached that final decision—you really *do* want a career in marketing or sales. It is with this vague certainty that all too many of you will race off, hunting for any firm willing to give you a job. You'll manage to get interviews at a couple and, smiling brightly, tell everyone you meet, "I want a career in marketing (sales, market research, etc.)." The interviewers, unfortunately, will all ask the same awkward question—"What *exactly* do you want to do at our company?"—and that will be the end of that.

It is simply not enough to narrow your job search to a general function. And so far, that's all you've done. You must now establish a specific career objective—the job you want to start, the career you want to pursue. Interviewers will *not* welcome you with open arms if you're still vague about your career goals. If you've managed to get an "informational interview" with an executive whose company currently has no job openings, what is he supposed to do with your resume after you leave? Who should he send it to for future consideration? Since *you* don't seem to know exactly what you want to do, how's *he* going to figure it out? Worse, he'll probably resent your asking him to function as your personal career counselor.

Remember, the more specific your career objective, the better your chances of finding a job. It's that simple and that important. Naturally, before you declare your objective to the world, check once again to make sure your specific job target matches the skills and interests you defined in your self evaluation. Do not consider this step final until you can summarize your job/career objective in a single, short, accurate sentence.

28

Targeting Prospective Employers & Networking For Success

As you move along the job search path, one fact will quickly become crystal clear—it is primarily a process of **elimination**: Your task is to consider and research as many options as possible, then—for good reasons—*eliminate* as many as possible, attempting to continually narrow your focus.

The essential first step is to establish some criteria to evaluate potential employers. This will enable you to identify your target companies, those for whom you'd really like to work. (This process, as we've pointed out, is not specific to any industry or field; the same steps, with perhaps some research resource variations, are applicable to any job, any company, any industry.)

Take a sheet of blank paper and divide it into three vertical columns. Title it "Target Company—Ideal Profile." Call the left-hand column "Musts," the middle column "Preferences," and the right-hand column "Nevers."

We've listed a series of questions below. After considering each question, decide whether a particular criteria *must* be met, whether you would simply *prefer* it, or *never* would consider it at all. If there are other criteria you consider important, feel free to add them to the list below and mark them accordingly on your Profile.

1. What are your geographical preferences? U. S.? Canada? Europe? Anywhere you can get a job???

2. If you prefer to work in the U.S. or Canada, what area, state(s) or province(s)? If overseas, what area or countries?

3. Do you prefer a large city, small city, town, or somewhere as far away from civilization as possible?

4. In regard to question 3, any specific preferences?

5. Do you prefer a warm or cold climate?

6. Do you prefer a large or small company? Define your terms (by sales, income, employees, offices, etc.).

7. Do you mind relocating right now? Do you want to work for a company with a reputation for *frequently* relocating top people?

8. Do you mind travelling frequently? What percent do you consider reasonable? (Make sure this matches the normal requirements of the job specialization you're considering.)

9. What salary would you *like* to receive (put in the "Preference" column)? What's the *lowest* salary you'll accept (in the "Must" column)?

10. Are there any benefits (such as an expense account, medical and/or dental insurance, company car, etc.) you must or would like to have?

11. Are you planning to attend graduate school at some point in the future; if so, is a tuition reimbursement plan important to you?

12. Do you feel a formal training program necessary?

13. What kinds of specific accounts would you prefer to work with? What specific types of products (if you have a choice)?

It's important to keep revising this new form, just as you should continue to update your Self-Evaluation Form. After all, it contains the criteria by which you will judge every potential employer. Armed with a complete list of such criteria, you're now ready to find all the companies that match them.

Targeting Individual Companies

To begin creating your initial list of targeted companies, start with the four chapters of our *Job Opportunities Databank*. These firms completed questionnaires we supplied, providing us (and you!) with a plethora of data concerning their overall operations, hiring practices, and other important information on entry-level job opportunities. All of the detailed information in these chapters was provided by the companies themselves. To our knowledge, it is available *only* in this *Career Directory.*

We have attempted to include information on those large and medium-sized companies that represent most of the entry-level jobs out there. But there are, of course, many other firms of all sizes and shapes that you may also wish to research. In the next section, we will discuss some other reference books you can use to obtain more information on the firms we've listed, as well as those we haven't.

Other Reference Tools

In order to obtain some of the detailed information you need, you will probably need to do further research, either in the library or by meeting and chatting with people familiar with the companies in which you're interested.

The most helpful book for you to study if you're hoping to work in marketing, sales or market research for a major corporation (on the "client side" of the business is the Standard Directory of Advertisers (the Advertiser Red Book). To check out ad agencies, use its companion, the Standard Directory of Advertising Agencies (the Agency Red Book). Your local library will probably have a copy of each (and, given their exorbitant cost, you probably shouldn't think of actually buying either one).

As you narrow your target list, you may want to check other sources, both advertising-oriented and general directories. The annual Ad Dollar Summary (available from Leading National Advertisers, 130 Madison Ave., 5th Floor, New York, NY 10002) is the book the industry uses to chart exact ad spending in all media (TV, radio, newspapers, magazines and outdoor). If you're considering a specific company, this book will give you a good feel for the amount they spend and the type of advertising you'd wind up working on.

A regionalized series of books which contains extensive information on both agencies and advertisers is Adweek's Directory of Advertising. It lists agencies, brands and client companies, media companies and service companies. It may well supply some additional information on targeted agencies or companies and should be available in your local library. There are six regional editions: West, Midwest, East, New England, Southwest and Southeast.

If you're particularly interested in working for a market research firm, the Green Book (International Directory of Marketing Research Houses and Services), published by the New York Chapter of the American Marketing Association, is an excellent companion to this *Directory*.

For more general research (pertinent to all companies), you might want to start with How To Find Information About Companies (Washington Researchers); the Encyclopedia of Business Information Sources (Gale Research, Book Tower, Detroit, MI 48226); and/or the Guide to American Directories (B. Klein Publications, P.O. Box 8503, Coral Springs, FL 33065), which lists directories for over 3,000 fields.

If you want to work for an association in marketing or one of its allied fields, we've listed all those in Appendix A. Other associations may be researched in the Encyclopedia of Associations (Gale Research Co.) or National Trade and Professional Associations of the United States (Columbia Books, Inc., 777 14th St., NW, Suite 236, Washington, DC 20005).

There are, in addition, many general corporate directories, biographical indexes, statistical abstracts, etc., etc.—from Gale Research, Dun & Bradstreet, Standard & Poor's, Ward's and others—which may give you additional information on major companies and their executives. These volumes—and more such directories seem to be published every month—should all be available in the reference (and/or business) section of your local library.

The trade magazines which you've been studying (and to which you've already subscribed) will offer a steady stream of information. Become as familiar as possible with individual companies, products, ad and marketing campaigns, issues, jargon, topics covered, etc.

One last note on potential sources of leads. The Oxbridge Directory of Newsletters, 7th Edition (available from Oxbridge Communications, 150 Fifth Ave., Suite 301, New York, NY 10011) lists details of more than 17,000 newsletters in a plethora of industries and might well give you some ideas and names. And the Professional Exhibits Directory (Gale Research Co.) lists more than 2,000 trade shows and conventions. Such shows are excellent places to "run into" sales reps, product managers, agency personnel, etc. and offer unexpected opportunities to learn about the business "from the horse's mouth."

Ask The Person Who Owns One

Some years ago, this advice was used as the theme for a highly successful automobile advertising campaign. The prospective car buyer was encouraged to find out about the product by asking the (supposedly) most trustworthy judge of all—someone who was already an owner.

You can use the same approach in your job search. You all have relatives or friends already out in the workplace—these are your best sources of information about those industries. Cast your net in as wide a circle as possible. Contact these valuable resources. You'll be amazed at how readily they will answer your questions. I suggest you check the criteria list at the beginning of this chapter to formulate your own list of pertinent questions. Ideally and minimally you will want to learn: how the industry is doing, what its long-term prospects are, the kinds of personalities they favor (aggressive, low key), rate of employee turnover, and the availability of training.

The Other Side Of The Iceberg

You are now better prepared to choose those companies that meet your own list of criteria. But a word of caution about these now-"obvious" requirements—they are not the only ones you need to take into consideration. And you probably won't be able to find all or many of the answers to this second set of questions in any reference book—they *are* known, however, by those persons already at work in the industry. Here is the list you will want to follow:

Promotion—If you are aggressive about your career plans, you'll want to know if you have a shot at the top. Look for companies that traditionally promote from within.

Training—Look for companies in which your early tenure will actually be a period of on-the-job training, hopefully ones in which training remains part of the long-term process. As new techniques and technologies enter the workplace, you must make sure you are updated on these skills. Most importantly, look for training that is craft- or function-oriented—these are the so-called **transferrable skills**, ones you can easily bring along with you from job-to-job, company-to-company, sometimes industry-to-industry.

Salary—Some industries are generally high paying, some not. But even an industry with a tradition of paying abnormally low salaries may have particular companies or job functions (like sales) within companies that command high remuneration. But it's important you know what the industry standard is.

Benefits—Look for companies in which health insurance, vacation pay, retirement plans, stock purchase opportunities, and other important employee benefits are extensive...and company paid. If you have to pay for basic benefits like medical coverage yourself, you'll be surprised at how expensive they are. An exceptional benefit package may even lead you to accept a lower-than-usual salary.

Unions—Make sure you know about the union situation in each industry you research. Periodic, union-mandated salary increases are one benefit non-union workers may find hard to match.

Making Friends And Influencing People

Networking is a term you have probably heard; it is definitely a key aspect of any successful job search and a process you must master. **Informational interviews** and **job interviews** are the two primary outgrowths of successful networking. **Referrals,** an aspect of the networking process, entail using someone else's name, creden-tials and recommendation to set up a receptive environment when seeking a job interview.

All of these terms have one thing in common: Each depends on the actions of other people to put them in motion.

So what *is* networking? *How* do you build your own network? And *why* do you need one in the first place? The balance of this chapter answers all of those questions and more.

Get your telephone ready. It's time to make some friends.

Not The World's Oldest Profession, But...

As Gekko, the high-rolling corporate raider, sneers in the movie *Wall Street:* "Any schmuck can analyze stock charts. What separates the players from the sheep is **information.**" Networking is the process of creating your own group of relatives, friends and acquaintances who can feed you the information *you* need to find a job—identifying where the jobs are and giving you the personal introductions and background data necessary to pursue them.

If the job market were so well-organized that details on all employment opportunities were immediately available to all applicants, there would be no need for such a process. Rest assured the job market is *not* such a smooth-running machine—most applicants are left very much to their own devices. Build and use your own network wisely and you'll be amazed at the amount of useful job intelligence you will turn up.

While the term networking didn't gain prominence until the 1970s, it is by no means a new phenomenon. A selection process that connects people of similar skills, backgrounds and/or attitudes—in other words, networking—has been in existence in a variety of forms for centuries. Attend any Ivy League school and you're automatically part of its very special centuries-old network.

Major law firms are known to favor candidates from a preferred list of law schools—the same ones the senior partners attended. Washington, D.C. and Corporate America have their own network—the same corporate bigwigs move back and forth from boardroom to Cabinet Room. The Academia-Washington connection is just as strong—notice the number of Harvard professors (e.g., Henry Kissinger, John Kenneth Galbraith) who call Washington their second home? No matter which party is in power, certain names just keep surfacing as Secretary of This or Undersecretary of That. No, networking is not new. It's just left its ivory tower and become a well-publicized process *anyone* can and should utilize in their lifelong career development.

And it works. Remember your own reaction when you were asked to recommend someone for a job, club or school office? You certainly didn't want to look foolish, so you gave it some thought and tried to recommend the best-qualified person that you thought would "fit in" with the rest of the group. It's a built-in screening process—what's more natural than recommending someone who's "our kind of _____?"

Creating The Ideal Network

As in most endeavors, there's a wrong way and a right way to network. The following tips will help you construct your own wide-ranging, information-gathering, interview-generating group—*your* network.

Diversify

Unlike the Harvard or Princeton network—confined to former graduates of each school—*your* network should be as diversified and wide-ranging as possible. You never know who might be in a position to help, so don't limit your group of friends. The more diverse they are, the greater the variety of information they may supply you with.

Don't Forget...

...to include everyone you know in your initial networking list: friends, relatives, social acquaintances, classmates, college alumni, professors, teachers; your dentist, doctor, family lawyer, insurance agent, banker, travel agent; elected officials in your community; ministers; fellow church members; local tradesmen; local business or social club officers. And everybody *they* know!

Be Specific

Make a list of the kinds of assistance you will require from those in your network, then make specific requests of each. Do they know of jobs at their company? Can they introduce you to the proper executives? Have they heard something about or know someone at the company you're planning to interview with next week?

The more organized you are, the easier it will be to target the information you need and figure out who might have it. Calling everyone and simply asking for "whatever help you can give me" is unfair to the people you're calling and a less effective way to garner the information you need.

Learn The Difference...

...between an **informational** interview and a **job** interview. The former requires you to cast yourself in the role of information gatherer; *you* are the interviewer and knowledge is your goal—about an industry, company, job function, key executive, etc. Such a meeting with someone already doing what you soon *hope* to be doing is by far the best way to find out everything you need to know...before you walk through the door and sit down for a formal job interview, at which time your purpose is more sharply defined: to get the job you're interviewing for.

If you learn of a specific job opening during an informational interview, you are in a position to find out details about the job, identify the interviewer and, possibly, even learn some things about him or her. In addition, presuming you get your contact's permission, you may be able to use his or her name as a referral. Calling up the interviewer and saying, "Joan Smith in your Research department suggested I contact you regarding openings for sales reps," is far superior to "Hello. Do you have any job openings at your company?"

(In such a case, be careful about referring to a specific job opening, even if your contact told you about it. It may not be something you're supposed to know about. By presenting your query as an open-ended question, you give your prospective employer the option of exploring your background without further commitment. If there is a job there and you're qualified for it, you'll find out soon enough.)

Don't Waste A Contact

Not everyone you call on your highly-diversified networking list will know about a job opening. It would be surprising if each one did. But what about *their* friends and colleagues? It's amazing how everyone knows someone who knows someone. Ask—you'll find that someone.

Value Your Contacts

If someone has provided you with helpful information or an introduction to a friend or colleague, keep him or her informed about how it all turns out. A referral that's panned out should be reported to the person who opened the door for you in the first place. Such courtesy will be appreciated...and may lead to more contacts. If someone has nothing to offer today, a call back in the future is still appropriate and may pay off.

The lesson is clear: Keep your options open, your contact list alive. Detailed records of your network—whom you spoke with, when, what transpired, etc.—will help you keep track of your overall progress and organize what can be a complicated and involved process.

Informational Interviews

You were, of course, smart enough to include John Fredericks, the bank officer who handled your dad's mortgage, on your original contact list. He knew you as a bright and concientious college senior; in fact, your perfect three-year repayment record on the loan you took out to buy that '77 Plymouth impressed him. When you called him, he was happy to refer you to his golfing buddy, Bob Jones, a marketing VP at Big Books, Inc. Armed with permission to use Fredericks' name and recommendation, you wrote a letter to Bob Jones, the gist of which went something like this:

> I am writing at the suggestion of Mr. Fredericks at Fidelity National Bank. He knows of my interest in book publishing, specifically in marketing, and, given your position at Big Books, thought you may be able to help me get a clearer understanding of it and how I might eventually be able to fit in.
>
> While I am majoring in marketing and minoring in English, I know I need to speak with professionals such as yourself to get a better understanding of the "big picture." If you could spare a half hour to meet with me, I'm certain I would be able to get enough information to give me the direction I need.
>
> I'll call your office next week in the hope that we can schedule a meeting.

Send a copy of this letter to Mr. Fredericks at the bank—it will refresh his memory should Mr. Jones call to inqure about you. Next step: the follow-up phone call. After you get Mr. Jones' secretary on the line, it will, with luck, go something like this:

> "Hello, I'm Mr. Paul Smith. I'm calling in reference to a letter I wrote to Mr. Jones requesting an appointment."
>
> "Oh, yes. You're the young man interested in our sales rep training program. Mr. Jones can see you on June 23rd. Will 10 A.M. be satisfactory?"
>
> "That's fine. I'll be there."

Well, the appointed day arrives. Well-scrubbed and dressed in your best (and most conservative) suit, you are ushered into Mr. Jones' office. He offers you coffee (you decline) and says that it is okay to light up if you wish to smoke (you decline). The conversation might go something like this:

> **You:** "Thank you for seeing me, Mr. Jones. I know you are busy and appreciate your taking the time to talk with me."
>
> **Jones:** "Well it's my pleasure since you come so highly recommended. I'm always pleased to meet someone interested in my field."
>
> **You:** "As I stated in my letter, my interest in book marketing is very real, but I'm having trouble seeing how all of my studies fit into the big picture. I think I'll be much better prepared to evaluate future job offers if I can learn how everything fits. May I ask you a few questions about the sales and marketing functions at Big Books?"

Mr. Jones relaxes. He realizes this is a knowledge hunt you are on, not a thinly-veiled job interview. Your approach has kept him off the spot—he doesn't have to be concerned with making a hiring decision. You've already gotten high marks for not putting him on the defensive. From this point on, you will be able to ask anything and everything you need to find out—not just about the sales and marketing functions at "book publishers" in general, but specifically about the training program at Big Books (which is what you're really interested in).

You should have made a detailed list of the questions you want answers to. Ask away. Take notes. What's happening in the field? What's happening at Big Books? Where can you fit in?—Don't be afraid to ask pointed questions like, "Given my course work (hand him your resume), where would I best fit in at a company like Big Books?"

After The Interview

The next step should be obvious: *Two* thank-you letters are required, one to Mr. Jones, the second to Mr. Fredericks. Get them both out immediately. (And see chapter 30 if you need help writing them.)

Keeping Track of The Interview Trail

Let's talk about record keeping again. If your networking works the way it's supposed to, this was only the first of many such interviews. Experts have estimated that the average person could develop a contact list of 250 people. Even if we limit your initial list to only 100, if each of them gave you one referral, your list would suddenly have 200 names. Presuming that it will not be necessary or helpful to see all of them, it's certainly possible that such a list could lead to 100 informational and/or job interviews! Unless you keep accurate records, by the time you're on No. 50, you won't even remember the first dozen!

So get the results of each interview down on paper. Use whatever format you're comfortable with. You should create some kind of file, folder or note card that is an "Interview Recap Record." It should be set up and contain something like the following:

Name: Big Books, Inc.

Address: 333 Broad St., NY, NY 10000

Phone: (212) 666-6666

Contact: Robert L. Jones

Type of Business: Hardcover & paper trade books—all subjects

Referral Contact: Mr. Fredericks, Fidelity National Bank

Date: June 23, 1990

At this point, you should add a one- or two-paragraph summary of what you found out at the meeting. Since these comments are for your eyes only, you should be both objective and subjective. State the facts—what you found out in response to your specific questions—but include your impressions—your estimate of the opportunities for further discussions, your chances for future consideration for employment.

"I Was Just Calling To..."

Find any logical opportunity to stay in touch with Mr. Jones. You may, for example, let him know when you graduate and tell him your Grade Point Average, carbon him on any letters you write to Mr. Fredericks, even send a congratulatory note if his company's year-end financial results are positive or if you read something in the local paper about his department or one of Big Books' titles. This type of follow up has the all-important effect of keeping you and your name in the forefront of others' minds. Out of sight *is* out of mind. No matter how talented you may be or how good an impression you made, you'll have to work hard to "stay visible."

There Are Rules, Just Like Any Game

It should already be obvious that the networking process is not only effective, but also quite deliberate in its objectives. There are two specific groups of people you must attempt to target: those who can give you information about an industry or career area and those who are potential employers. The line between these groups may often blur. Don't be concerned—you'll soon learn when (and how) to shift the focus from interview*er* to interview*ee*.

To simplify this process, follow a single rule: Show interest in the field or job area under discussion, but wait to be asked about actually working for that company. During your informational interviews, you will be surprised at the number of times the person you're interviewing turns to you and asks, "Would you be interested in...?" Consider carefully what's being asked and, if you *would* be interested in the position under discussion, make your feelings known.

What's It All About (Alfie)?

- To unearth current information about the industry, company and pertinent job functions. Remember: Your knowledge and understanding of broad industry trends, financial health, hiring opportunities, and the competitive picture are key.

- To investigate each company's hiring policies—who makes the decisions, who the key players are (personnel, staff managers), whether there's a hiring season, whether they prefer applicants going direct or through recruiters, etc.

- To sell yourself—discuss your interests and research activities—and leave your calling card, your resume.

- To seek out advice on refining your job search process.

- To obtain the names of other persons (referrals) who can give you additional information on where the jobs are and what the market conditions are like.

- To develop a list of follow-up activities that will keep you visible to key contacts.

If The Process Scares You

Some of you will undoutedly be hesitant about, even fear, the networking process. It is not an unusual response—it is very human to want to accomplish things "on your own," without anyone's help. Understandable and commendable as such independence might seem, it is, in reality, an impediment if it limits your involvement in this important process. Networking has such universal application because *there is no other effective way to bridge the gap between job applicant and job.* Employers are grateful for its existence. You should be, too.

Whether you are a first-time applicant or reentering the work force now that the children are grown, the networking process will more than likely be your point of entry. Sending out mass mailings of your resume and answering the help wanted ads may well be less personal (and, therefore, "easier") approaches, but they will also be far less effective. The natural selection process of the networking phenomenon is your assurance that water does indeed seek its own level—you will be matched up with companies and job opportunities in which there is a mutual fit.

Six Good Reasons To Network

Many people fear the networking process because they think they are "bothering" others with their own selfish demands. Nonsense! There are good reasons—six of them, at least—why the people on your networking list will be *happy* to help you:

1) *Some day you will get to return the favor.* An ace insurance salesman built a successful business by offering low-cost coverage to first-year medical students. Ten years later, these now-successful practitioners remembered the company (and person) that helped them when they were just getting started. He gets new referrals every day.

2) *They, too, are seeking information.* If you sense that your "brain is being picked" about the latest case studies being used in your marketing courses, be forthcoming with your information. Why not let the interviewer "audit" your course? It may be the reason he or she agreed to see you in the first place.

3) *Internal politics*—Some people will see you simply to make themselves appear powerful, implying to others in their organization that they have the authority to hire (they may or may not), an envied prerogative.

4) *They're "saving for a rainy day"*—Executives know that it never hurts to look and that maintaining a backlog of qualified candidates is a big asset when the floodgates open and supervisors are forced to hire quickly.

5) *They're just plain nice*—Some people will see you simply because they feel it's the decent thing to do or because they just can't say "no."

6) *They are looking themselves*—Some people will see you because they are anxious to do a friend (whoever referred you) a favor. Or because they have another friend seeking new talent, in which case you represent a referral *they* can make (part of their own continuing network process). You see, networking never *does* stop—it helps them and it helps you.

Before you proceed to the next chapter, begin making your contact list. You may wish to keep a separate sheet of paper or note card on each person (especially the dozen or so you think are most important), even a separate telephone list to make your communications easier and more efficient. However you set up your list, be sure to keep it up to date—it won't be long before you'll be calling each and every name on the list.

29

Preparing Your Resume

Your resume is a one- or two-page summary of you—your education, skills, employment experience, and career objective(s). It is *not* a biography—just a quick way to identify and describe you to potential employers. Most importantly, its *real* purpose is to *sell* you to the company you want to work for. It must set you apart from all the other applicants (those competitors) out there.

So, as you sit down to formulate your resume, remember you're trying to present the pertinent information in a format and manner that will convince an executive to grant you an interview, the prelude to any job offer. (If you feel you need more help in resume preparation, or even in the entire job search area, we recommend <u>Your First Resume</u> by Ronald W. Fry.)

An Overview Of Resume Preparation

- **Know what you're doing**—your resume is a personal billboard of accomplishments. It must communicate your specific worth to a prospective employer.

- **Your language should be action-oriented,** full of "doing"-type words. And less is better than more. Be concise and direct; don't worry about complete sentences.

- **Be persuasive.** In those sections that allow you the freedom to do so, don't hesitate to communicate your worth in the strongest language. This does *not* mean a long list of self-congratulatory superlatives; it *does* mean truthful claims about your abilities and the evidence (educational, experiential) that supports them.

- **Don't be cheap or gaudy.** Don't hesitate to spend the few extra dollars necessary to present a professional-looking resume. Do avoid outlandish (and generally ineffective) gimmicks like over-sized or brightly-colored paper.

- **Find an editor.** Every good writer needs one, and you are *writing* your resume. At the very least, it will offer you a second set of eyes proofreading for embarrassing typos. But if you are fortunate enough to have a professional in the field—a recruiter or personnel executive—critique a draft, grab the opportunity.

- **If you're the next Michaelangelo,** so multi-talented that you can easily qualify for jobs in different career areas, don't hesitate to prepare two or more completely different resumes. This will enable you to change the emphasis on your education and skills according to the specific career objective on each resume, a necessary alteration that will correctly target each one.

- **Choose the proper format.** There are only three we recommend—chronological, functional and combination. It's important you use the one that's right for you.

The Records You Need

The resume-writing process begins with the assembly and organization of all the personal, educational and employment data from which you will choose the pieces that actually end up on paper. If this information is properly organized, writing your resume will be a relatively easy task, a simple process of just shifting data from one format (record-keeping sheets) to another (the resume format you'll use later in this chapter, including a fill-in-the-blanks form).

As you will soon see, there is a lot of information you'll need to keep track of. In order to avoid a fevered search for important information, take the time right now to designate a single location in which to store all your records. My recommendation is either a filing cabinet or an expandable pocket portfolio. The latter is less expensive, yet it will still enable you to sort your records into an unlimited number of more-manageable categories.

Losing important report cards, citations, letters, etc., is easy to do if your life's history is scattered throughout your room or, even worse, your house! While copies of many of these items may be obtainable, why put yourself through all that extra work? Making good organization a habit will ensure that all the records you need to prepare your resume will be right where you need them *when* you need them.

For each of the categories summarized below, designate a separate file drawer or, at the very least, file folder in which pertinent records can be kept. Your own notes are important, but keeping actual report cards, award citations, letters, etc. is even more so. Here's what your record-keeping system should include:

Transcripts (Including GPA And Class Rank Information)

Transcripts are your school's official record of your academic history, usually available, on request, from your high school's guidance office or college registrar's office.

Your college may charge you for copies and "on request" doesn't mean "whenever you want"—you may have to wait some time for your request to be processed (so *don't* wait until the last minute!).

Your school-calculated GPA (Grade Point Average) is on the transcript. Most schools calculate this by multiplying the credit hours assigned to each course times a numerical grade equivalent (e.g., "A" = 4.0, "B" = 3.0, etc.), then dividing by total credits/courses taken. Class rank is simply a listing of GPAs, from highest to lowest.

Employment Records

Details on every part-time or full-time job you've held, including:

- Each employer's name, address and telephone number
- Name of supervisor
- Exact dates worked
- Approximate numbers of hours per week
- Specific duties and responsibilities
- Specific skills utilized
- Accomplishments, honors
- Copies of awards, letters of recommendation

Volunteer Activities

Just because you weren't paid for a specific job—stuffing envelopes for the local Republican candidate, running a car wash to raise money for the homeless, manning a drug hotline—doesn't mean that it wasn't significant or that you shouldn't include it on your resume. So keep the same detailed notes on these volunteer activities as you have on the jobs you've held:

- Each organization's name, address and telephone number
- Name of supervisor
- Exact dates worked
- Approximate numbers of hours per week
- Specific duties and responsibilities
- Specific skills utilized
- Accomplishments, honors
- Copies of awards, letters of recommendation

Extracurricular Activities

List all sports, clubs or other activities in which you've participated, either inside or outside school. For each, you should include:

- Name of activity/club/group
- Office(s) held
- Purpose of club/activity
- Specific duties/responsibilities
- Achievements, accomplishments, awards

Honors And Awards

Even if some of these honors are previously listed, the following specific data on every honor or award you receive should be kept in your awards folder:

- Award name
- Date and from whom received
- What it was for
- Any pertinent details

Military Records

Complete military history, if pertinent, including:

- Dates of service
- Final rank awarded
- Duties and responsibilities
- All citations and awards
- Details on specific training and/or special schooling
- Skills developed
- Specific accomplishments

Creating Your First Resume

There are a lot of options about what to include or leave out. In general, we suggest you always include the following data:

- Your name, address and telephone number
- Pertinent educational history (grades, class rank, activities, etc.)
- Pertinent work history
- Academic honors
- Memberships in organizations
- Military service history (if applicable)

You have the option of including the following:

- Your career objective
- Personal data
- Hobbies
- Summary of qualifications

And you should *never* include the following:

- Photographs or illustrations (of yourself or anything else) unless they are required by your profession—e.g., actors' composites
- Why you left past jobs
- References
- Salary history or present salary objectives/requirements (if salary history is requested in an ad, include it in your cover letter)
- Feelings about travel or relocation

Special note: There is definitely a school of thought that discourages any mention of personal data—marital status, health, etc.—on a resume. While I am not vehemently opposed to including such information, I am not convinced it is particularly necessary, either.

As far as hobbies go, I would only include such information if it were in some way pertinent to the job/career you're targeting. Your love of reading is pertinent if, for example, you are applying for a part-time job at a library. But including details on the joys of "hiking, long walks with my dog and Isaac Asimov short stories" is rarely correct.

Maximizing Form And Substance

Your resume should be limited to a single page if possible, two at most. When you're laying out the resume, try to leave a reasonable amount of "white space"—generous margins all around and spacing between entries. It should be typed or printed (not Xeroxed) on 8 1/2" x 11" white, cream or ivory stock. The ink should be black or, at most, a royal blue.

Don't scrimp on the paper quality—use the best bond you can afford. And since printing 100 or even 200 copies will cost little more than 50, if you do decide to print your resume, *over*estimate your needs, and opt for the highest quantity you think you may need. Prices at various "quick print" shops are not exorbitant; the quality look printing affords will leave the right impression.

Use Power Words For Impact

Be brief. Use phraseology rather than complete sentences. Your resume is a summary of your talents, not a term paper. Choose your words carefully and use "power words" whenever possible. "Organized" is more powerful than "put together;" "supervised" better than "oversaw;" "formulated" better than "thought up."

Strong words like these can make the most mundane clerical work sound like a series of responsible, professional positions. And, of course, they will tend to make your resume stand out. Here's a starter list of words that you may want to use in your resume:

achieved	administered	advised
analyzed	applied	arranged
budgeted	calculated	classified
communicated	completed	computed
conceptualized	coordinated	critiqued
delegated	determined	developed
devised	directed	established
evaluated	executed	formulated
gathered	generated	guided
implemented	improved	initiated
instituted	instructed	introduced
invented	issued	launched
lectured	litigated	lobbied
managed	negotiated	operated
organized	overhauled	planned
prepared	presented	presided
programmed	promoted	recommended
researched	reviewed	revised
reorganized	regulated	selected
solved	scheduled	supervised
systematized	taught	tested
trained	updated	utilized

Choose The Right Format

There is not a lot of mystery here—your background will generally lead you to the right format. For an entry-level job applicant with limited work experience, the **chronological** format, which organizes your educational and employment history by date (most recent first) is the obvious choice.

For older or more experienced applicants, either the **functional**—which emphasizes the duties and responsibilities of all your jobs over the course of your career—or **combination**—halfway between chronological and functional—may be more suitable. While I have tended to emphasize the chronological format in this chapter, one of the other two may well be the right one for you.

Here's What To Avoid

In case we didn't stress them enough, here are some reminders of what to avoid:

- **Be brief and to the point**—Two pages if absolutely necessary, one page if at all possible. Never longer!

- **Don't be fancy.** Multi-colored paper and all-italic type won't impress employers, just make your resume harder to read (and easier to discard). Use plain white or ivory paper, blue or black ink and an easy-to-read standard typeface.

- **Forget rules about sentences.** Say what you need to say in the fewest words possible; use phrases, not drawn-out sentences.

- **Stick to the facts.** Don't talk about your dog, vacation, etc.

- **Resumes should never be blind.** A cover letter should *always* accompany a resume and that letter should always be directed to a specific person.

- **Almost doesn't count.** Your resume *must* be perfect—proofread everything as many times as necessary to catch any misspellings, grammatical errors, strange hyphenations or typos.

- **This is your sales tool**. Your resume is, in many cases, as close to you as an employer will ever get. Make sure it includes the information necessary to sell yourself the way you want to be sold!

- **Spend the money for good printing.** Soiled, tattered or poorly reproduced copies speak poorly of your own self-image. Spend the money and take the time to make sure your resume is the best presentation you've ever made.

- **Help the reader,** by organizing your resume in a clear-cut manner so key points are easily gleaned.

On the following two pages, I've included two samples of well-constructed student resumes that you can use as guides as you prepare your own.

Sample Chronological Resume

LINDSAY TAYLOR FRY

HOME ADDRESS: SCHOOL ADDRESS:
80 Stemmons Freeway,   4240 Hill St.,
Dallas, TX 87540   Los Angeles, CA 90410
(214)788-0000   (213)001-0100

OBJECTIVE   A position offering challenge and responsibility in
                        agency marketing research

EDUCATION   U.C.L.A., Los Angeles, CA
1986-1990   Graduating in June, 1990, with a B.A. degree (Marketing);
                        Deans List four years; Summa cum laude.

                        Fields of study include: marketing and advertising
                        theory, research, business law, economics, mass
                        communications, statistical analysis and research
                        methodology.

                        Graduate courses in advertising theory and policies,
                        consumer behavioral theory, sales management.

1982-1986   Greg Wright High School, Los Angeles, CA

                        National Honor Society; Senior Class President;
                        United Way Club Head Fund Raiser.

WORK
EXPERIENCE   1989: JIM CANNON, INC., Los Angeles, CA
(Summers)   Administrative assistant in Research Department:
                        Trained in behavioral research techniques;
                        Responsible for record keeping, expense reports,
                        public relations, lab report dissemination,
                        correspondence.

                        1986 - 1988: KISCHTRONICS, San Diego, CA

                        Basic sales and management training at this major
                        research and development facility. Duties included
                        billing, inventory control, shipping and distribution,
                        lab maintenance and delivery schedules.

Sample Functional Resume

JIM BEAM
76 Cortlandt St.,
New York, NY 10017
(212)555-1111

Career Objective: A position as an entry-level account executive
at a major metropolitan ad agency

SUMMARY

I am completing my degree in journalism, specializing in marketing, at University State. For two summers, I interned as an assistant account executive (with copywriting responsibilities) for a local advertising agency. I also have two year's experience selling advertising space (and supervising a staff of three salespeople) on my college newspaper and one year's experience in a bookstore. All of these jobs have convinced me I will be successful in advertising account work.

EXPERIENCE

Summer, 1988 & 89: Intern, Kay Silver & Associates, Inc.
Summer, 1987 : Intern, Committee to Re-elect Kim Kerr

1988/89 & 1989/90 school years: Ad Director, *The Daily Planet*
1987/88 school year: Salesman, Joe's University Book Store

EDUCATION

B.A. Journalism (Marketing) University State - June, 1990
(summa cum laude)

PROFESSIONAL MEMBERSHIPS AND BUSINESS SKILLS

Member of the Young Professionals Division of the Advertising Club of New York. Skills: Sales, media placement, typing (50 wpm), word processing, computer literate.

PERSONAL

Age: 21
Health: Excellent
Language Skills: Fluent (read/write/speak) in German and French

References Available Upon Request

30

Writing Better Letters

Stop for a moment and review your resume draft. It is undoubtedly (by now) a near-perfect document that instantly tells the reader the kind of job you want and why you are qualified. But does it say anything personal about you? Any amplification of your talents? Any words that are ideally "you?" Any hint of the kind of person who stands behind that resume?

If you've prepared it properly, the answers should be a series of ringing "no's"—your resume should be a mere sketch of your life, a bare-bones summary of your skills, education and experience.

To the general we must add the specific. That's what your letters must accomplish—adding the lines, colors and shading that will help fill out your self portrait. This chapter will cover the kinds of letters you will most often be called upon to prepare in your job search. There are essentially nine different types you will utilize again and again, based primarily on what each is trying to accomplish. I've included at least one well-written example of each at the end of this chapter.

Before you put pencil to paper to compose any letter, there are five key questions you must ask yourself:

- **Why** are you writing it?
- To **Whom**?
- **What** are you trying to accomplish?.
- **Which** lead will get the reader's attention?
- **How** do you organize the letter to best accomplish your objectives?

Why?

There should be a single, easily-definable reason you are writing any letter. This reason will often dictate what and how you write—the tone and flavor of the letter—as well as what you include or leave out.

Have you been asked in an ad to amplify your qualifications for a job, provide a salary history and college transcripts? Then that (minimally) is your objective in writing. Limit yourself to following instructions and do a little personal selling—but very little. Including everything asked for and a simple, adequate cover letter is better than writing a "knock-'em, sock-'em" letter and omitting your salary history.

If, however, you are on a networking search, the objective of your letter is to seek out contacts who will refer you for possible informational or job interviews. In this case, getting a name and address—a referral—is your stated purpose for writing. You have to be specific and ask for this action.

You will no doubt follow up with a phone call, but be certain the letter conveys what you are after. Being vague or oblique won't help you. You are after a definite yes or no when it comes to contact assistance. The recipient of your letter should know this. As they say in the world of selling, at some point you have to ask for the order.

Who?

Using the proper "tone" in a letter is as important as the content—you wouldn't write a letter to your television repairman using the same words and style you would employ in a letter to the director of personnel of a major company. Properly addressing the person or persons you are writing is as important as what you say to them.

Some hints to utilize: the recipient's job title and level, his or her hiring clout (if they are just a pass along conduit, save your selling for the next step up the ladder), the kind of person they are (based on your knowledge of their area of involvement).

For example, it pays to sound technical with technical people—in other words, use the kinds of words and language which they use on the job. If you have had the opportunity to speak with them, it will be easy for you. If not, and you have formed some opinions as to their types then use these as the basis of the language you employ. The cardinal rule is to say it in words you think the recipient will be comfortable hearing, not in the words you might otherwise personally choose.

What?

What do you have to offer that company? What do you have to contribute to the job, process or work situation that is unique and/or of particular benefit to the recipient of your letter?

For example, if you were applying for a sales position and recently ranked number one in a summer sales job, then conveying this benefit is logical and desirable. It is a factor you may have left off your resume. Even if it was listed in your skills/accomplishment section of the resume, you can underscore and call attention to it in your letter. Repetition, when it is properly focused, can be a good thing.

Which?

Of all the opening sentences you can compose, which will immediately get the reader's attention? If your opening sentence is dynamic, you are already fifty percent of the way to your end objective—having your entire letter read. Don't slide into it. Know the point you are trying to make and come right to it.

How?

While a good opening is essential, how do you organize your letter so that it is easy for the recipient to read in its entirety? This is a question of *flow*—the way the words and sentences naturally lead one to another, holding the reader's interest until he or she reaches your signature.

If you have your objective clearly in mind, this task is easier than it sounds: Simply convey your message(s) in a logical sequence. End your letter by stating what the next steps are—yours and/or the reader's.

One More Time

Pay attention to the small things. Neatness still counts. Have your letters typed. Spend a few extra dollars and have some personal stationary printed.

And most important, make certain that your correspondence goes out quickly. The general rule is to get a letter in the mail during the week in which the project comes to your attention or in which you have had some contact with the organization. I personally attempt to mail follow-up letters the same day as the contact; at worst, within 24 hours.

When To Write

- To answer an ad
- To prospect (many companies)
- To inquire about specific openings (single company)
- To obtain a referral
- To obtain an informational interview
- To obtain a job interview
- To say "thank you"
- To accept or reject a job offer
- To withdraw from consideration for a job

In some cases, the letter will accompany your resume; in others, it will need to stand alone. Each of the above circumstance is described in the pages that follow. I have included at least one sample of each type of letter at the end of this chapter.

Answering An Ad

Your eye catches an ad in the Positions Available Section of the Sunday paper for an assistant publicist. It tells you that the position is in a large publishing company and that, though some experience would be desirable, it is not required. Well, you possess *those* skills. The ad asks that you send a letter and resume to a Post Office Box. No salary is indicated, no phone number given. You decide to reply.

Your purpose in writing—the objective (why?)—is to secure a job interview. Since no individual is singled out for receipt of the ad, and since it is a large company, you assume it will be screened by Personnel.

Adopt a professional, formal tone. You are answering a "blind" ad, so you have to play it safe. In your first sentence, refer to the ad—including the place and date of publication and the position outlined. (Chances are this company is running more than one ad on the same date and in the same paper, so you need to identify the one to which you are replying.) Tell the reader what (specifically) you have to offer that company. Include your resume, phone number and the times it is easiest to reach you. Ask for the order—tell them you'd like to have an appointment.

Blanket Prospecting Letter

In June of this year you will graduate from a specialized four-year insurance college. You seek a position (internship or full-time employment) in a major insurer's underwriting department. You have decided to write to fifty top insurance companies, sending each a copy of your resume. You don't know which, if any, have job openings.

Such blanket mailings are effective given two circumstances: 1) You must have an exemplary record and a resume which reflects it, and 2) You must send out a goodly number of packages, since the response rate to such mailings is very low.

A blanket mailing doesn't mean an impersonal one—you should *always* be writing to a specific executive. If you have a referral, send a personalized letter to that person. If not, do *not* simply mail a package to the Personnel department; identify the department head and *then* send a personalized letter. And make sure you get on the phone and follow up each letter within about ten days. Don't just sit back and wait for everyone to call you. They won't.

Just Inquiring

The inquiry letter is a step above the blanket prospecting letter; it's a "cold-calling" device with a twist. You have earmarked a company (and a person) as a possibility in your job search based on something you have read about them. Your general research tells you that it is a good place to work. Although you are not aware of any specific openings, you know that they employ entry-level personnel with your credentials.

While ostensibly inquiring about any openings, you are really just "referring yourself" to them in order to place your resume in front of the right person. This is what I would call a "why not?" attempt at securing a job interview. Its effectiveness depends on their actually having been in the news. This, after all, is your "excuse" for writing.

Networking

It's time to get out that folder marked "Contacts" and prepare a draft networking letter. The lead sentence should be very specific, referring immediately to the friend, colleague, etc. "who suggested I write you about..." Remember: Your objective is to secure an informational interview, pave the way for a job interview, and/or get referred to still other contacts.

This type of letter should not place the recipient in a position where a decision is necessary; rather, the request should be couched in terms of "career advice." The second paragraph can then inform the reader of your level of experience. Finally, be specific about seeking an appointment.

Unless you have been specifically asked by the referring person to do so, you will probably not be including a resume with such letters. So the letter itself must highlight your credentials, enabling the reader to gauge your relative level of experience. For entry-level personnel, education, of course, will be most important.

For An Informational Interview

Though the objectives of this letter are similar to those of the networking letter, they are not as personal. These are "knowledge quests" on your part and the recipient will most likely not be someone you have been referred to. The idea is to convince the reader of the sincerity of your research effort. Whatever selling you do, if you do any at all, will arise as a consequence of the meeting, not beforehand. A positive response to this type of request is in itself a good step forward. It is, after all, exposure, and amazing things can develop when people in authority agree to see you.

Thank-You Letters

Although it may not always seem so, manners *do* count in the job world. But what counts even more are the simple gestures that show you actually care—like writing a thank-you letter. A well-executed, timely thank-you note tells more about your personality than anything else you may have sent. It says something about the way you were brought up—whatever else your resume tells them, you are, at least, polite, courteous and thoughtful.

Thank-you letters may well become the beginning of an all-important dialogue that leads directly to a job. So be extra careful in composing them, and make certain that they are custom made for each occasion and person.

The following are the primary situations in which you will be called upon to write some variation of thank-you letter:

- After a job interview

- After an informational interview

- Accepting a job offer

- Responding to rejection: While optional, such a letter is appropriate if you have been among the finalists in a job search or were rejected due to limited experience. Remember: Some day you'll *have* enough experience; make the interviewer want to stay in touch.

- Withdrawing from consideration: Used when you decide you are no longer interested in a particular position. (A variation is usable for declining an actual job offer.) Whatever the reason for writing such a letter, it's wise to do so and thus keep future lines of communication open.

In Response To An Ad

10 E. 89th Street
New York, N.Y. 10028
December 3, 1990

The <u>New York Times</u>
P.O. Box 7520
New York, N.Y. 10128

Dear Sir or Madam:

This letter is in response to your advertisement for an assistant publicist which appeared in the December 2nd issue of the *New York Times*.

I have the qualifications you are seeking. I graduated magna cum laude from Emerson Junior College with a degree in public relations and a minor in journalism.

I wrote for the Emerson newspaper—the <u>Collegian</u>—during all four years. During my senior year, when I was editor-in-chief, we won four awards for editorial excellence—three more than Emerson had ever won before.

For the past three summers, I have worked for Little Local PR, a firm specializing in publishing accounts. This position has provided me with hands-on experience in the public relations field, as well as the chance to use and hone my writing, communication and interpersonal skills.

My resume is enclosed. I would like to have the opportunity to meet with you personally to discuss your requirements for the position. I can be reached at (212) 785-1225 between 8:00 a.m. and 5:00 p.m. and at (212) 785-4221 after 5:00 p.m. I look forward to hearing from you.

Sincerely,

Karen Weber

Enclosure: Resume, Clips

Prospecting Letter

Kim Kerr
8 Robutuck Hwy.
Hammond, IN 54054
555-875-2392

December 14, 1990

Mr. Fred Jones
Vice President—Underwriting
Alcott & Alcott
One Lakeshore Drive
Chicago, Illinois

Dear Mr. Jones:

The name of Alcott & Alcott continually pops up in our classroom discussions of outstanding insurance companies. Given my interest in insurance as a career and underwriting as a specialty, I've taken the liberty of enclosing my resume.

As you can see, I have just completed a very comprehensive four years of study at the College of Insurance which included courses in all lines of insurance, underwriting, rating, etc. Though my resume does not indicate it, I will be graduating in the top 10% of my class, with honors.

I will be in the Chicago area on June 29 and will call your office to see when it is convenient to arrange an appointment.

Sincerely yours,

Kim Kerr

Inquiry Letter

42 7th Street
Ski City, Vermont 85722
September 30, 1990

Ms. Crystal Igotmine
President
Really Big Ad & PR, Inc.
521 West Elm Street
Indianapolis, IN   83230

Dear Ms. Igotmine:

I just completed reading the article in the October issue of <u>Fortune</u> on your company's record-breaking quarter. Congratulations!

Your innovative approach to recruiting minorities is of particular interest to me because of my background in advertising and minority recruitment.

I am interested in learning more about your work as well as the possibilities of joining your firm. My qualifications include:

- B.A. in Psychology
- Research on minority recruitment
- Publicity Seminar participation (Univ. of Virginia)
- Reports preparation on creative writing, education and minorities

I will be in Connecticut during the week of October 10 and hope your schedule will permit us to meet briefly to discuss our mutual interests. I will call your office next week to see if such a meeting can be arranged.

I appreciate your consideration.

Sincerely yours,

Ronald W. Sodidie

Networking Letter

Richard A. Starky
42 Bach St., Musical City, IN 20202   **317-555-1515**

May 14, 1990

Ms. Michelle Fleming
Vice President
Financial Planning Associates
42 Jenkins Avenue
Fulton, Mississippi 23232

Dear Ms. Fleming:

Sam Kinnison suggested I write you. I am interested in an entry-level editorial position, but <u>not</u> with a publishing company. Sam felt it would be mutually beneficial for us to meet and talk.

I have been educated and trained as an accountant and have just over two years' part-time experience in bookkeeping, accounting, auditing and tax work. But I also worked on the college newspaper throughout my undergraduate career. I am particularly interested in finding a way to mesh my interest in journalism with my training in finance.

I know from Sam how similar our backgrounds are— the same training, the same interest in journalism. And, of course, I am aware of how successfully you have managed to mesh these interests— fourteen awards for newsletter excellence in fifteen years!

As I begin my job search during the next few months, I am certain your advice would help me. Would it be possible for us to meet briefly? My resume is enclosed.

I will call your office next week to see when your schedule would permit such a meeting.

Sincerely,

Richard A. Starky

To Obtain An Informational Interview

16 NW 128th Street
Raleigh, North Carolina 75755
December 2, 1990

Mr. Johnson B. McClure
Vice President—Trading
SellThemGoldMines Brokerage, Inc.
484 Smithers Road
Awkmont, North Carolina 76857

Dear Mr. McClure:

I'm sure a good deal of the credit for your company's 23% jump in trading volume last year is attributable to the highly-motivated sales staff you have recruited during the last three years. I hope to obtain an entry-level position for a company just as committed to growth.

I have four years of sterling sales results to boast of, experience acquired while working my way through college. I believe my familiarity with the precious metals market, sales experience and Bachelor's degree in economics from American University have properly prepared me for a career in precious metals trading.

As I begin my job search, I am trying to gather as much information and advice as possible before applying for positions. Could I take a few minutes of your time next week to discuss my career plans? I will call your office on Monday, December 12, to see if such a meeting can be arranged.

I appreciate your consideration and look forward to meeting you.

Sincerely,

Karen R. Burns

After An Informational Interview

LAZELLE WRIGHT
921 West Fourth Street
Steamboat, Colorado 72105
303-303-3030

May 21, 1990

Mr. James R. Payne
Marketing Manager
Proctor's Gamble, Inc.
241 Snowridge
Ogden, Utah 72108

Dear Mr. Payne:

Jinny Bastienelli was right when she said you would be most helpful in advising me on a career in consumer product marketing.

I appreciated your taking the time from your busy schedule to meet with me. Your advice was most helpful and I have incorporated your suggestions into my resume. I will send you a copy next week.

Again, thanks so much for your assistance. As you suggested, I will contact Joe Simmons at Conglomerate, Inc. next week in regards to a possible opening with his company.

Sincerely,

Lazelle Wright

After A Job Interview

1497 Lilac Street
Old Adams, MA 01281
October 5, 1990

Mr. Rudy Delacort
Director of Personnel
We Publish Everything, Inc.
175 Boylston Avenue
Ribbit, Massachusetts 02857

Dear Mr. Delacort:

Thank you for the opportunity to interview yesterday for the sales trainee position. I enjoyed meeting you and Cliff Stoudt and learning more about WPEI.

Your organization appears to be growing in a direction which parallels my interests and career goals. The interview with you and your staff confirmed my initial positive impressions of WPEI, and I want to reiterate my strong interest in working for you.

I am convinced my prior experience as ad sales director for my school's daily newspaper, my Business College training in marketing and finance, and my summer sales experience working with a variety of products would enable me to progress steadily through your training program and become a productive member of your sales team.

Again, thank you for your consideration. If you need any additional information from me, please feel free to call.

Yours truly,

Hugh Beaumont

cc: Mr. Cliff Stoudt
       New Projects Unit

Accepting A Job Offer

1497 Lilac Street
Old Adams, MA 01281
October 5, 1990

Mr. Rudy Delacort
Director of Personnel
We Publish Everything Inc.
175 Boylston Avenue
Ribbit, Massachusetts 02857

Dear Mr. Delacort:

I want to thank you and Mr. Stoudt for giving me the opportunity to work for WPEI. I am very pleased to accept the position as a sales rep trainee with your New Projects Unit. The position entails exactly the kind of work I want to do, and I know that I will do a good job for you.

As we discussed, I shall begin work on January 5, 1991. In the interim I shall complete all the necessary employment forms, obtain the required physical examination and locate housing.

I plan to be in Ribbit within the next two weeks and would like to deliver the paperwork to you personally. At that time, we could handle any remaining items pertaining to my employment. I'll call next week to schedule an appointment with you.

Sincerely yours,

Edward J. Haskell

cc: Mr. Cliff Stoudt
    New Projects Unit

Withdrawing From Consideration

1497 Lilac Street
Old Adams, MA 01281
October 5, 1990

Mr. Rudy Delacort
Director of Personnel
We Publish Everything, Inc.
175 Boylston Avenue
Ribbit, Massachusetts 02857

Dear Mr. Delacort:

It was indeed a pleasure meeting with you and Mr. Stoudt last week to discuss your needs for a sales rep trainee in your New Projects Unit. Our time together was most enjoyable and informative.

As I discussed with you during our meetings, I believe one purpose of preliminary interviews is to explore areas of mutual interest and to assess the fit between the individual and the position. After careful consideration, I have decided to withdraw from consideration for the position.

My decision is based primarily upon the one factor we discussed in some detail—the position would simply require more travel than I am able to accept, given my other responsibilities.

I want to thank you for interviewing me and giving me the opportunity to learn about your needs. You have a fine staff and and I would have enjoyed working with them.

Yours truly,

Barbara Billingsly

cc: Mr. Cliff Stoudt
New Projects Unit

In Response To Rejection

1497 Lilac Street
Old Adams, MA 01281
October 5, 1990

Mr. Rudy Delacort
Director of Personnel
We Publish Everything, Inc.
175 Boylston Avenue
Ribbit, Massachusetts   02857

Dear Mr. Delacort:

Thank you for giving me the opportunity to interview for the sales rep trainee position. I appreciate your consideration and interest in me.

Although I am disappointed in not being selected for your current vacancy, I want you to know that I appreciated the courtesy and professionalism shown to me during the entire selection process. I enjoyed meeting you, Cliff Stoudt, and the other members of your sales staff. My meetings confirmed that WPEI would be an exciting place to work and build a career.

I want to reiterate my strong interest in working for you. Please keep me in mind if a similar position becomes available in the near future.

Again, thank you for the opportunity to interview and best wishes to you and your staff.

Sincerely yours,

Anthony Dow

cc: Mr. Cliff Stoudt
    New Projects Unit

31

Questions For You,
Questions For Them

You've done days of research, contacted everyone you've known since kindergarten, compiled a professional-looking and -sounding resume, and written brilliant letters to the handful of companies your research has revealed are perfect matches for your own strengths, interests and abilities. Unfortunately, all of this preparatory work will be meaningless if you are unable to successfully convince one of those firms to hire you.

If you were able set up an initial meeting at one of these companies, your resume and cover letter obviously peaked *someone's* interest. Now you have to traverse the last minefield—the job interview itself. It's time to make all that preparation pay off.

This chapter will attempt to put the interview process in perspective, giving you the "inside story" on what to expect and how to handle the questions and circumstances that arise during the course of a normal interview...and even many of those that surface in the bizarre interview situations we have all sometimes experienced.

Why Interviews Shouldn't Scare You

Interviews shouldn't scare you. The concept of two (or more) persons meeting to determine if they are right for each other is a relatively logical and certainly not apparently frightening idea. As important as research, resumes, letters and phone calls are, they are inherently impersonal. The interview is your chance to really see and feel the company firsthand—"up close and personal," as Howard Cosell used to crow—so think of it as a positive opportunity, your chance to succeed.

That said, many of you will still be put off by the inherently inquisitive nature of the process. Though many questions *will* be asked, interviews are essentially experiments in chemistry. Are you right for the company? Is the company right for you? Not just on paper—*in the flesh*. If you decide the company *is* right for you, *your* purpose is simple and clearcut—to convince the interviewer that you are the right person for the job, that you will fit in, and that you will be an asset to the company now and in the future. The interviewer's purpose is equally simple—to decide whether he or she should buy what you're selling.

This chapter will focus on the kinds of questions you are likely to be asked, how to answer them, and the questions you should be ready to ask of the interviewer. By removing the workings of the interview process from the "unknown" category, you will reduce the fear it engenders.

But all the preparation in the world won't completely eliminate your sweaty palms, unless you can convince yourself that the interview is an important, positive life experience from which you will benefit...even if you don't get the job. Approach it with a little enthusiasm, calm yourself, and let your personality do the rest. You will undoubtedly spend an interesting hour, one that will teach you more about yourself. It's just another step in the learning process you've undertaken.

What To Do First

Start by setting up a calendar on which you can enter and track all your scheduled appointments. When you schedule an interview with a company, ask them how much time you should allow for the appointment. Some require all new applicants to fill out numerous forms and/or complete a battery of intelligence or psychological tests—all before the first interview. If you've only allowed an hour for the interview—and scheduled another at a nearby firm ten minutes later—the first time you confront a three-hour test series will effectively destroy any schedule.

Some companies, especially if the first interview is very positive, like to keep applicants around to talk to other executives. This process may be planned or, in a lot of cases, a spontaneous decision by an interviewer who likes you and wants you to meet some other key decision makers. Other companies will tend to schedule such a series of second interviews on a separate day. Find out, if you can, how the company you're planning to visit generally operates. Otherwise, especially if you've traveled to another city to interview with a number of firms in a short period of time, a schedule that's too tight will fall apart in no time at all.

If you need to travel out-of-state to interview with a company, be sure to ask if they will be paying some or all of your travel expenses. (It's generally expected that you'll be paying your own way to firms within your home state.) If they don't offer—and you don't ask—presume you're paying the freight.

Even if the company agrees to reimburse you, make sure you have enough money to pay all the expenses yourself. While some may reimburse you immediately, the majority of firms may take from a week to a month to forward you an expense check.

What Color Shirts Does He Like?

The research you did to find these companies is nothing compared to the research you need to do now that you're beginning to narrow your search. If you followed our detailed suggestions when you started targeting these firms in the first place, you've already amassed a lot of information about them. If you didn't do the research *then*, you sure better decide to do it *now*. Study each company as if you were going to be tested on your detailed knowledge of their organization and operations. Here's what you should know about each company you plan to visit:

The Basics

1. The address of (and directions to) the office you're visiting
2. Headquarters location (if different)
3. Some idea of domestic and international branches

4. Relative size (compared to other similar companies)
5. Annual billings, sales and/or income (last two years)
6. Subsidiary companies; specialized divisions
7. Departments (overall structure)
8. Major accounts, products or services

The Subtleties

1. History of the firm (specialties, honors, awards, famous names)
2. Names, titles and backgrounds of top management
3. Existence (and type) of training program
4. Relocation policy
5. Relative salaries (compared to other companies in field or by size)
6. Recent developments concerning the the company and its products or services (from your trade magazine and newspaper reading)
7. Everything you can learn about the career, likes and dislikes of the person(s) interviewing you

The amount of time and work necessary to be *this* well prepared for an interview is considerable. It will not be accomplished the day before the interview. You may even find some of the information you need to be unavailable on short notice.

(Is it really so important to do all this? Well, **somebody out there is going to.** *And if you happen to be interviewing for the same job as that other, well-prepared, knowledgeable candidate, who do* **you** *think will impress the interviewer more?)*

As we've already discussed, if you give yourself enough time, most of this information is surprisingly easy to obtain. In addition to the reference sources we previously covered (see Appendix B, too), the company itself can probably supply you with a great deal of data. A firm's annual report—which all publicly-owned companies must publish yearly for their stockholders—is a virtual treasure trove of information. Write each company and request copies of their last two annual reports. A comparison of sales, income and other data over this period may enable you to discover some interesting things about their overall financial health and growth potential. Many libraries also have collections of annual reports from major corporations.

Attempting to learn about your interviewer is a chore, the importance of which is underestimated by most applicants (who then, of course, don't bother to do it). Being one of the exceptions may get you a job. Use the biographical references available in your local library. If he or she is listed in any of these sources, you'll be able to learn an awful lot about his or her background. In addition, find out if he or she has written any articles that have appeared in the trade press or, even better, books on his or her area(s) of expertise. Referring to these writings during the course of an interview, without making it *too* obvious a compliment, can be very effective. We all have egos and we all like people to talk about us. The interviewer is no different from the rest of us. You might also check to see if any of your networking contacts worked with him or her at his current (or a previous) company and can help "fill you in."

Selection Vs. Screening Interviews

The process to which the majority of this chapter is devoted is the actual *selection interview*, usually conducted by the person to whom the new hire will be reporting. But there is another process—the *screening interview*—which many of you may have to survive first.

Screening interviews are usually conducted by a member of the personnel department. Though they may not be empowered to hire, they *are* in a position to screen out or eliminate those candidates they feel (based on the facts) are not qualified to handle the job. These decisions are not usually made on the basis of personality, appearance, eloquence, persuasiveness or any other subjective criteria, but rather by clicking off yes or no answers against a checklist of skills. If you don't have the requisite number, you will be eliminated from further consideration. This may seem arbitrary, but it is a realistic and often necessary way for corporations to minimize the time and dollars involved in filling even the lowest jobs on the corporate ladder.

Remember, screening personnel are not looking for reasons to *hire* you; they're trying to find ways to *eliminate* you from the job search pack. Resumes sent blindly to the personnel department will usually be subjected to such screening; you will be eliminated without any personal contact (an excellent reason to construct a superior resume and *not* send out blind mailings).

If you are contacted, it will most likely be by telephone. When you are responding to such a call, keep these three things in mind: 1). It *is* an interview; be on your guard. 2). Answer all questions honestly. And 3). Be enthusiastic. You will get the standard questions from the interviewer—his or her attempts to "flesh out" the information included on your resume and/or cover letter. Strictly speaking, they are seeking out any negatives which may exist. If your resume is honest and factual (and it should be), you have no reason to be anxious, because you have nothing to hide.

Don't be nervous—be glad you were called and remember your objective: to get past this screening phase so you can get on to the real interview.

The Day Of The Interview

On the day of the interview, wear a conservative (not funereal) business suit—*not* a sports coat, *not* a "nice" blouse and skirt. Shoes should be shined, nails cleaned, hair cut and in place. And no low-cut or tight-fitting dresses (especially on the men).

It's not unusual for resumes and cover letters to head in different directions when a company starts passing them around to a number of executives. If you sent them, both may even be long gone. So bring along extra copies of your resume and your own copy of the cover letter that originally accompanied it.

Whether or not you make them available, we suggest you prepare a neatly-typed list of references (including the name, title, company, address and phone number of each person). You may want to bring along a copy of your high school or college transcript, especially if it's something to brag about. (Once you get your first job, you'll probably never use it—or be asked for it—again, so enjoy it while you can!)

On Time Means Fifteen Minutes Early

Plan to arrive fifteen minutes before your scheduled appointment. If you're in an unfamiliar city or have a long drive to their offices, allow extra time for the unexpected delays that seem to occur with mind-numbing regularity on important days.

Arriving early will give you some time to check your appearance, catch your breath, check in with the receptionist, learn how to correctly pronounce the interviewer's name, and get yourself organized and battle ready.

Arriving late does not make a sterling first impression. If you are only a few minutes late, it's probably best not to mention it or even excuse yourself. With a little luck, everybody else is behind schedule and no one will notice. However, if you're more than fifteen minutes late, have an honest (or at least *serviceable)* explanation ready and offer it at your first opportunity. Then drop the subject as quickly as possible and move on to the interview.

The Eyes Have It

When you meet the interviewer, shake hands firmly. People notice handshakes and often form a first impression based solely on them.

Ask for a business card. This will make sure you get the person's name and title right when you write your follow-up letter. You can staple it to the company file for easy reference as you continue your networking.

Try to maintain eye contact with the interviewer as you talk. This will indicate you're interested in what he or she has to say. Sit straight. Avoid smoking.

Should coffee or a soft drink be offered, you may accept (but should do so only if the interviewer is joining you).

Keep your voice at a comfortable level, and try to sound enthusiastic (without imitating Charleen Cheerleader). Be confident and poised, and provide direct, accurate and honest answers to the trickiest questions.

And, as you try to remember all this, just be yourself, and try to act like you're comfortable and almost enjoying this whole process!

Don't Name Drop...Conspicuously

A friendly relationship with other company employees may have provided you with valuable information prior to the interview, but don't flaunt such relationships. The interviewer is interested only in how you will relate to him or her and how well he or she surmises you will fit in with the rest of the staff. Name dropping may smack of favoritism. And you are in no position to know who the interviewer's favorite (or *least* favorite) people are.

On the other hand, if you have established a complex network of professionals through informational interviews, attending trade shows, reading trade magazines, etc., it is perfectly permissable to refer to these people, their companies, conversations you've had, whatever. It may even impress the interviewer with the extensiveness of your preparation.

Fork On The Left, Knife On The Right

Interviews are sometimes conducted over lunch, though this is not usually the case with entry-level people. If it does happen to you, though, try to order something in the middle price range, neither filet mignon nor a cheeseburger.

Do not order alcohol. If your interviewer orders a carafe of wine, you may share it. Otherwise, alcohol should be considered *verboten*, under any and all circumstances. Then hope your mother taught you the correct way to eat and talk at the same time. If not, just do your best to maintain your poise.

The Importance Of *Last* Impressions

There are some things interviewers will always view with displeasure: street language, complete lack of eye contact, insufficient or vague explanations or answers, a noticeable lack of energy, poor interpersonal skills (i.e., not listening or the basic inability to carry on an intelligent conversation), and a demonstrable lack of motivation.

Every impression may count. And the very *last* impression an interviewer has may outweigh everything else. So, before you allow an interview to end, summarize why you want the job, why you are qualified, and what, *in particular,* you can offer their company.

Then, take some action. If the interviewer hasn't told you about the rest of the interview process and/or where you stand, ask him or her. Will you be seeing other people that day? If so, ask for some background on anyone else with whom you'll be interviewing. If there are no other meetings that day, what's the next step? When can you expect to hear from them about coming back?

When you return home, file all the business cards, copies of correspondence and notes from the interview(s) with each company in the appropriate files. Finally, but most importantly, ask yourself which firms you really want to work for and which you are no longer interested in. This will quickly determine how far you want the process at each to develop before you politely tell them to stop considering you for the job.

Immediately send a thank-you letter to each executive you met. These should, of course, be neatly-typed business letters, not handwritten notes (unless you are most friendly, indeed, with the interviewer and want to *stress* the "informal" nature of your note). If you are still interested in pursuing a position at their company, tell them in no uncertain terms. Reiterate why you feel you're the best candidate and tell each of the executives when you hope (expect?) to hear from them.

On The 8th Day God Created Interviewers

Though most interviews will follow a relatively standard format, there will undoubtedly be a wide disparity in the skills of the interviewers you meet. Many of these executives (with the exception of the Personnel staff) will most likely not have extensive interviewing experience, have limited knowledge of interviewing techniques, use them infrequently, be hurried or harried by the press of other duties or not even view your interview as critically important.

Rather than studying standardized test results or utilizing professional evaluation skills developed over many years of practice, these non-professionals react intuitively—their initial (first five minutes) impressions are often the lasting and overriding factors they remember. So you must sell yourself …fast.

The best way to do this is to try to achieve a comfort level with your interviewer. Isn't establishing rapport—through words, gestures, appearance common interests, etc. —what you try to do in *any* social situation? It's just trying to know one another better. Against this backdrop, the questions and answers will flow in a more natural way.

The Set Sequence

Irrespective of the competence levels of the interviewer, you can anticipate an interview sequence roughly as follows:

- Greetings
- Social niceties (small talk)
- Purpose of meeting (let's get down to business)
- Broad questions/answers

- Specific questions/answers
- In-depth discussion of company, job and opportunity
- Summarizing information given & received
- Possible salary probe (dependent upon level of achievement)
- Summary/indication as to next steps

When you look at this sequence closely, it is obvious that once you have gotten past the greeting, social niceties and some explanation of the job (in the "getting down to business" section), the bulk of the interview will be questions—yours and the interviewer's. In this question and answer session, there are not necessarily any right or wrong answers, only good and bad ones.

It's Time To Play Q & A

You can't control the "chemistry" between you and the interviewer—do you seem to "hit it off" right from the start or never connect at all? Since you *can't* control such a subjective problem, it pays to focus on what you *can* —the questions you will be asked, your answers and the questions *you* had better be prepared to ask.

Not surprisingly, many of the same questions pop up in interview after interview, regardless of company size, type or location. I have chosen the thirteen most common—along with appropriate hints and answers for each—for inclusion in this chapter. Remember: There are no right or wrong answers to these questions, only good and bad ones.

Substance counts more than speed when answering questions. Take your time and make sure that you listen to each question—there is nothing quite as disquieting as a lengthy, well-thoughtout answer that is completely irrelevant to the question asked. You wind up looking like a programmed clone with stock answers to dozens of questions who has, unfortunately, pulled the wrong one out of the grab bag.

Once you have adequately answered a specific question, it *is* permissible to go beyond it and add more information if doing so adds something to the discussion and/or highlights a particular strength, skill, course, etc. But avoid making lengthy speeches just for the sake of sounding off.

Study the list of questions (and hints) that follow, and prepare at least one solid, concise answer for each. Practice with a friend until your answers to these most-asked questions sound intelligent, professional and, most important, unmemorized and unrehearsed.

"Why do you want to be in this field?"

Using your knowledge and understanding of the particular field, explain why you find the business exciting and where and how you see yourself fitting in.

"Why do you think you will be successful in this business?"

Using the information from your self evaluation and the research you did on that particular company, formulate an answer which marries your strengths to theirs and to the characteristics of the position for which you're applying.

"Why did you choose our company?"

This is an excellent opportunity to explain the extensive process of education and research you've undertaken. Tell them about your strengths and how you match up with their firm. Emphasize specific things about their company that led you to seek an interview. Be a salesperson—be convincing.

"What can you do for us?"

Construct an answer that essentially lists your strengths, the experience you have which will contribute to your job performance, and any other unique qualifications that will place you at the head of the applicant pack. Be careful: This is a question specifically designed to *eliminate* some of that pack. Sell yourself. Be one of the few called back for a second interview.

"What position here interests you?"

If you're interviewing for a specific position, answer accordingly. If you want to make sure you don't close the door on other opportunities of which you might be unaware, you can follow up with your own question: "I'm here to apply for your Sales Training Program. Is there another position open for which you feel I'm qualified?"

If you've arranged an interview with a company without knowing of any specific openings, use the answer to this question to describe the kind of work you'd like to do and why you're qualified to do it. Avoid a specific job title, since they will tend to vary from firm to firm.

If you're on a first interview with the personnel department, just answer the question. They only want to figure out where to send you.

"What jobs have you held and why did you leave them?"

Or the direct approach: "Have you ever been fired?" Take this opportunity to expand on your resume, rather than precisely answering the question by merely recapping your job experiences. In discussing each job, point out what you liked about it, what factors led to your leaving and how the next job added to your continuing professional education. If you *have* been fired, say so. It's very easy to check.

"What are your strengths and weaknesses?"

Or *"What are your hobbies (or outside interests)?"* Both questions can be easily answered using the data you gathered to complete the self-evaluation process. Be wary of being too forthcoming about your glaring faults (nobody expects you to volunteer every weakness and mistake), but do *not* reply, "I don't have any." They won't believe you and, what's worse, *you* won't believe you. After all, you did the evaluation—you know it's a lie!

Good answers to these questions are those in which the interviewer can identify benefits for him- or herself. For example: "I consider myself an excellent planner. I am seldom caught by surprise and I prize myself on being able to anticipate problems and schedule my time to be ahead of the game. I devote a prescribed number of hours each week to this activity. I've noticed that many people just react. If you plan ahead, you should be able to cut off most problems before they arise."

You may consider disarming the interviewer by admitting a weakness, but doing it in such a way as to make it relatively unimportant to the job function. For example: "Higher mathematics has never been my strong suit. Though I am competent enough, I've always envied my friends with a more mathematical bent. In sales, though, I haven't found this a liability. I'm certainly quick enough in figuring out how close I am to monthly quotas and, of course, I keep a running record of commissions earned."

"Do you think your extracurricular activities were worth the time you devoted to them?"

This is a question often asked of entry-level candidates. One possible answer: "Very definitely. As you see from my resume, I have been quite active in the Student Government and French Club. My language fluency allowed me to spend my junior year abroad as an exchange student, and working in a functioning government gave me firsthand knowledge of what can be accomplished with people in the real world. I suspect my marks would have been somewhat higher had I not taken on so many activities outside of school, but I feel the balance they gave me contributed significantly to my overall growth as a person."

"What are your career goals?"

Interviewers are always seeking to probe the motivations of prospective employees. Nowhere is this more apparent than when the area of ambition is discussed. The high key answer to this question might be; "Given hard work, company growth and a few lucky breaks along the way, I'd look forward to being in a top executive position by the time I'm 35. I believe in effort and the risk/reward system—my research on this company has shown me that it operates on the same principles. I would hope it would select its future leaders from those people who displaying such characteristics."

"At some future date would you be willing to relocate?"

Pulling up one's roots is not the easiest thing in the world to do, but it is often a fact of life in the corporate world. If you're serious about your career (and such a move often represents a step up the career ladder), you will probably not mind such a move. Tell the interviewer. If you really *don't* want to move, you may want to say so, too—though I would find out how probable or frequent such relocations would be before closing the door while still in the interview stage.

Keep in mind that as you get older, establish ties in a particular community, marry, have children, etc., you will inevitably feel less jubilation at the thought of moving once a year or even "being out on the road." So take the opportunity to experience new places and experiences while you're young. If you don't, you may never get the chance.

"How did you get along with your last supervisor?"

This question is designed to understand your relationship with (and reaction to) authority. Remember: Companies look for team players, people who will fit in with their hierarchy, their rules, their ways of doing things. An answer might be: "I prefer to work with smart, strong people who know what they want and can express themselves. I learned in the military that in order to accomplish the mission, someone has to be the leader and that person has to be given the authority to lead. Someday I aim to be that leader. I hope then my subordinates will follow me as much and as competently as I'm ready to follow now."

"What are your salary requirements?"

If they are at all interested in you, this question will probably come up. The danger is that you may price yourself too low or, even worse, right out of a job you want. Since you will have a general idea of industry figures for that position (and may even have an idea of what that company tends to pay new people for the position), why not refer to a *range* of salaries, such as $20,000 - $25,000?

If the interviewer doesn't bring up salary at all, it's doubtful you're being seriously considered, so you probably don't need to even bring the subject up. (If you know you aren't getting the job or aren't interested in it if offered, you may try to nail down a salary figure in order to be better prepared for the next interview.)

"Tell me about yourself"

Watch out for this one! It's often one of the first questions asked. If you falter here, the rest of the interview could quickly become a downward slide to nowhere. Be prepared, and consider it an opportunity to combine your answers to many of the previous questions into one concise description of who you are, what you want to be and why that company should take a chance on you. Summarize your resume—briefly—and expand on particular courses or experiences relevant to the firm or position. Do *not* go on about your hobbies or personal life, where you spent your summer vacation, or anything that is not relevant to securing that job. You may explain how that particular job fits in with your long-range career goals and talk specifically about what attracted you to their company in the first place.

The Not-So-Obvious Questions

Every interviewer is different and, unfortunately, there are no rules saying he or she has to use all or any of the "basic" questions covered above. But we think the odds are against his or her avoiding *all* of them. Whichever of these he or she includes, be assured most interviewers do like to come up with questions that are "uniquely theirs." It may be just one or a whole series—questions developed over the years that he or she feels help separate the wheat from the chaff.

You can't exactly prepare yourself for questions like, "What would you do if...(fill in the blank with some obscure occurrence)?" "Tell me about your father," or "What's your favorite ice cream flavor?" Every interviewer we know has his or her favorites and all of these questions seem to come out of left field. Just stay relaxed, grit your teeth (quietly) and take a few seconds to frame a reasonably intelligent reply.

Some questions may be downright inappropriate. Young women, for example, may be asked about their plans for marriage and children. Don't call the interviewer a chauvinist (or worse). And don't point out that the question may be a little outside the law—the nonprofessional interviewer may not realize such questions are illegal, and a huffy response may confuse, even anger, him or her.

Whenever any questions are raised about your personal life—and this question surely qualifies—it is much more effective to respond that you are very interested in the position and have no reason to believe that your personal life will preclude you from doing an excellent job.

"Do *You* Have Any Questions?"

It's the last fatal question on our list, often the last one an interviewer throws at you after an hour or two of grilling. Unless the interview has been very long and unusually thorough, you probably *should* have questions—about the job, the company, even the industry. Unfortunately, by the time this question off-handedly hits the floor, you are already looking forward to leaving and may have absolutely nothing to say.

Preparing yourself for an interview means more than having answers for some of the questions an interviewer may ask. It means having your *own* set of questions—at least five or six—for the interviewer. The interviewer is trying to find the right person for the job. *You're* trying to find the right job. So you should be just as curious about him or her and the company as he or she is about you. Here's a short list of questions you may consider asking on any interview:

1. What will my typical day be like?
2. What happened to the last person who had this job?
3. Given my attitude and qualifications, how would you estimate my chances for career advancement at your company?
4. Why did you come to work here? What keeps you here?
5. If you were I, would you start here again?
6. How would you characterize the management philosophy of your firm?
7. What characteristics do the successful_____ at your company have in common (fill in the blank with an appropriate title)?
8. What's the best (and worst) thing about working here?
9. On a scale of 1 to 10, how would you rate your company—in terms of salaries, benefits and employee satisfaction—in comparison to similar firms?

Testing & Applications

Though not part of the selection interview itself, job applications and psychological testing are often part of the pre-interview process. You should know something about them.

The job application is essentially a record-keeping exercise—simply the transfer of work experience and educational data from your resume to a printed applications form.Though taking the time to recopy data may seem like a waste of time, some companies simply want the information in a particular order on a standard form. One difference: Applications often require the listing of references and salary levels achieved. Be sure to bring your list of references with you to any interview (so you can transfer the pertinent information), and don't lie about salary history; it's easily checked.

Many companies now use a variety of psychological tests as additional mechanisms to screen out undesirable candidates. Although their accuracy is subject to question, the companies that use them obviously believe they are effective at identifying applicants whose personality makeups would preclude their participating positively in a given work situation, especially those at the extreme ends of the behavior spectrum.

Their usefulness in predicting job accomplishment is considered limited. If you are normal (like the rest of us), you'll have no trouble with these tests and may even find them amusing. Just don't try to outsmart them—you'll just wind up outsmarting yourself.

Section 3

Job Opportunities Databanks

32

Major Corporation Listings

This section consists of four chapters In this chapter, we have listed hundreds of major corporations across the United States that we believe are representative of every major industry. For each of these, we have included address and phone information and the person to contact regarding entry-level employment. In many cases, we also included information on total employment, the average number of entry-level people hired each year for marketing and sales positions, and whether or not the company offers internships in marketing, marketing research, sales, advertising and/or public relations. These listings are an excellent place to start your search for an entry-level job in any industry

In chapter 33, we've listed similar information on the top market research (supplier) firms, including more details on actual entry-level opportunities.

And in chapters 34 and 35, we have included more detailed information on the top advertising and public relations firms for those of you considering agency careers. *Note that for the first time, information on the largest ad and PR agencies across Canada is also included here.* If you are most interested in these two areas, we'd suggest you purchase either the *Advertising Career Directory* or *Public Relations Career Directory* (from which this information was extracted). Each of these volumes includes articles by over two dozen top professionals and more detailed information at those firms listed here...plus listings of many other firms that were *not* reproduced in this volume.

Two final notes: First, despite our every attempt to ensure the accuracy of the information we've included, time marches on...and so do contacts. In other words, there will be mistakes in these listings—the very day they're published—just because things change and, in some companies, change very quickly. But we think you'll find that the vast majority of this previously-unpublished information will remain credible until it is updated in 1992 in a fourth edition.

You'll find the listings to be self-explanatory, we believe, throughout the next four chapters. **One important point: A "?" following the "average entry-level hiring" entry means** *they tend to hire entry-level people;* **they were just unable to come up with any specific number.**

Lastly, previous editions of this *Career Directory* have also included information on summer and school-year internships. At the request of the librarians, counselors, professors and students who utilize these Directories, we have now published this internship data (and, in fact, increased three-fold the amount of information included in each internship listing) in a completely separate series of books—our *Internships Series.*

Volume 1 of this series lists internship programs at hundreds of major advertising agencies, PR firms, corporations and market research firms in the United States *and Canada.* It is available in a new second edition for 1990.

Companies Requesting No Listing

Admar Research, Inc.
Allegheny International, Inc.
Bally Manufacturing Corp.
Beatrice/Hunt-Wesson
Brown & Williamson Tobacco Corp.

CBS Inc.
Decisions Center, Inc.
National Analysts
A.C. Nielsen Company
Daniel Yanklovich Group

Major Corporation Listings

THE ACADEMY OF PRODUCTIVE PERFORMANCE
200 Lindenwood Drive
Malvern, PA 19355
215-251-0250

Employment Contact: Gil Ostrander, Chairman of the Board
Average Entry-Level Hiring: ?
Internships: No

ADOLPH COORS COMPANY
311 Tenth Street
Golden, CO 80401
303-279-6565

Employment Contact: Tonia Hamilton, Personnel Department
Total Employees: 10,000+ (250 in sales, 100 in marketing, 50 in promotion, 20 in advertising)
Average Entry-Level Hiring: 20-30
Internships: Yes

AETNA LIFE & CASUALTY
151 Farmington Avenue
Hartford, CT 06156
203-273-0123

Employment Contact: Theresa Y. Tanguay

Total Employees: 45,000
Averge Entry-Level Hiring: 75-100 (Hartford area)
Internships: Yes

ALBERTO-CULVER COMPANY
2525 Armitage Avenue
Melrose Park, IL 60160
708-450-3000

Employment Contact: Albert Swayne, VP-Personnel
Average Entry-Level Hiring: ?
Internships: No

ALLIED PRODUCTS CORP.
10 South Riverside Plaza
Chicago, IL 60606
312-454-1020

Employment Contact: Leo Simmermeyer
Average Entry-Level Hiring: ?
Internships: No

ALLIED-SIGNAL INC.
P.O. Box 2245R
Morristown, NJ 07962
201-455-3997

Employment Contact: Don Redlinger, VP-Human Resources

Total Employees: 115,000 (worldwide)
Average Entry-Level Hiring: ?
Internships: No

AMERICAN BRANDS, INC.
1700 East Putnam Avenue
Old Greenwich, CT 06870
203-698-5000

Employment Contact: Dennis D. Doherty, Manager-
Human Resources
Average Entry-Level Hiring: ?
Internships: No

**AMERICAN EXPRESS -TRAVEL RELATED
SERVICES**
American Express Tower
World Financial Center
New York, NY 10285
212-640-2573

Employment Contact: Personnel Dept. or Barbara
Kurz, Dir. of Graduate Program
Average Entry-Level Hiring: 50
Internships: Yes

AMERICAN HOME PRODUCTS
685 Third Avenue
New York, NY 10017
212-878-5301

Comments: Does not hire entry-level college
graduates.

AMERICAN INTERNATIONAL GROUP
72 Wall Street
New York, NY 10270
212-770-3585

Employment Contact: Patricia Toro
Total Employees: 29,000
Average Entry-Level Hiring: ?
Internships: No

AMERICAN MOTORS
See listing for Chrysler Corporation

ANHEUSER-BUSCH COMPANIES INC.
1 Busch Place
St. Louis, MO 63118
314-577-2000

Employment Contact: Employment Services
Total Employees: 44,000 nationwide
Average Entry-Level Hiring: 0
Internships: No

APPLE COMPUTER, INC.
20525 Mariani Avenue
Mailstop 39A
Cupertino, CA 95014
408-974-3010

Employment Contact: College Relations
Average Entry-Level Hiring: 70
Internships: Yes

ARA SERVICES
1101 Market Street
Philadelphia, PA 19107
215-238-3000

Employment Contact: Kim Meyerson or Lisa Staley,
Human Resources Specialists
Total Employees: 120,000 worldwide
Average Entry-Level Hiring: 6-9
Internships: No
*Note: Information is for headquarters only—
Contact individual offices for information on
opportunities at each.*

ARCHER DANIELS MIDLAND CO.
4666 Faries Parkway
Decatur, IL 62526
217-424-5200

Employment Contact: Sheila Witts-Manweiler
Total Employees: 10,000 worldwide
Internships: Yes

ASLAC
1932 Wynnton Road
Columbus, GA 31999
404-323-3431

Total Employees: 1,500 (in home office)
Average Entry-Level Hiring: 0
Internships: No

AVIS, INC.
900 Old Country Road
Garden City, NY 11530
516-222-3000

Employment Contact: Carol Tromba, Personnel
Manager
Average Entry-Level Hiring: 10-15
Internships: No

BAXTER HEALTHCARE CORPORATION
1 Baxter Parkway
Deerfield, IL 60015
708-948-2000

Employment Contact: Connie King
Total Employees: 50,000

Average Entry-Level Hiring: ?
Internships: No

BEATRICE COMPANY
2 North LaSalle Street
Chicago, IL 60602
312-782-3820

Employment Contact: Kate Wollensak
Average Entry-Level Hiring: 0
Internships: No

BELL & HOWELL COMPANY
5215 Old Orchard Road
Skokie, IL 60077
708-470-7100

Employment Contact: Cheryl Haas, Corporate
Human Resources Manager
Average Entry-Level Hiring: ?
Internships: No

BEVERLY ENTERPRISES
873 South Fair Oaks Avenue
Pasadena, CA 91105
818-577-6111

Employment Contact: Molly Burgett
Total Employees: 109,000 nationwide
Average Entry-Level Hiring: 0
Internships: No

BLOOMINGDALE'S
59th & Lexington
New York, NY 10022
212-705-2000

Employment Contact: Lloyd Lvell, VP-Personnel
Total Employees: 6,000
Average Entry-Level Hiring: ?
Internships: No

BORDEN, INC.
180 East Broad Street
Columbus, OH 43215
614-225-4000

Employment Contact: Carl Braun
Average Entry-Level Hiring: 0
Internships: No

BRANIFF
7701 Lemmon Avenue
P.O. Box 7035
Dallas, TX 75209
214-358-6011

Employment Contact: Steve Vinciguerra, Recruitment Office

Internships: No

BRISTOL MYERS COMPANY
345 Park Avenue
New York, NY 10154
212-546-4000

Employment Contact: Human Resources
Average Entry-Level Hiring: ?
Internships: No

BRITISH AIRWAYS
75-20 Astoria Blvd.
Jackson Heights, NY 11370
718-397-4000

Employment Contact: Human Resources Department
Total Employees: 1,700 (U. S.)
Internships: No

BROWN GROUP
8400 Maryland Avenue—Box 29
St. Louis, MO 63105
314-854-2432

Employment Contact: Corporate Personnel Dept.
Total Employees: 30,000
Internships: No

BWIA INTERNATIONAL
118-35 Queens Blvd.
Forest Hills, NY 11375
718-520-8100

Employment Contact: Pam Campbell
Total Employees: 35,000
Internships: No

CALVIN KLEIN JEANS
205 West 39th Street
New York, NY 10018
212-719-2600

Employment Contact: Tina Olson, Personnel
Average Entry-Level Hiring: ?
Internships: No

CAMPBELL SOUP COMPANY
Campbell Place
Camden, NJ 08103-1799
609-342-4800

Employment Contact: John Dieleuterio, Director of
Human Resources; Carl Stinnett, VP-Marketing &
Sales
Total Employees: 32,000
Average Entry-Level Hiring: As needed.
Internships: Offered on an "as needed" basis.

CANADIAN PACIFIC HOTELS CORP.
1 University Avenue—Suite 1400
Toronto, ON M5J 2P1
416-367-7111

Employment Contact: Bonnie Holbrook, Director of Corporate Recruitment
Corporate-Level Internships: No

CHANNEL HOME CENTERS
945 Route 10
Whippany, NJ 07981
201-887-7000

Employment Contact: Marc Hettinger, VP-Human Resources
Average Entry-Level Hiring: 2
Internships: No

CHESAPEAKE CORPORATION
1021 East Cary
James Center—22nd Floor
Richmond, VA 23218
804-843-5268

Employment Contact: Joanne Boroughs, Manager of Employment Administration
Average Entry-Level Hiring: 5-6
Internships: Yes

CHRYSLER CORPORATION
12000 Chrysler Drive
Highland Park, MI 48288-1919
313-956-5252/1268

Employment Contact: John W. Stone, College Relations & Recruiting
Total Employees: 148,000 worldwide
Average Entry-Level Hiring: 300 (corporate only)
Internships: Yes

CHUBB
15 Mountain View Road—Box 1615
Warren, NJ 07061
201-580-2000

Employment Contact: Tripp Sheehan, National Recruit Coordinator
Average Entry-Level Hiring: 300
Internships: Yes

CIGNA CORP.
900 Cottage Grove Road
Bloomfield, CT 06002
203-726-6000

Employment Contact: University Relations Department

Total Employees: 50,000 worldwide
Average Entry-Level Hiring: 200
Internships: Yes

C.I.T. GROUP
650 C.I.T. Drive
Livington, NJ 07039
201-740-5485

Employment Contact: Eileen Greenwald, Personnel Representative
Average Entry-Level Hiring: 2-5 (in Marketing/Sales)
Internships: Yes

CLAIROL, INC.
345 Park Avenue
New York, NY 10154
212-546-5000

Employment Contact: Allison Rubeli, VP-Human Resources
Average Entry-Level Hiring: ?
Internships: No

COLGATE-PALMOLIVE COMPANY
300 Park Avenue
New York, NY 10022
212-310-2829

Employment Contact: John Garrison, Human Resources
Average Entry-Level Hiring: ?
Internships: Yes

CONSOLIDATED FREIGHTWAYS
Old Danbury Road
Wilton, CT 06897
203-762-8601

Employment Contact: Kelly Copeland, Human Resource Coordinator
Average Entry-Level Hiring: ?
Internships: No

CONSOLIDATED NATURAL GAS
4 Gateway Center
CNG Tower
Pittsburgh, PA 15222
412-227-1064

Employment Contact: Katrina Burkett, Personnel Manager; or Personnel Managers at the following addresses:

> **East Ohio Gas Company**
> 1201 East 55th Street—P.O. Box 5759
> Cleveland, OH 44101-0759

People's Natural Gas Company
625 Liberty Avenue
Pittsburgh, PA 15222-3197

CNG Transmission
445 West Main
Clarksburg, W. VA 26302-2450

CNG Producing Company
1 Canal Place—Suite 3100
New Orleans, LA 70130

Total Employees: 7,550
Average Entry-Level Hiring: 100
Internships: Yes

CONTROL DATA CORPORATION
P.O. Box 0
Minneapolis, MN 55440
612-853-8100

Employment Contact: Human Resources
Average Entry-Level Hiring: ?
Internships: Yes

COURTYARD BY MARRIOTT
1 Marriott Drive
Washington, DC 20058
800-638-6707

Employment Contact: Manager of Employment
Corporate-Level Internships: Yes

DATA GENERAL CORPORATION
4400 Computer Drive
Westborough, MA 01580
617-366-8911

Employment Contact: K. Holids, Manager of
Corporate Employment
Average Entry-Level Hiring: ?
Internships: No

DAYS INNS OF AMERICA, INC.
2751 Buford Highway, NE
Atlanta, GA 30324
404-325-4000

Employment Contact: Michael Lapenta, District
Director
Average Entry-Level Hiring: ?
Internships: No

DEAN WITTER REYNOLDS INC.
5 World Trade Center—8th Floor
New York, NY 10048
212-392-2222

Employment Contact: Jack O'Connor, Personnel
Manager

Average Entry-Level Hiring: 0
Internships: No

DIGITAL EQUIPMENT CORPORATION
146 Main Street
Maynard, MA 01754
617-897-5111

Employment Contact: John Sims, VP-Personnel
Average Entry-Level Hiring: ?
Internships: No

DISNEYLAND
1313 Harbor Blvd.
Anaheim, CA 92803
714-490-3272

Employment Contact: Professional Staffing Dept.
Total Employees: 10,000
Average Entry-Level Hiring: ?
Internships: Yes

DOW CHEMICAL USA
2020 Dow Center
Midland, MI 48674
517-636-3005

Employment Contact: Mr. Barton Bowser, Supervisor of Marketing Recruiting
Total Employees: 23,000 nationwide, 50,000
worldwide
Average Entry-Level Hiring: 40
Internships: Yes

Other Employment Contacts: University Relations
or Dow Chemical USA at following addresses:

     Mideast Applicant Center
     P.O. Box 1713
     Midland, MI 48674

     Southwest Applicant Center
     Building 120
     Freeport, TX 77541

     Southeast Applicant Center
     P.O. Box 150-C
     Tlaquemine, LA 70764

DOW JONES
200 Liberty Street
New York, NY 10281
212-416-2000

Employment Contact: College Recruiting
Total Employees: 38,000
Internships: Yes

E.I. DUPONT DE NEMOURS & COMPANY
1007 Market Street
Wilmington, DE 19898
302-774-1000

Employment Contact: Dr. Robert Armstrong,
Manager-Professional Staffing
Total Employees: 140,000
Average Entry-Level Hiring: 800
Internships: Yes

EMERY WORLDWIDE
See listing under new name: Consolidated Freightways

EQUIFAX
1600 Peachtree Street—Box 4081
Atlanta, GA 30302
404-885-8000

Employment Contact: Mitchell King
Total Employees: 17,000
Average Entry-Level Hiring: 10-20
Internships: No

EXXON CORPORATION
1251 Avenue of the Americas
New York, NY 10020
212-333-1000

Employment Contact: Nina Benavides, Human Resources
Average Entry-Level Hiring: ?
Internships: No

FARMERS GROUP
4680 Wilshire Blvd.,
Los Angeles, CA 90010
213-932-3200

Employment Contact: Kathy Bollinger
Total Employees: 16,000 employees, 15,000 agents
Average Entry-Level Hiring: 120 Corporate, 100 Regional
Internships: Yes

FEDERAL EXPRESS CORPORATION
P.O. Box 727
Memphis, TN 38194
901-369-3600

Employment Contact: Carole Presley, VP-Corp. Marketing
Average Entry-Level Hiring: ?
Internships: No

FIREMAN'S FUND
777 San Marid Drive
Novato, CA 94998
415-899-3705

Employment Contact:

Central Employment Services
Fireman's Fund Insurance Companies
4040 Civic Center Drive
San Rafael, CA 94903

Total Employees: 11,000
Average Entry-Level Hiring: 20
Internships: No

THE FIRESTONE TIRE & RUBBER COMPANY
1200 Firestone Parkway
Akron, OH 44317
216-379-7000

Employment Contact: Donald L. Groninger, VP-Human Resources
Average Entry-Level Hiring: ?
Internships: No

FISHER FOODS, INC.
5300 Richmond Road
Bedford Heights, OH 44146
216-292-7000

Employment Contact: Dorne Chadsey, Training & Recruitment Coordinator
Average Entry-Level Hiring: ?
Internships: No

FMC CORPORATION
200 East Randolph Drive
Chicago, IL 60601
312-861-6000

Employment Contact: Lawrence P. Holleran, Director-Human Resources
Average Entry-Level Hiring: ?
Internships: No

FORD MOTOR COMPANY
The American Road—Box 1899
Dearborn, MI 48121
313-322-3000

Employment Contact: Peter J. Petillo, VP-Employee Relations
Total Employees: 370,000
Average Entry-Level Hiring: 500
Internships: Yes

FRITO-LAY INC.
P.O. Box 660634
Dallas, TX 75266
214-351-7000

Employment Contact: W. Leo Kiely, Sr VP-Sales &
Marketing
Average Entry-Level Hiring: ?
Internships: No

GAF CORPORATION
1361 Alps Road
Wayne, NJ 07470
201-628-3000

Employment Contact: Gerald Whitmore, VP-
Human Resources
Average Entry-Level Hiring: ?
Internships: No

E & J GALLO WINERY
P.O. Box 1130
Modesto, CA 95353
209-579-3111

Employment Contact: Albion Fenderson, Executive
VP-Marketing
Average Entry-Level Hiring: ?
Internships: No

GEICO INSURANCE
Geico Plaza
Washington, DC 20076
301-986-3000
or:
4520 Willard Avenue
Chevy Chase, MD 20015

Employment Contact: Deborah Lipsey, College
Relations Recruiting Specialist
Total Employees: 68,000
Average Entry-Level Hiring: 300
Internships: Yes

GENERAL DYNAMICS CORPORATION
Pierre LaClede Center
7734 Forsyth Street—21st Floor
St. Louis, MO 63105
314-889-8200

Comments: No entry-level positions at headquarters. Contact the following division offices for
information on entry-level opportunities at each:

    Cessna Aircraft Company
    P.O. Box 7704
    Wichita, KS 67277
    316-946-7466
    Employment Contact: Phil Kusnerus

    Convair Division
    P.O. Box 85357
    San Diego, CA 92138
    619-573-8792
    Employment Contact: Lee C. Kelley

    Data Systems Division
    12101 Woodcrest Executive Drive
    St. Louis, MO 63141
    314-851-8929
    Employment Contact: Cindy Rosburg

    DSD—Central Center
    P.O. Box 748
    Fort Worth, TX 76101
    817-737-1590
    Employment Contact: David E. Marchman

    DSD—Eastern Center
    100 Winnenden Road
    Norwich, CT 06360
    203-823-2395
    Employment Contact: Joan P. Evans-Hunter

    DSD—Ponoma Valley Center
    P.O. Box 2507
    Ponoma, CA 91769
    714-868-2113
    Employment Contact: Ellen Ploeger

    DSD—Western Center
    P.O. Box 85808
    San Diego, CA 92138
    619-573-3974
    Employment Contact: Joe Navarro

    Electric Boat Division
    Eastern Point Road
    Department 641
    Groton, CT 06340
    203-446-6579
    Employment Contact: Fred Pendlebury

    Electronics Division
    P.O. Box 85106
    San Diego, CA 92138
    619-573-5501
    Employment Contact: Mike Chick

    Fort Worth Division
    P.O. Box 748
    Fort Worth, TX 76101
    817-777-5751
    Employment Contact: Elizabeth Polak

GD Services Company
P.O. Box 12598
St. Louis, MO 63141
314-851-4053
Employment Contact: Bernie M. Landau

Land Systems Division
P.O. Box 2071
Warren, MI 48090-2071
313-825-4296
Employment Contact: Donna Thompson

Material Service Corporation
222 North LaSalle
Chicago, IL 60601
312-372-3600 (X2712)
Employment Contact: Ed Wilverding

Ponoma Division
P.O. Box 2507
Ponoma, CA 91769
714-868-4392
Employment Contact: Rich W. Love

Ponoma/Camden Operations
Airport Industrial Park
East Camden, AR 71701
501-574-4304
Employment Contact: Glendle Griggs

Space Systems Division
P.O. Box 85990
San Diego, CA 92138
619-573-9441
Employment Contact: Sue Dehesa

Valley Systems Division
P.O. Box 50-800
Ontario, CA 91761-1085
714-945-8446
Employment Contact: Mark V. Cvikota

Corporate Office
Pierre Laclede Center
St. Louis, MO 63105
314-889-8406
Employment Contact: Kathie McCloskey

General Dynamics Corp.
Pierre Laclede Center
St. Louis, MO 63105
314-889-8440/8437
Employment Contact: John M. Elmers

GENERAL ELECTRIC
3135 Easton Turnpike
Fairfield, CT 06431
203-373-2028 or:

General Electric Company
Recruiting and University Development
1285 Boston Avenue
Bridgeport, CT 06602

Employment Contact:

> Jim Clark, Educational Communications
> Manager
> General Electric—E2B1
> Fairfield, CT 06431

Total Employees: 220,000 nationwide, 300,000 worldwide
Average Entry-Level Hiring: 200
Internships: Yes

GENERAL FOODS CORPORATION
250 North Street
White Plains, NY 10625
914-335-2500

Employment Contact: Susan Lynch Gannor, Manager of College Recruiting
Average Entry-Level Hiring: ?
Internships: Yes

THE B. F. GOODRICH COMPANY
3925 Embassy Parkway
Akron, OH 44313
216-374-2000

Employment Contact: Dale Wagers, Manager of Corporate Resources
Total Employees: 12,000
Average Entry-Level Hiring: ?
Internships: No

GOODYEAR TIRE & RUBBER
1144 East Market Street
Akron, OH 44316
216-796-2121

Employment Contact: Dave Jones
Total Employees: 5,000
Average Entry-Level Hiring: 15
Internships: No

HAMPTON INNS INC.
6799 Great Oaks Road—Suite 100
Memphis, TN 38138
901-756-2811

Employment Contact: Personnel
Corporate-Level Internships: No

HERSHEY FOODS CORPORATION
19 Chocolate Avenue
Hershey, PA 17033
717-534-4000

Employment Contact: Michael Bailey, Manager of Staffing/Employee Services
Total Employees: 6,000
Average Entry-Level Hiring: ?
Internships: No

HILTON HOTELS CORPORATION
9336 Civic Center Drive—P.O. Box 5587
Beverly Hills, CA 90210
213-278-4321

Employment Contact: Personnel
Corporate-Level Internships: No

HILTON INTERNATIONAL/
VISTA INTERNATIONAL
605 Third Avenue
New York, NY 10158
212-973-2200

Employment Contact: Edwin Zephirin
Corporate-Level Internships: No

HOFFMANN-LA ROCHE INC.
340 Kingsland Street
Nutley, NJ 07110
201-235-5000

Employment Contact: Donald Hollander
Average Entry-Level Hiring: ?
Internships: No

HOLIDAY INNS
3796 Lamar Avenue
Memphis, TN 38118
901-362-4881

Employment Contact: Personnel
Corporate-Level Internships: Yes

HONEYWELL
Honeywell Plaza
Minneapolis, MN 55408
612-870-5200

Employment Contact: Ernie Von Heimburg, Mgmt. Corporate/University Relations; Fosten A. Boyle, VP-Human Resources
Total Employees: 58,000 nationwide, 79,000 worldwide
Average Entry-Level Hiring: 450
Internships: No

HOUSEHOLD INTERNATIONAL
2700 Sanders Road
Prospect Heights, IL 60070
312-564-6396

Employment Contact: Sharon Kvam, Employment Manager
Total Employees: 22,000
Average Entry-Level Hiring: Varies
Internships: Yes

HUMANA, INC.
P.O. Box 1438
Louisville, KY 40201
502-580-3416

Employment Contact: Michael Hanley, Director of Corporate Employment
Average Entry-Level Hiring: ?
Internships: No

HYATT HOTELS
200 West Madison Plaza
Chicago, IL 60606
312-750-1234

Employment Contact: Chuck Palid
Corporate-Level Internships: Yes

INGERSOLL-RAND COMPANY
200 Chestnut Ridge Road
Woodcliff Lake, NJ 07675
201-573-0123

Employment Contact: R.G. Ripston, VP-Human Resources
Average Entry-Level Hiring: ?
Internships: No

INTERNATIONAL BUSINESS MACHINES CORPORATION
Old Orchard Road
Armonk, NY 10504
914-765-1900

Employment Contact: Robert Lange, Director of Employment/Personnel Systems (IBM, 2000 Purchase Street, Purchase, NY 10577)
Total Employees: 225,000
Average Entry-Level Hiring: 30-150
Internships: Yes

ITT CORPORATION
320 Park Avenue
New York, NY 10022
212-752-6000

Employment Contact: Ralph W. Pausig, VP/Director of Personnel

Average Entry-Level Hiring: ?
Internships: No

J.C. PENNEY COMPANY, INC.
14841 North Dallas Parkway
Dallas, TX 75240-6740
214-591-2316

Employment Contact: John A Wells, Director of Corporate Marketing; or:

George Neely—Northeast
2000 Oxford
Bethel Park, PA 15102

Ron Varnodo—Southeast
715 Peachtree NE
Atlanta, GA 30308

Don Brewer—Northwest
650 Woodfield Drive
Schaumburg, IL 60173

Joe Hunter—Southwest
6131 Orangethorpe Avenue
Buena Park, CA 90624

Total Employees: 185,000
Average Entry-Level Hiring: 1,500
Internships: Yes

JOHN HANCOCK MUTUAL LIFE INSURANCE
John Hancock Place
Boston, MA 02117
617-421-6000

Employment Contact: Lynn Rosenstein, Dir-Human Resources
Average Entry-Level Hiring: ?
Internships: No

KENTUCKY FRIED CHICKEN CORPORATION
P.O. Box 32070
Louisville, KY 40232
502-456-8300

Employment Contact: Robert Vavrina, VP-Human Resources
Average Entry-Level Hiring: ?
Internships: Yes

K MART CORPORATION
3100 West Big Beaver Road
Troy, MI 48084
313-643-1000

Employment Contact: B.E. Thomas, Sr. VP-Personnel & Management Development
Average Entry-Level Hiring: ?
Internships: No

KNOTT'S BERRY FARM
8039 Beach Blvd.
Buena Park, CA 90620
714-220-5170

Employment Contact: Lisa Moncaio
Total Employees: 3,500
Internships: Yes

KRAFT INC (INDUSTRIAL FOODS GROUP)
6410 Poplar Avenue
Memphis, TN 38119
901-766-2100

Employment Contact: Frank D. Donovan, VP-Sales & Marketing
Average Entry-Level Hiring: ?
Internships: No

KRAFT INC (US RETAIL FOOD GROUP)
Kraft Court
Glenview, IL 60025
708-998-2000

Employment Contact: Dan Dressel, Sr. VP-Human Resources
Average Entry-Level Hiring: ?
Internships: No

KROGER
1014 Vine Street
Cincinnati, OH 45202
513-762-4261

Employment Contact: Human Resource Director
Total Employees: 100,000
Internships: Yes

LEVER BROTHERS COMPANY
390 Park Avenue
New York, NY 10022
212-688-6000

Employment Contact: P. Edward Bohlender, VP-Personnel
Average Entry-Level Hiring: ?
Internships: No

LEVI STRAUSS & COMPANY
P.O. Box 7215
San Francisco, CA 94120
415-544-6000

Employment Contact: Gwendoline Geer, Employment Manager
Average Entry-Level Hiring: ?
Internships: Yes

LIBERTY MUTUAL INSURANCE GROUP
171-175 Berkeley Street
Boston, MA 02117
617-357-9500

Employment Contact: Director of College Relations
Total Employees: 23,000
Average Entry-Level Hiring: 500
Internships: Yes

ELI LILLY & COMPANY
Lilly Corporate Center
Indianapolis, IN 46285
317-261-2000

Employment Contact: Conrad McKinney, Manager-Recruiting
Average Entry-Level Hiring: 5-15
Internships: No

R.H. MACY & COMPANY, INC.
151 West 43rd Street
New York, NY 10001
212-560-3600

Employment Contact: A. David Brown, Sr VP-Personnel
Average Entry-Level Hiring: ?
Internships: No

MARRIOTT CORPORATION
Marriott Drive
Washington, DC 20058
301-380-1203

Employment Contact: Clifford J. Ehrlich, Sr VP-Human Resources
Average Entry-Level Hiring: ?
Internships: Yes

MASSACHUSETTS MUTUAL LIFE INSURANCE COMPANY
1295 State Street
Springfield, MA 01111
413-788-8411

Employment Contact: Celeste Freeman, Associate Director
Average Entry-Level Hiring: ?
Internships: No

MATTEL, INC.
5150 Rosecrans Avenue
Hawthorne, CA 90250
213-978-5150

Employment Contact: Jack Sage, Sr. VP/Human Resources

Average Entry-Level Hiring: ?
Internships: No

MCI COMMUNICATIONS CORPORATION
1133 19th Street—NW
Washington, DC 20036
202-872-1600

Employment Contact: John Zimmerman, VP-Human Resources
Average Entry-Level Hiring: ?
Internships: No

MEAD JOHNSON & COMPANY, INC.
2400 Pennsylvania Street
Evansville, IN 47721
812-429-5000

Employment Contact: E. Lynn Johnson, VP-Personnel
Average Entry-Level Hiring: ?
Internships: No

MERCK & COMPANY, INC.
P.O. Box 2000
Rahway, NJ 07065
201-574-4000

Employment Contact: Walter R. Trosin, VP-Human Resources
Average Entry-Level Hiring: ?
Internships: No

MERCK, SHARP & DOHME
A division of Merck & Company, Inc.
P.O. Box 2000
Rahway, NJ 07065
201-574-6221

Employment Contact: Alaina Love, Manager of College Relations.
Total Employees: 32,000 (including 1,600 in sales, 250 in marketing, 40 in promotion and 70 in advertising).
Average Entry-Level Hiring: ?
Internships: Yes

METROPOLITAN LIFE INSURANCE COMPANY
1 Madison Avenue
New York, NY 10010
212-578-2211

Employment Contact: Catharine Rein, VP-Human Resources; Judith Gaechter
Total Employment: 33,000
Average Entry-Level Hiring: 70
Internships: Yes

MIDWAY AIRLINES
5959 South Cicero Avenue
Chicago, IL 60638
312-838-0001

Employment Contact: Employment Department
Internships: No

MONY FINANCIAL SERVICES
1740 Broadway
New York, NY 10019
212-708-2000

Employment Contact: Russ Austin, Manager of Human Resources
Average Entry-Level Hiring: ?
Internships: No

MORTON THIOKOL, INC.
110 North Wacker Drive
Chicago, IL 60606
312-807-2000

Employment Contact: Hugh C. Marx, VP-Human Resources
Average Entry-Level Hiring: ?
Internships: No

MUTUAL BENEFIT LIFE INSURANCE CO.
520 Broad Street
Newark, NJ 07102
201-481-8000

Employment Contact: Jean M. Lilley, Personnel Consultant
Average Entry-Level Hiring: Varies
Internships: No

MUTUAL OF OMAHA INSURANCE COMPANY
Mutual of Omaha Plaza
Omaha, NE 68175
402-807-2000

Employment Contact: John R. Dixon, Director of Personnel
Average Entry-Level Hiring: ?
Internships: No

NATIONAL BROADCASTING COMPANY, INC.
30 Rockefeller Plaza
New York, NY 10112
212-664-4444

Employment Contact: Eugene McGuire, Executive VP-Personnel
Average Entry-Level Hiring: ?
Internships: No

NATIONAL CAR RENTAL SYSTEM, INC.
7700 France Avenue South
Minneapolis, MN 55435
612-830-2121

Employment Contact: Dick Forsman, Director of Human Resources
Average Entry-Level Hiring: ?
Internships: No

NAVISTAR INTERNATIONAL CORPORATION
401 North Michigan Avenue
Chicago, IL 60611
312-836-2000

Employment Contact: Tom Kent, Staff VP-Management Training
Average Entry-Level Hiring: ?
Internships: No

NCR CORPORATION
1700 South Patterson Blvd.
Dayton, OH 45479
513-445-5000

Employment Contact: James E. McElwain, VP-Personnel Resources
Average Entry-Level Hiring: ?
Internships: No

NORTH AMERICAN PHILIPS CORPORATION
100 East 42nd Street
New York, NY 10017
212-850-5000

Employment Contact: Robert Banks, Recruiting
Average Entry-Level Hiring: ?
Internships: No

NORTHWEST AIRLINES, NWA, INC.
Staffing Division MS-A3200
Minneapolis—St. Paul International Airport
St. Paul, MN 55111
612-726-4262

Employment Contact: Jim Dixie
Total Employees: 38,000
Internships: Yes

OHIO CASUALTY
136 North Third Street
Hamilton, OH 45025
513-867-3000

Employment Contact: Marge Brown, Employment Supervisor
Average Entry-Level Hiring: 10-20
Internships: No

ONEIDA LTD.
Kenwood Avenue
Sherrill, NY 13461
315-361-3000

Employment Contact: Michael Reilly, Employment
Manager
Total Employees: 2,000
Average Entry-Level Hiring: 5-10
Internships: No

PACE MANAGEMENT SERVICE CORP.
2346 South Lynhurst E-105
Indianapolis, IN 46241
317-243-2224

Employment Contact: Lawrence A. Olivia, Director
of Resource Development
Corporate-Level Internships: Yes

PACIFIC BELL
633 Folsom Street—Room 103
San Francisco, CA 94107
415-542-8369

Employment Contact: Personnel Department
Total Employees: 68,000
Average Entry-Level Hiring: 15-25
Internships: Yes

PAN AMERICAN WORLD AIRWAYS INC.
Miami International Airport
P.O. Box 59-2055AMF
Miami, FL 33159
212-880-6369

Employment Contact: Ellen Schikuma, Corporate
Recruiting
Total Employees: 30,000
Internships: Yes

PARAMOUNT COMMUNICATIONS
15 Columbus Circle
New York, NY 10023
212-373-8000

Employment Contact: Betty Panarella, Sr. VP-
Human Resources
Average Entry-Level Hiring: ?
Internships: No

PEPSI-COLA U.S.A.
Anderson Hill Road
Purchase, NY 10577
914-253-2000

Employment Contact: Michael Feiner, VP-
Personnel

Average Entry-Level Hiring: ?
Internships: No

PHILIP MORRIS COMPANIES, INC.
120 Park Avenue
New York, NY 10017
212-880-5000

Employment Contact: William O'Connor, VP-
Human Resources
Average Entry-Level Hiring: ?
Internships: No

PHILLIPS PETROLEUM COMPANY
Fourth & Keeler
Bartlesville, OK 74004
918-661-6600

Employment Contact: S.R. Thomas, VP-Human
Resources
Average Entry-Level Hiring: ?
Internships: No

POLAROID CORPORATION
549 Technology Square
Cambridge, MA 02139
617-577-2000

Employment Contact: Owen J. Gaffney, Group VP-
Human Resources
Average Entry-Level Hiring: ?
Internships: No

PONDEROSA INC.
Box 578
Dayton, OH 45401
513-454-2400

Employment Contact: Harry Leidy, Manager-
Human Resources
Total Employees: 20,000
Average Entry-Level Hiring: 5
Internships: Yes

PRINCIPAL MUTUAL LIFE INSURANCE
711 High
Des Moines, IA 50307
515-247-5111

Employment Contact: Carol Ward, Senior
Professional Recruiter
Total Employees: 10,000
Average Entry-Level Hiring: 200
Internships: No

PROCTER & GAMBLE
One Procter & Gamble Plaza
Cincinnati, OH 45202
513-983-6293

Employment Contact: See below for individual contacts listed by area of specialization:

Advertising: Brand Management:

Advertising Department
The Procter & Gamble Co.,
P.O. Box 599
Cincinnati, OH 45201
Contact: Stanley M. Haude, Recruiting Manager

Purchasing Management:

Corporate Purchases Division
The Procter & Gamble Co., GO TN-5
P.O. Box 599
Cincinnati, IH 45201
Contact: Assoc. Manager of Personnel Development

General Customer Services Management:

The Procter & Gamble Distributing Co., GO TN-10
P.O. Box 85525
Cincinnati, OH 45201
Contact: General Customer Services Recruiting Manager

Financial Management:

Finance Division
The Procter & Gamble Co., GO TE-15
P.O. Box 599
Cincinnati, OH 45201
Contact: Associate Director—Personnel

Management Systems:

The Procter & Gamble Co., GO TN-15
P.O. Box 599
Cincinnati, OH 45201
Contact: Management Systems Recruiting

Market Research:

The Procter & Gamble Co., GO C-8
P.O. Box 599
Cincinnati, OH 45201
Contact: Personnel Manager, Market Research Dept.

Sales Management:

The Procter & Gamble Distributing Co.
Contact: Regional Personnel Manager at addresses below:

100 Walnut Avenue
Clark, NJ 07066

P.O. Box 105085
Atlanta, GA 30348

2000 Oxford Drive—Suite 240
Bethel Park, PA 15102

1801 S. Meyers Road—Suite 500
Oakbrook Terrace, IL 60181

P.O. Box 1910
Dallas, TX 75221

P.O. Box 5977
Orange, CA 92667

PRUDENTIAL INSURANCE COMPANY
56 North Livingston Avenue
Roseland, NJ 07068
201-716-8306

Employment Contact: Charles Robbins, Assoc. Employment Manager
Total Employees: 85,000
Average Entry-Level Hiring: 500
Internships: Recruits mainly through Employment Centers on campuses.

PUBLIC SERVICE INDIANA
1000 East Main Street
Plainfield, IN 46168
317-838-1472

Employment Contact: Jerry Land
Total Employees: 4,300
Average Entry-Level Hiring: 10
Internships: Yes

THE QUAKER OATS COMPANY
321 North Clark
Chicago, IL 60610
312-222-7111

Employment Contact: Lawrence M. Baytos, VP-Human Resources
Total Employees: 20,000
Average Entry-Level Hiring: ?
Internships: No

RADISSON HOTEL CORP.
12805 State Highway 55
Minneapolis, MN 55441
612-540-5526

Employment Contact: John R. Burns, Director of Human Resource Development or Marilee Johnson, Manager of Employment
Corporate-Level Internships: No

RALSTON PURINA COMPANY
Checkerboard Square
St. Louis, MO 63164
314-982-1000

Employment Contact: Barbara Cant, Manager-Personnel Services
Average Entry-Level Hiring: ?
Internships: No

RAMADA INNS, INC.
P.O. Box 590
Phoenix, AZ 85001
602-273-4000

Employment Contact: Thomas W. Davidson, VP-Human Resources
Average Entry-Level Hiring: ?
Internships: No

RED ROOF INNS
4355 Davidson Road
Hilliard, OH 43026
614-876-3433

Employment Contact: Doug Bruce
Corporate-Level Internships: Yes

THE RESIDENCE INN CO.
A subsidiary of the Marriott Corp.
1 Marriott Drive
Washington, DC 20058
800-638-6707

Employment Contact: Personnel
Corporate-Level Internships: Yes

A.H. ROBBINS COMPANY, INC.
P.O. Box 26609
Richmond, VA 23261
804-257-2000

Employment Contact: For pharmaceutical sales—
Shirley Hess (ext. 2072); Consumer Products/
Marketing & Sales—John Neurohr (ext. 2721).
Average Entry-Level Hiring: ?
Internships: No

ROSES STORES
P.H. Rose Building
218 Garnett Street
Henderson, NC 27536
919-492-8111

Employment Contact: Bob Hilton
Total Employees: 22,000
Average Entry-Level Hiring: 250
Internships: No

SARA LEE CORPORATION
3 First National Plaza
Chicago, IL 60602
312-726-2600

Employment Contact: Karen Batenic, Director of Human Resources
Average Entry-Level Hiring: ?
Internships: No

SEARLE LABORATORIES
5200 Old Orchard Road
Skokie, IL 60077
708-982-7000

Employment Contact: Margie McCarthy, Employment Specialist
Average Entry-Level Hiring: ?
Internships: No

SHAKLEE CORPORATION
444 Market Street
San Francisco, CA 94111
415-954-3000

Employment Contact: Neil Barnhart, Director of Personnel
Average Entry-Level Hiring: ?
Internships: No

SHERATON CORP.
60 State Street
Boston, MA 02109
617-367-3600

Employment Contact: Brett Hutchens
Corporate-Level Internships: Yes

SIGNATURE INNS, INC.
P.O. Box 50703
Indianapolis, IN 46250
317-577-1111

Employment Contact: Cindi Rosecrans, Training Coordinator; John Ewing, Director of Training.
Average Entry-Level Hiring: 50
Corporate-Level Internships: No

THE SOUTHLAND CORPORATION
2711 North Haskell
Dallas, TX 75204
214-828-7011

Employment Contact: Wanda Williams, Personnel Manager
Average Entry-Level Hiring: ?
Internships: No

SPIEGEL
1515 West 22nd Street
Oak Brook, IL 60521
312-986-8800

Total Employees: 5,200 total; 1,500 executives
Average Entry-Level Hiring: 25
Internships: Yes

STATE FARM MUTUAL INSURANCE
1 State Farm Plaza
Bloomington, IL 61701
309-766-2311

Employment Contact: Dallas T. Reynolds, VP-Personnel
Average Entry-Level Hiring: ?
Internships: No

STERLING DRUG INC.
90 Park Avenue
New York, NY 10016
212-907-2000

Employment Contact: Theresa Girsch, Employment Manager
Average Entry-Level Hiring: ?
Internships: No

ST. PAUL COMPANIES
385 Washington Street
St. Paul, MN 55102
612-228-5840

Employment Contact: Bill Bush, Employment Rep.
Total Employees: 14,000 worldwide
Average Entry-Level Hiring: 150
Internships: Yes

STRAWBRIDGE AND CLOTHIER
(Department Store Division)
801 Market Street
Philadelphia, PA 19107
215-629-7817

Employment Contact: Charlotte Waterbury, Mgr. of Exec. Recruitment and Placement
Total Employees: 12,000 in 33 retail stores, including 4,000 in sales, 1,000 in marketing, 25 in promotion and 45 in advertising.
Average Entry-Level Hiring: ?
Internships: Yes

SUPER VALU STORES
P.O. Box 990
Minneapolis, MN 55440

Employment Contact: Steve Frederick, Management Recruiter

Total Employees: 35,000 (mainly warehousing)
Average Entry-Level Hiring: 10 (at corporate level)
Internships: No

TANDEM COMPUTERS INC.
19333 Vallco Parkway
Cupertino, CA 95014
408-725-6000

Employment Contact: Jan E. Jensen, VP-Human Resources
Average Entry-Level Hiring: ?
Internships: No

TOYS R US
395 West Passaic Street
Rochelle Park, NJ 07662
201-599-7865

Employment Contact: Richard Cudrin, Director Human Resources
Average Entry-Level Hiring: NA
Internships: Co-op program.

TRANSAMERICA
1150 South Olive Street
Los Angeles, CA 90015
213-742-3431

Employment Contact: Employment Department
Average Entry-Level Hiring: ?
Internships: Yes

TRUSTHOUSE FORTE HOTELS
1973 Friendship Drive
El Cajon, CA 92020
619-448-1884

Employment Contact: Barbara Radcliffe
Corporate-Level Internships: No

20TH CENTURY INSURANCE COMPANY
6301 Owensmouth Avenue
Woodland Hills, CA 91367
818-704-3760

Employment Contact: Human Resources
Total Employees: 1,650
Average Entry-Level Hiring: 25
Internships: No

UNITED AIRLINES
P.O. Box 66100
Chicago, IL 60666
312-952-4201

Employment Contact: Mr. Gene Krop, Employment Manager

Total Employees: 65,000
Internships: Yes

UNITED OF OMAHA LIFE INSURANCE CO.
Mutual Of Omaha Plaza
Omaha, NE 68175
402-342-7600

Employment Contact: NA
Total Employees: 65,000
Average Entry-Level Hiring: 120
Internships: Now developing a program.

UNITED TECHNOLOGIES
United Technologies Bldg.
Hartford, CT 06101
203-678-4806

Employment Contact: C. J. Livesay, University Relations, at above address or contacts at the divisions/subsidiaries below:

> Guy Courcy
> Pratt & Whitney
> East Hartford, CT
>
> Jeff O'Dell
> Hamilton Standard
> Winsorlock, CT 06096
>
> Joel Slaskey
> Sikorsky
> Stratford, CT
>
> Sam Aconford
> Otis
> Farmington, CT 06032
>
> Bob Currier
> Carrier
> Syracuse, NY
>
> Barry James
> Norton Systems
> Norwalk, CT

USF&G
100 Light Street
Baltimore, MD 21202
301-547-3000

Employment Contact: Phil Ostrander
Total Employees: 12,000
Average Entry-Level Hiring: 15-20
Internships: No

U.S. WEST
7800 East Orchard Road
Englewood, CO 80111
305-741-8454

Employment Contact: Judy Smith, Staffing Mgr.
Total Employees: 68,000
Average Entry-Level Hiring: 30
Internships: Yes

WALGREEN
200 Wilmot Road
Deerfield, IL 60015
312-405-5886

Employment Contact: Richard Heaton, Consultant/Personnel Recruiter
Total Employees: 50,000
Average Entry-Level Hiring: 204
Internships: Yes

WALT DISNEY WORLD RESORT
PO Box 10000
Lake Buena Vista, FL 32830-1000
407-828-2850

Employment Contact: Donna Palmer
Total Employees: 33,000
Average Entry-Level Hiring: ?
Internships: Yes

WESTIN HOTELS
2001 Sixth Avenue
Seattle, WA 98121
206-443-5000

Employment Contact: College Relations Manager
Corporate-Level Internships: No

WINNEBAGO INDUSTRIES, INC.
P.O. Box 152
Forest City, IA 50436
515-582-3535

Employment Contact: Larry Kluckhohn, Personnel Mgr.
Average Entry-Level Hiring: ?
Internships: Yes

WYNDHAM HOTELS & RESORTS
3200 Trammell Crow Center
2001 Ross Avenue
Dallas, TX 75201-2997
214-978-4578

Employment Contact: Elizabeth Brannon, Staffing and Development Manager
Corporate-Level Internships: Yes

YELLOW FREIGHT SYSTEM, INC.
10990 Roe Avenue
Overland Park, KS 66207
913-345-3000

Employment Contact: Jody Kramer, Human
Resources Department Analyst.

Total Employees: 23,400, including 1,000 in sales, 30
in marketing, 2 in promotion and 3 in advertising
functions.

Average Entry-Level Hiring: ?

Internships: Yes

ZALE CORP.
901 West Walnut Hill Lane
Irving, TX 75038
214-580-4988

Average Entry-Level Hiring: 0

33

Market Research (Supplier) Firm Listings

This chapter features information on the top 35-odd market research firms in the U.S. and Canada. A more extensive listing of such firms is available from the American Marketing Association in two of its annual publications: its <u>Marketing Services Guide</u> (which is also the AMA Membership Directory) and the <u>Green Book: the International Directory of Marketing Research Houses and Services</u>. (The latter volume is published by the New York chapter.)

We have listed pertinent entry-level opportunities (with the correct contact noted as *Employment Contact)* and whether or not internships are available, though as these listings will soon make clear, most such firms do *not* hire new people right out of college and offer few internships. If entry-level jobs *are* available, we noted the *Average Entry-Level Hiring* (a yearly number) and specific job titles with educational/skills requirements where available (under either *Comments* or *Opportunities).*

If other information, such as total employees, specialties, etc. was available on specific companies, it was noted separately.

Listings begin on the following page.

ARBITRON RATINGS
142 West 57th
New York, NY 10019
212-887-1300

Employment Contact: Roberta DePolo, Personnel
Total Employees: 100+
Average Entry-Level Hiring: ?
Internships: No

ASI MARKET RESEARCH, INC.
7655 Sunset Blvd.
Los Angeles, CA 90046
213-876-6600

Employment Contact: Shirley Raphael, Personnel
Director
Opportunities: Marketing Research—College
degree required; 2-3 years experience.
Internships: No

BURKE MARKETING RESEARCH
800 Broadway
Cincinnati, OH 45202
513-852-8585

Employment Contact: Anne Schwing, Director of
Human Resources
Internships: No

CHILTON RESEARCH SERVICES INC.
201 King of Prussia Road
Radnor, PA 19089
215-964-4218

Employment Contact: Marilyn McLaughlin,
Manager of Employment
Opportunities: All beginning positions require a
college degree and at least 1-2 years experience.
Internships: No

**COMPUSEARCH MARKET & SOCIAL
RESEARCH**
330 Front Street West—Suite 1100
Toronto, ON M5V 3S7
416-348-9180

Employment Contact: Debbie Coughtrey, Dir. of
Corporate Communications
Total Employees: 65
Average Entry-Level Hiring: 3-5
Opportunities: Sales Rep., Researchers—College
degree (business preferred). Administrative staff—
High school degree required.
Internships: No

CUSTOM RESEARCH, INC.
10301 Wayzata Blvd.—Box 26695
Minneapolis, MN 55426-0695
612-542-0800

Employment Contact: Ilene Taylor, Personnel
Director
Opportunities: Assistants in Marketing Research—
College degree required and at least 2-3 years
experience.
Internships: No

DATA DEVELOPMENT CORPORATION
600 Third Avenue
New York, NY 10016
212-633-1100

Employment Contact: Linda Amrani, VP-
Operations
Total Employees: 50
Average Entry-Level Hiring: 1
Opportunities: Clerks—High school graduates.
Mailroom (proofreading)—No requirements
specified. Accounting Asst.—College degree; no
experience necessary.
Internships: No

DECISION RESEARCH CORPORATION
33 Hayden Avenue
Lexington, MA 02173
617-861-7350

Employment Contact: Janet Pozen, Personnel
Director
Total Employees: 60
Opportunities: Data Processing Asst. and Mar-
keting & Sales Asst. positions require a college
degree and at least 1-2 years experience.
Internships: No

DIMARK MARKETING SERVICES, INC.
66-K-1485 Portagee Avenue
Winnipeg, MB R3G 0W4
204-783-4924

Employment Contact: Kathy Heffernan, General
Manager

DUN & BRADSTREET CANADA LTD.
5770 Huron Torio Street
Mississagua, ON A5R 3G5
416-568-6000

Employment Contact: Jenny Watson, Human
Resource Rep.
Total Employees: 400
Average Entry-Level Hiring: 50

Opportunities: Sales Rep. Trainee—College degree (sales, business); prior experience. Business Analysts— No requirements specified.
Internships: No

EHRHART-BABIC ASSOCIATES, INC.
120 Route 9W
Englewood Cliffs, NJ 07632
201-461-6700

Employment Contact: Donald W. Harkin, Sr. Vice President
Total Employees: 85
Average Entry-Level Hiring: 1
Internships: No

ELRICK AND LAVIDGE, INC.
A subsidiary of Equifax, Inc.
10 South Riverside Plaza
Chicago, IL 60606-3232
312-726-0666

Employment Contact: Shirley L. Sandkam, Admininstrative Assistant
Total Employees: 203
Opportunities: Marketing and Sales Assistants—College degree required as well as 2+ years experience.
Internships: No

THE GALLUP ORGANIZATION, INC..
53 Bank Street—Box 310
Princeton, NJ 08542
609-924-9600

Employment Contact: Dean J. Maitlen, Exec. VP-Sales & Marketing
Average Entry-Level Hiring: 1-2
Opportunities: Marketing and Sales Assistants—College degree required; no experience necessary.
Internships: No

LOUIS HARRIS AND ASSOCIATES, INC.
630 Fifth Avenue
New York, NY 10111
212-698-9600

Employment Contact: Humphrey Taylor, President
Opportunities: Beginning positions in Research require a college degree and 2-3 years experience.
Internships: No

HARTE-HANKS
65 Route 4 East
Riveredge, NJ 07661
201-342-8800

Employment Contact: Denise Sheehan

Total Employees: 200
Opportunities: Telemarketing—College degree required plus two years experience.
Internships: No

IMS AMERICA
600 West Germantown Pike
Plymouth Meeting, PA 19462
215-834-4590

Employment Contact: Dee Grosso
Total Employees: 2,000
Opportunities: Marketing Support Analyst ($20,000)—Provide analytical and client support to account executives. Technical Analyst ($20,000)—Provide internal user support to all company personnel regarding work processing and software PC packages to expedite work-load. Programmer Trainee ($22,000)—Responsible for providing coding and system analysis, IBM/COBOL/BATCH. Associate Accountant ($20,000)—Provide analytical support regarding general accounting principles to senior accountant. Depending on job discipline, there is a mix of departmental, human resources and independent studies/training.
Internships: Yes

INFORMATION RESOURCES
150 North Clinton
Chicago, IL 60606
312-726-1221

Employment Contact: Gary Tackett, Recruiter
Total Employees: 2,500
Internships: No

KAPULER MARKETING RESEARCH
3436 North Kennicott Avenue
Arlington Heights, IL 60004
312-870-6730

Employment Contact: Josh Goldspiel
Total Employees: 400
Opportunities: Beginning positions in Marketing and Sales Research require a college degree and at least 2-3 years experience.
Internships: Yes

M/A/R/C INC.
P.O. Box 650083
Dallas, TX 75265-0080
214-506-3400

Employment Contact: Sharon Olson, Human Resources Director
Total Employees: 480

Average Entry-Level Hiring: 1-3

Opportunities: Clerks—High school graduates. Marketing Asst., Asst. Account Executive—College degree; no experience required.

Internships: Yes

MARKET FACTS, INC.
676 North St. Clair Street
Chicago, IL 60611
312-280-9100

Employment Contact: Lynn Quettrochi, Personnel Director (312-524-2001)

Total Employees: 1,000

Average Entry-Level Hiring: 30

Opportunities: Field Interviewing, Account Group, Consumer Mail Panel—College degree; no experience required.

Internships: No

MARKET OPINION RESEARCH
243 West Congress—Suite 1000
Detroit, MI 48226-3298
313-963-2414

Employment Contact: Dolores Allor, Personnel

Total Employees: 75

Opportunities: Research Analyst and Juniors in the Accounting Dept—College degree required; at least two years experience.

Internships: Yes

McCOLLUM/SPIELMAN RESEARCH
235 Great Neck Road
Great Neck, NY 11021
516-482-0310

Employment Contact: Dorothy Brown, Personnel Dir

Total Employees: 50

Opportunities: Marketing Research Analyst—College degree required and at least 2-3 years experience.

Internships: No

MEDIAMARK RESEARCH INC.
341 Madison Avenue
New York, NY 10017
212-599-0444

Employment Contact: Renata Ranges, Office Manager

Total Employees: 58

Average Entry-Level Hiring: 0

Opportunities: Marketing Asst.—College degree; no experience required.

Internships: No

MENDON ASSOCIATES, INC.
201 Duffern Street—Suite 302
Toronto, ON M6K 1Y9
416-537-7363

Employment Contact: George DeMendonza, President

Total Employees: 11

Average Entry-Level Hiring: 2

Opportunities: Programmer—No requirements specified.

Internships: No

THE NPD GROUP
900 West Shore Road
Port Washington, NY 11050
516-625-0700

Employment Contact: Harriet Abrams, Human Resources

Total Employees: 700

Average Entry-Level Hiring: 20-25

Comments: Company promotes from within.

Internships: No

OXTOBY-SMITH, INC.
150 East 58th Street
New York, NY 10155
212-614-0040

Employment Contact: Ruth Cowan, Personnel Director

Total Employees: 100

Average Entry-Level Hiring: 0

Internships: No

RESPONSE ANALYSIS CORPORATION
377 Wall Street—P.O. Box 158
Princeton, NJ 08542
609-921-3333

Employment Contact: Kim Hart, Personnel Administrator

Total Employees: 64

Average Entry-Level Hiring: 0

Opportunities: Data Processing—College degree required and at least two years experience.

Internships: No

SIMMONS MARKET RESEARCH BUREAU
219 East 42nd Street
New York, NY 10017
212-916-8900

Employment Contact: William Stetter, Controller

Total Employees: 190

Average Entry-Level Hiring: 0
Internships: No

STARCH INRA HOOPER, INC.
566 East Boston Post Road
Mamaroneck, NY 10543
914-698-0800

Employment Contact: Robert Bishop, Personnel Director
Total Employees: 225
Average Entry-Level Hiring: 0
Opportunities: Positions in Field Research and Writing/Project Work require a college degree and 1-2 years experience.
Internships: No

WALKER RESEARCH, INC.
3939 Priority Way South Drive
P.O. Box 80432
Indianapolis, IN 46280-0432
317-843-3939

Employment Contact: Tami Kaltenbach, Human Resources
Total Employees: 231
Average Entry-Level Hiring: 5-10
Internships: No

WESTAT
1650 Research Blvd.
Rockville, MD 20850
301-251-1500

Employment Contact: Patricia Smith, Personnel Director
Total Employees: 1,000
Average Entry-Level Hiring: 3-5
Opportunities: Clerks—High school graduates; no experience. Programmer Analyst—College degree required; 1-2 years experience.
Internships: No

WINONA RESEARCH, INC.
8200 Humboldt Avenue South
Minneapolis, MN 55431
612-881-5400

Employment Contact: Clyde Drees, Personnel Director
Total Employees: 200
Average Entry-Level Hiring: 0
Opportunities: Field Dept., Data Dept.—College degree required; at least 1-2 years experience.
Internships: No

THE WIRTHLIN GROUP
(formerly Decision/Making/Information)
1363 Beverly Road
McLean, VA 22101
703-556-0001

Employment Contact: Rosemary Hidalgo, Director of Personnel
Total Employees: 65 (headquarters only)
Average Entry-Level Hiring: 2-3 (nationwide)
Comments: Entry-level people must have MBA in Marketing.
Internships: No

YANKELOVICH, SKELLY & WHITE/ CLANCY, SHULMAN, INC.
Eight Wright Street
Westport, CT 06880
203-227-2700

Employment Contact: Human Resource Department
Total Employees: 100
Average Entry-Level Employment: 10
Opportunities: Entry-level employees begin as analysts. Must have a college degree; preferrably in Business, Marketing or Statistics.
Internships: Yes

34

Selected Ad Agency Job Listings: United States & Canada

If you are interested in a career at an advertising agency, our first recommendation is that you consult our *Advertising Career Directory*, available in a brand-new fourth edition. In addition to two dozen articles by top agency pros (only five of which were excerpted in this volume), it includes detailed listings of agencies throughout the U.S. and Canada seeking entry-level people.

We have excerpted *some* of those listings here, though we have limited them to the very largest agencies only and have not listed the detailed "Opportunities" included in our *Advertising Career Directory*. Do note that this is the first time that information on Canadian agencies has also been included.

Despite our every attempt to ensure the accuracy of the information we've included, time marches on...and so do contacts.

In other words, there will be mistakes in these listings—the very day they're published—just because things change and, in some agencies, change very quickly. But we think you'll find that the vast majority of this previously-unpublished information will remain credible until it is updated in 1992.

Lastly, previous editions of this *Career Directory* have also included information on summer and school-year internships.

At the request of the librarians, counselors, professors and students who utilize these Directories, we have now published this internship data (and, in fact, increased three-fold the amount of information included in each internship listing) in a completely separate series of books—our *Internships Series*.

Volume 1 of this series lists internship programs at hundreds of major advertising agencies, PR firms and corporations in the United States and Canada. It is available in a new second edition for 1990.

Selected listings begin on the next page.

Ad Agency Entry-Level Job Listings

AC&R ADVERTISING, INC.
A member of Saatchi & Saatchi USA Affiliates
16 East 32nd Street
New York, NY 10016
212-685-2500

Employment Contact: Patricia Shelton, VP/Dir.of Human Resources; Robin Ornstein, Personnel Rep.

Total Employees: 320

Average Entry-Level Hiring: 30

Internships: No

ALLY & GARGANO, INC.
805 Third Avenue
New York, NY 10022
212-688-5300

Employment Contact: Paulette Barlanera, VP-Office Services & Personnel

Total Employees: 260

Average Entry-Level Hiring: 0

Opportunities: Applicants with experience only.

Internships: No

BARNHART & COMPANY
455 Sherman—Suite 500
Denver, CO 80203
303-744-3211

Employment Contact: Steve Fay, Chief Financial Officer

Total Employees: 48

Average Entry-Level Hiring: 3

Internships: Yes

THE BCP GROUP LIMITED
1000 Sherbrooke Street West—21st Floor
Montreal, PQ H3A 3G9
514-285-1414

Employment Contact: Prefontaine Chrftane, Personnel Agent

Total Employees: 140

Average Entry-Level Hiring: 5

Internships: No

BHN ADVERTISING & PUBLIC RELATIONS
910 North 11th Street
St. Louis, MO 63101
314-241-1200

Employment Contact: Kay Going, Media Director

Total Employees: 65

Average Entry-Level Hiring: 1-2

Internships: Yes

THE BLOOM COMPANIES
3500 Maple
Dallas, TX 75219
214-443-9900

Employment Contact: Diane Bynum, Personnel Dir.

Total Employees: 200

Average Entry-Level Hiring: 1-2

Internships: No

LEO BURNETT COMPANY, INC.
35 West Wacker Drive
Chicago, IL 60601
312-220-5959

Employment Contact: Wayne Johnson, Creative Recruiting Dept.

Total Employees: 1,961

Average Entry-Level Hiring: 50-70

Internships: No

THE BURNS GROUP, INC.
1575 Sheland Tower
Minneapolis, MN 55426
612-334-6000

Employment Contact: Susan Kroska, Personnel Administrator

Total Employees: 188

Average Entry-Level Hiring: 2-3

Internships: Yes

HAROLD CABOT & COMPANY, INC.
One Constitution Plaza
Boston, MA 02129
617-242-6200

Employment Contact: Edmund C. Fitzmaurice, Sr. VP

Total Employees: 125

Average Entry-Level Hiring: 0-1

Internships: No

CAMPBELL-MITHUN-ESTY ADVERTISING
A subsidiary of Saatchi & Saatchi
222 South Ninth Street
Minneapolis, MN 55402
612-347-1000

Employment Contact: Account Svces: Robert Seper, Director of Human Resources; Media: Sharon Moe, Human Resources Administrator

Total Employees: 430

Average Entry-Level Hiring: 5-10 (varies each yr.)

Comments: Send cover letter and resume to appropriate contact. <u>No phone calls.</u>

Internships: No

CAMPBELL-MITHUN-ESTY ADVERTISING
A subsidiary of Saatchi & Saatchi
100 East 42nd Street
New York, NY 10017
212-692-6200

Employment Contact: Hal Simpson, Senior VP/Dir. of Human Resources

Total Employees: 185

Average Entry-Level Hiring: 0

Comments: Rarely available, entry-level openings tend to be in the areas of accounting and media.

Internships: No

CARGILL, WILSON & ACREE, INC.
A subsidiary of The Omnicom Group
3060 Peachtree Road NW, 1 Buckhead Plaza
Atlanta, GA 30305
404-364-8700

Employment Contact: Denise Steiner, Sr. VP/Director Creative Services

Total Employees: 40

Average Entry-Level Hiring: 5

Internships: Yes

COLLE & MCVOY, INC.
7900 International Drive—Suite 700
Minneapolis, MN 55425
612-851-2500

Employment Contact: Bob Hettlinger—VP/Director Human Resources;

Creatives—Jon Anderson, Executive Creative Director;

Public Relations—Doug Spong, Sr. VP/Director Public Relations

Total Employees: 104

Average Entry-Level Hiring: 2-4

Comments: "We suggest sending a cover letter and resume to contact. Exploratory interviews are conducted as time permits. When an opening occurs, resume file is the first source used to identify candidates for interviews.

Agency conducts monthly informational meetings for public relations and account services entry-level candidates."

Internships: Yes (positions filled locally)

COMMERCIAL ASSOCIATES/ROSS ROY LTD.
1737 Walker Road
Windsor, ON M8Y 4R8
519-258-7584

Employment Contact: Claudette Munger, Human Resource Manager

Total Employees: 80

Average Entry-Level Hiring: ?

Internships: No

FRANK J. CORBETT INC.
211 East Chicago Avenue—Suite 1100
Chicago, IL 60611
312-664-5310

Employment Contact: Department heads

Total Employees: 80

Average Entry-Level Hiring: 3

Internships: No

CRAMER KRASSELT COMPANY
733 North Van Buren Street
Milwaukee, WI 53202
414-227-3500

Employment Contact: Paul Counsell, Executive VP or Department Heads—Account Services: Paul Bentley; Creative: Neil Casey; Media Services: Donald Pom or Donald Clow; Research: James Shampley

Total Employees: 170

Average Entry-Level Hiring: 2-3

Internships: No

CV ADVERTISING
One Eglinton Avenue East—Suite 500
Toronto, ON M4P 3A1
416-486-6695

Employment Contact: Department Heads

Total Employees: 48

Average Entry-Level Hiring: 1-2

Internships: No

DAILEY & ASSOCIATES
A subsidiary of the Interpublic Group of Companies
3055 Wilshire Blvd.
Los Angeles, CA 90010
213-386-7823

Employment Contact: Mrs. Toby J. Burke, Director of Personnel Administration

Total Employees: 200

Average Entry-Level Hiring: 3

Internships: No

D'ARCY MASIUS BENTON & BOWLES, INC.
909 Third Avenue
New York, NY 10022
212-758-6200

Employment Contact: Karen Schiller, Personnel Dir.
Total Employees: 6,200
Average Entry-Level Hiring: 50
Suggestions: "If you are looking for an entry-level job post-graduation, send us your resume the January *before* you graduate."
Internships: Yes

DCA ADVERTISING
A division of Dentsu—Tokyo, Japan
1114 Avenue of the Americas
New York, NY 10036
212-703-1433

Employment Contact: Personnel
Internships: Yes

DDB-NEEDHAM WORLDWIDE, INC.
437 Madison Avenue
New York, NY 10022
212-415-2000

Employment Contact: Ms. Mariam Saytell
Internships: Yes

DEACON DAY ADVERTISING
20 Richmond Street East—7th Floor
Toronto, ON M5C 2R9
416-362-8600

Employment Contact: Chris Chow, Office Mgr
Total Employees: 22
Average Entry-Level Hiring: 5
Internships: No

DELLA FEMINA, MCNAMEE WCRS
WCRS (Holding Company)
500 North Michigan Avenue
Chicago, IL 60611
312-222-1313

Employment Contact: Arlene Hamilton Office Mgr.
Total Employees: 45
Average Entry-Level Hiring: 6
Internships: Yes

W. B. DONER & COMPANY ADVERTISING
25900 Northwestern Highway
Southfield, MI 48075
313-354-9700

Employment Contact: *Creative*—Paula Bettendorf, Recruitment-Creative; *All Others*—Dianne Lemaux, Asst. Personnel Manager

Total Employees: 575
Average Entry-Level Hiring: 7 (3 in Creative, 4 in other areas)
Internships: Yes

DUGAN/FARLEY COMMUNICATIONS
600 East Cressant Avenue
Upper Saddle River, NJ 07458
201-934-0720

Employment Contact: Ginny Raimann, Vice Pres.
Total Employees: 65
Average Entry-Level Hiring: 5
Internships: No

EARLE PALMER BROWN
100 Colony Square, Ste. 2400
Atlanta, GA 30361
404-881-8585

Employment Contact: Judy Perdew, Personnel Dir.
Total Employees: 50
Average Entry-Level Hiring: 0
Internships: Yes

EPSILON
50 Cambridge Street
Burlington, MA 01803
617-273-0250

Employment Contact: Mary Richards Griffin, Head of Human Resources
Total Employees: 400
Average Entry-Level Hiring: 12
Internships: No

EVANS COMMUNICATIONS
4 Triad Center, #750
Salt Lake City, UT 84180
801-364-7000

Employment Contact: Regional managers of offices in: Atlanta, Denver, Los Angeles, Phoenix, Pittsburgh, Portland, San Francisco, and Seattle.
Total Employees: 289
Average Entry-Level Hiring: ?
Internships: No

FAHLGREN & SWINK
A division of Lintas: New York
P.O. Box 1628
Parkersburg, WV 26101
304-424-3591

Employment Contact: Director of Human Resources
Total Employees: 320

Average Entry-Level Hiring: 4
Internships: Yes

FCB/RONALDS-REYNOLDS
1500 West Georgia Street—Suite 450
Vancouver, BC V6G 2Z6
604-684-8311

Employment Contact: Ken Bates, VP/Director of Client Services
Total Employees: 30
Average Entry-Level Hiring: Varies
Internships: Yes

FOOTE, CONE & BELDING
11601 Wilshire Blvd.
Los Angeles, CA 90025
213-312-7000

Employment Contact: Melissa Germaine, Personnel Administrator
Total Employees: 185
Average Entry-Level Hiring: 10-20
Internships: Yes

FOOTE, CONE & BELDING
1255 Battery Street
San Francisco, CA 94111
415-398-5200

Employment Contact: Personnel Department
Total Employees: 300
Average Entry-Level Hiring: ?
Internships: Yes

FOOTE, CONE & BELDING DIRECT MARKETING
245 Eglinton East, Suite 300
Toronto, ON M4P 3C2
416-483-3600

Employment Contact: Janice Anderson, Personnel Coordinator
Total Employees: 200
Average Entry-Level Hiring: 3-4
Internships: No

GARDNER ADVERTISING COMPANY, INC.
Branch office of Wells, Rich, Greene, Inc
10 South Broadway
St. Louis, MO 63102
314-444-2000

Employment Contact: Peggy Fessler, Act. Supervisor
Total Employees: 100
Average Entry-Level Hiring: 5+

Comments: "We usually do interviewing only when there is an opening. All resumes are forwarded to pertinent departments and kept on file for 6 months."
Internships: Yes

GOODWIN, DANNEBAUM, LITTMAN & WINGFIELD, INC.
5400 Westheimer Court—Suite 900
Houston, TX 77056
713-622-7676

Employment Contact: Barry Silverman, President
Total Employees: 85
Average Entry-Level Hiring: 2
Internships: No

GREY ADVERTISING INC.
777 Third Avenue
New York, NY 10017
212-546-2000

Employment Contact: James Brink, VP/Associate Director Personnel
Total Employees: 2,000 (in NY)
Average Entry-Level Hiring: 50
Suggestions: "Send resume and cover letter giving specific objective and long-range career goals."
Internships: No

HENDERSON ADVERTISING
P.O. Box 2247
Greenville, SC 29602
803-271-6000

Employment Contact: Department Heads
Total Employees: 100
Average Entry-Level Hiring: 2
Internships: Yes

INGALLS, QUINN & JOHNSON
855 Boylston Street
Boston, MA 02116
617-437-7000

Employment Contact: Kate Kelly, Office Manager Personnel
Total Employees: 300
Average Entry-Level Hiring: 15
Internships: Yes

JORDAN ASSOCIATES
1000 West Wilshire—Suite 428
Oklahoma City, OK 73116
405-840-3201

Employment Contact: Jeanette L. Gamba, President
Total Employees: 52

Average Entry-Level Hiring: 3-4
Internships: Yes

KELLER-CRESCENT COMPANY
1100 East Louisiana Street
Evansville, IN 47701
812-464-2461

Employment Contact: Allen R. Mounts, VP-Human Resources
Total Employees: 550
Average Entry-Level Hiring: 7
Internships: Yes

KELLEY ADVERTISING, INC.
Park Place—3rd Floor
Hamilton, ON L7N 3E4
416-525-3610

Employment Contact: Phyllis Montgomery, Corporate Financial Operator
Total Employees: 35
Average Entry-Level Hiring: 5
Internships: Yes

KELLY ADVERTISING, INC.
20 Dundas Street West—Suite 1030
Toronto, ON M5G 2C2
416-977-2125

Employment Contact: Denise Marshall, Account Director
Total Employees: 25
Average Entry-Level Hiring: 3-4
Internships: No

KETCHUM ADVERTISING
A division of Ketchum Communications Inc.
6 PPG Place
Pittsburgh, PA 15222
412-456-3500

Employment Contact: Joyce Adler, Personnel Mgr.
Total Employees: 3,500
Average Entry-Level Hiring: 50
Internships: Yes

LAWRENCE & SCHILLER
3932 South Willow Avenue
Sioux Falls, SD 57105
605-338-8000

Employment Contact: Craig Lawrence, Partner
Total Employees: 41
Average Entry-Level Hiring: 1-2
Internships: Yes

AL PAUL LEFTON COMPANY
Rohm/Haas Building
Independence Mall West
Philadelphia, PA 19106
215-923-9600

Total Employees: 155
Internships: Yes

LEVENSON, LEVENSON & HILL
P.O. Box 619507
DFW Airport, TX 75261
214-556-0944

Employment Contact: Candice Ramsey, Office Mgr.
Total Employees: 65
Average Entry-Level Hiring: 2
Internships: Yes

LEVINE, HUNTLEY, SCHMIDT & BEAVER, INC.
250 Park Avenue
New York, NY 10177
212-545-3500

Employment Contact: Rose Marie Lyddan, Director of Personnel/Office Manager
Total Employees: 90
Internships: Yes

LINTAS: CAMPBELL EWALD
30400 Van Dyke
Warren, MI 48093
313-574-3400

Employment Contact: Human Resource Department
Total Employees: 900
Average Entry-Level Hiring: 15-25
Internships: No

LINTAS: NEW YORK
(formerly SSC&B: Lintas)
1 Dag Hammarskjold Plaza
New York, NY 10017
212-605-8000

Employment Contact: Patricia Ransom, Personnel Manager; Mariann Millar, Creative Management
Total Employees: 600
Average Entry-Level Hiring: 40
Internships: Yes

LONG, HAYMES & CARR, INC.
140 Charlois Blvd.—P.O. Box 5627
Winston-Salem, NC 27113
919-765-3630

Employment Contact: Department Heads
Total Employees: 140

Average Entry-Level Hiring: 15
Suggestions: "Please send cover letter and resume to our Personnel dept. for interviewing consideration. Portfolio needed for creative positions."
Internships: Yes

L.G.F.E., INC. (Lord, Geller, Frederico, Einstein)
A subsidiary of WPP Group PLC
655 Madison Avenue
New York, NY 10021
212-421-6050

Employment Contact: Emilie Schaum, VP/Director of Personnel & Administration
Total Employees: 94
Average Entry-Level Hiring: 3-5
Comments: "Applicants most likely to succeed present themselves as mature, high energy and enthusiastic when approaching work."
Internships: Yes

LORD, SULLIVAN & YODER ADVERTISING
250 Old Wilson Bridge Road
P.O. Box 800
Columbus, OH 43085-0800
614-846-8500

Employment Contact: Jo Ella Fosco, Administrative Assistant
Total Employees: 80
Average Entry-Level Hiring: 0
Internships: No

LOWE MARSCHALK
1345 Avenue of the Americas
New York, NY 10105
212-708-8800

Employment Contact: Peter Detels, VP
Total Employees: 365
Average Entry-Level Hiring: 3-4
Comments: People with experience only.
Internships: Yes

MACLAREN ADVERTISING
Atrium on the Bay
Toronto, ON M5G 2H1
416-977-2244

Employment Contact: Nancy Carroll, Personnel Officer
Total Employees: 318
Average Entry-Level Hiring: Varies.
Internships: No

McCANN-ERICKSON ADVERTISING OF CANADA, LTD.
Waterpark Place
10 Bay Street—13th Floor
Toronto, ON M5J 2S3
416-594 6000

Employment Contact: Cheryl Fry, Manager of Human Resources
Total Employees: 260
Average Entry-Level Hiring: 6-10
Internships: No

McKIM ADVERTISING LTD.
600-237 Eighth Avenue SE
Calgary, AB T2G 5C3
403-234-7400

Employment Contact: Chris Bedford, Manager
Total Employees: 28
Average Entry-Level Hiring: Varies
Internships: No

McKIM ADVERTISING LTD.
Rene Levesque West—Floor 28
Montreal, PQ H3B 2L2
514-861-8421

Employment Contact: Francine Lepage, Administration Manager
Total Employees: 40+
Average Entry-Level Hiring: ?
Internships: No

McKIM ADVERTISING LTD.
2 Bloor Street West
Toronto, ON M4W 3R6
416-960-1722

Employment Contact: JoAnne Porter, Head of Personnel
Total Employees: 200
Average Entry-Level Hiring: ?
Internships: No

MARC AND COMPANY, INC.
4 Station Square—Suite 500
Pittsburgh, PA 15219
412-562-2000

Employment Contact: Theadora Ftaklas, Personnel Director
Total Employees: 94
Average Entry-Level Hiring: 4
Internships: Yes

MEDICUS INTERCON INTERNATIONAL, INC
A subsidiary of D'Arcy Masius Benton & Bowles
909 Third Avenue
New York, NY 10022
212-826-0760

Employment Contact: Personnel Department
Total Employees: 375
Average Entry-Level Hiring: 3-5
Internships: Yes

MILLS HALL WALBORN & ASSOCIATES
29125 Chagrin Blvd.
Cleveland, OH 44122
216-646-9400

Employment Contact: Gloria Zupancit, Office Mgr.
Total Employees: 40
Average Entry-Level Hiring: 3-5
Internships: No

MULLEN ADVERTISING
P.O. Box 2700
Wenham, MA 01982
508-468-1155

Employment Contact: Department Heads
Total Employees: 90
Average Entry-Level Hiring: 0
Internships: Yes

N. W. AYER INCORPORATED
Worldwide Plaza
825 Eighth Avenue
New York, NY 10019-7498
212-708-5000

Employment Contact: Brenda Rotola, Personnel
Recruiter
Average Entry-Level Hiring: 20
Internships: No

OGILVY & MATHER WORLDWIDE
2 East 48th Street
New York, NY 10017
212-237-4000

Employment Contact: Nan Keenan, VP/Manager
Account Management
Total Employees: 8,500
Average Entry-Level Hiring: 10-12
Internships: Yes

OGILVY & MATHER
101 Sixth Avenue SW—Suite 850
Calgary, AB P2P 3P4
403-262-6852

Employment Contact: Mark Pigott, Mging Director

Total Employees: 22
Average Entry-Level Hiring: 0
Internships: No

PNMD
1610 St. Catherine Street West
Suite 500
Montreal, PQ H3H 2S2
514-939-4100

Employment Contact: Joy Meyer, Administrative
Assistant
Total Employees: 55
Average Entry-Level Hiring: 4
Internships: No

PRINGLE DIXON PRINGLE
245 Peachtree Center—Suite 1500
Marquis 1 Tower
Atlanta, GA 30303
404-688-6720

Employment Contact: Susan Johnson, Jr. Account
Executive
Total Employees: 40
Average Entry-Level Hiring: ?
Internships: Yes

PUBLICITE LEO BURNETT LTD.
175 Bloor Street East
Toronto, ON M4W 3L9
416-925-5997

Employment Contact: Dave Teller; Ruth Jackson,
Senior Secretary; Jim McKenzy, President
Total Employees: 165
Average Entry-Level Hiring: 3
Internships: No

ROSENTHAL, GREENE AND CAMPBELL
7910 Woodmont Avenue
Bethesda, MD 20815
301-657-3400

Employment Contact: Sheila Campbell, President
Total Employees: 38
Average Entry-Level Hiring: 10
Internships: Yes

ROSS ROY, INC.
100 Bloomfield Hills Parkway
Bloomfield Hills, MI 48013
313-433-6000

Employment Contact: Lori Taylor, VP-Human
Resources
Total Employees: 955

Average Entry-Level Hiring: 25
Internships: No

SAATCHI & SAATCHI ADVERTISING
375 Hudson Street
New York, NY 10014
212-704-7291

Employment Contact: Linda Seale, Executive VP/
Human Resources Director
Total Employees: 1,300
Average Entry-Level Hiring: ?
Internships: No

SAATCHI & SAATCHI COMPTON HAYHURST
55 Eglinton Avenue East
Toronto, ON M4T 1G9
416-487-4371

Employment Contact: Department Heads
Total Employees: 142
Average Entry-Level Hiring: 50
Internships: No

SAFFER ADVERTISING INC.
180 Lesmill Road
Don Mills, ON M3B 2T5
416-449-7961

Employment Contact: Personnel Department
Total Employees: 165
Average Entry-Level Hiring: ?
Internships: No

SMITH/GREENLAND ADVERTISING, INC.
555 West 57th Street
New York, NY 10019
212-757-3200

Employment Contact: Rita Greenland, Personnel
Director
Total Employees: 110
Suggestions: "Enclose with your resume and cover
letter a stamped, self-addressed postcard with 2
boxes: The first box reads 'We have a position
available. Please telephone for an interview
appointment.' The second box reads: 'We have no
positions open at this time but would like you to
telephone for an interview for future opportunities."
Internships: No

SPIRO & ASSOCIATES
100 South Broad Street
Philadelphia, PA 19110
215-851-9600

Employment Contact: Anne Kelley, Office Manager
Total Employees: 150

Average Entry-Level Hiring: 2-4
Suggestions: "Send resume in advance."
Internships: Yes

TAYLOR BROWN, SMITH & PERRAULT
4544 Post Oak Place—Suite 264
Houston, TX 77027
713-877-1220

Employment Contact: Patsy Perrault, Executive VP/
Media Director
Total Employees: 52
Average Entry-Level Hiring: 5
Internships: Yes

J. WALTER THOMPSON
A subsidiary of the WPP Group PLC
466 Lexington Avenue
New York, NY 10017
212-210-6993 or 6988

Employment Contact: Mellisa Statmore
Total Employees: 7,380
Average Entry-Level Hiring: Varies
Internships: Yes

VALENTINE-RADFORD, INC.
911 Main Street—Suite 11
Kansas City, MO 64105
816-842-5021

Employment Contact: Cindy Kitchen, Personnel
Total Employees: 150
Average Entry-Level Hiring: ?
Internships: Yes

VAN SANT, DUGDALE & COMPANY, INC.
The World Trade Center
Baltimore, MD 21202
301-539-5400

Employment Contact: Kenneth E. Mayhorne,
Chairman and CEO
Total Employees: 80
Average Entry-Level Hiring: 0
Internships: No

VICKERS & BENSON PROMOTIONAL SVCS.
1133 Yonge Street
Toronto, ON M4T 2Z3
416-926-4380

Employment Contact: Rose Galluzzo,
Payroll/Personnel Manager
Total Employees: 220
Average Entry-Level Hiring: 30-40%
Internships: No

WUNDERMAN INTERNATIONAL INC.
60 Bloor Street West
Toronto, ON M4W 3B8
416-921-9050

Employment Contact: Department Heads
Total Employees: 50
Average Entry-Level Hiring: Depends on what is happening in the industry.
Internships: No

YOUNG & RUBICAM INC.
285 Madison Avenue
New York, NY 10017
212-210-3000

Employment Contact: Steven Nisberg, Manager of Employment
Total Employees: 11,000
Average Entry-Level Hiring: 75-100
Suggestions: "Send resume and cover letter first, 2-3 week reply by mail, interviews by appointment only."
Internships: Yes

Selected Public Relations
Job Listings: U.S. & Canada

As noted in the previous chapter, the following listings include *abridged* information on *selected* PR agencies and corporate and association PR departments throughout the United States and, for the first time, selected agencies across Canada. Those of you heading towards a public relations career should consult our *Public Relations Career Directory,* available in a brand-new fourth edition, for far more extensive advice and information. Note especially that PR firms in Canada are decidedly smaller and less numerous than their U.S. counterparts.

AGNEW CARTER McCARTHY INC.
One Exeter Plaza
Boston, MA 02116
617-437-7722

Type: PR agency
Employment Contact: Carol Garrity, Office Mgr
Total Employees: 30
Average Entry-Level Hiring: 5-6
Internships: Yes

ALLSTATE
Allstate Plaza South G.I.C.
Northbrook, IL 60062
312-291-5000

Type: Corporation
Employment Contact: Rick Warren, Employment Mgr.
Total Employees: 50,000
Employees Involved In PR: 100
Average Entry-Level Hiring: 50
Internships: No

AMERICAN BANKERS ASSOCIATION
1120 Connecticut Avenue NW
Washington, D.C. 20036
202-663-5000

Type: Trade Association
Employment Contact: Larry Weekly, Group Director
Total Employees: 400
Employees Involved In PR: 15
Average Entry-Level Hiring: 2-4
Internships: No

AMERICAN BAR ASSOCIATION
750 North Lake Shore Drive
Chicago, IL 60645
312-988-5000

Type: Professional Association
Employment Contact: Brian Garvy, Human Resources
Total Employees: 700
Employees Involved In PR: 18
Average Entry-Level Hiring: 1

Comments: "Resumes and screening initially go through the Human Resources Department."
Internships: No

AMERICAN COUNCIL OF LIFE INSURANCE
1850 K Street NW
Washington, DC 20006
202-624-2000

Type: Trade Association
Employment Contact: Lorraine K. Branson, Personnel Administrator
Total Employees: 273
Employees Involved In PR: ?
Average Entry-Level Hiring: 2
Internships: No

AMERICAN EXPRESS COMPANY
American Express Tower
World Financial Center
New York, NY 10285
212-640-2000 or 5656

Type: Corporation
Employment Contact: Lorraine Coyle, Corporate Headquarters Human Resources
Total Employees: 70,536 worldwide
Employees Involved In PR: 75
Average Entry-Level Hiring: 0
Comments: Do not hire entry-level candidates in PR.
Internships: No

AMERICAN HEART ASSOCIATION
7320 Greenville Avenue
Dallas, TX 75231
214-373-6300

Type: Nonprofit Health Corporation
Employment Contact: Larry Joyce, Personnel Mgr.
Total Employees: 285
Average Entry-Level Hiring: 6-10
Internships: No

AMERICAN RED CROSS
17th and D Street NW
Washington, DC 20006
202-639-3200

Type: Nonprofit Corporation
Employment Contact: Virginia Pa, Director of Media Coordination
Total Employees: 400
Average Entry-Level Hiring: 10-12
Internships: No

BADER RUTTER & ASSOCIATES
13555 Bishop's Court
Brookfield, WI 53183
414-784-7200

Type: PR dept. of ad agency
Employment Contact: Lyle E. Orwig, Vice President/Director of PR
Expertise: Business-to-business (agricultural, industrial, consumer)
Total Employees: 100
Employees Involved In PR: 28
Average Entry-Level Hiring: 2-3
Suggestions: "Send resume and three samples of your best writing."
Comments: "Internships are extremely important."
Internships: No

BAKER LOVICK ADVERTISING
350 Seventh Ave.—Suite 2200
Calgary, AB T2P 3TS
403-262-6161

Employment Contact: Brenda Barrett, Office Manager
Total Employees: 85
Average Entry-Level Hiring: 1
Internships: No

BANKAMERICA CORPORATION
P.O. Box 37000, #3124
San Francisco, CA 99137
415-622-2775 or 7324

Type: Corporation
Employment Contact: Ronald E. Rhody, Senior Vice President
Total Employees: 56,000
Employees Involved In PR: 50
Average Entry-Level Hiring: 0
Internships: No

BEATRICE COMPANIES
Two North LaSalle Street
Chicago, IL 60602
312-782-3820

Type: Corporation
Employment Contact: Kate Wollensak, Compensation Analyst
Comments: While company has had entry-level PR hiring and an internship program in the past, it is in the process of changing many of its policies. The future of its programs is uncertain and no applicable information is otherwise available.
Internships: No

BERGER & ASSOCIATES CANADA INC.
100 University Avenue—Suite 1004
Toronto, ON M5J 1V6
416-599-8454

Employment Contact: Brian Chadderton, Senior VP
Total Employees: 14
Average Entry-Level Hiring: 1
Internships: No
Note: Other offices in Montreal, Ottawa, Calgary and Edmonton.

BOZELL, INC.
75 Rockefeller Plaza—6th Floor
New York, NY 10010
212-484-7400

Type: PR agency
Employment Contact: Linda Blanc, Sr. VP & General Manager
Expertise: Consumer
Total Employees: 60
Average Entry-Level Hiring: ?
Internships: Yes

BRISTOL-MYERS COMPANY
345 Park Avenue
New York, NY 10154
212-546-4341

Type: Corporation
Employment Contact: Thomas McCann, VP-Corporate Communications
Total Employees: 1,500
Internships: No

BRUM & ANDERSON PUBLIC RELATIONS, INC.
425 Lumber Exchange Blvd.
Minneapolis, MN 55402
612-871-8877

Type: PR agency
Employment Contact: Barbara Kirklock, Director of Administration
Expertise: Marketing, Corporate Affairs, Public Affairs, Technical
Total Employees: 40
Average Entry-Level Hiring: 1
Internships: Yes

BURSON-MARSTELLER
230 Park Avenue South
New York, NY 10003
212-614-5127

Type: PR agency
Employment Contact: Randy Essner, Human Resources Executive

Expertise: Corporations, Consumer, Business & Health
Total Employees: 704 (in NY)
Average Entry-Level Hiring: 4-6
Internships: Yes

BURSON-MARSTELLER
80 Bloor Street West
Toronto, ON M5S 2V1
416-964-8300

Employment Contact: Brenadine Sach
Total Employees: 100

BURTON CAMPBELL, INC.
100 Colony Square
Atlanta, GA 30361
404-881-8585

Type: PR dept. of ad agency
Employment Contact: Judy Purdue, Dir of Operations
Expertise: Editorial Services, Media Relations, Placement
Total Employees: 500
Average Entry-Level Hiring: 5
Internships: No

CAMPBELL SOUP COMPANY
Campbell Place
Camden, NJ 08103-1799
609-342-6426

Type: Corporation
Employment Contact: James H. Moran, Director of Public Relations
Total Employees: 1,750
Employees Involved In PR: 20
Average Entry-Level Hiring: ?
Internships: No

CARTER HAWLEY HALE STORES, INC.
550 South Flower Street
Los Angeles, CA 90071
213-620-0150

Type: Corporation
Employment Contact: Bill Dombrowski, VP-Corporate Affairs
Total Employees: 57,000
Employees Involved In PR: 50
Average Entry-Level Hiring: 5
Internships: No

CENEX
P.O. Box 64089
Street Paul, MN 55164
612-451-4930

Type: Corporation
Employment Contact: Chuck Jones, Human Resources Manager
Total Employees: 2,850 worldwide
Employees Involved In PR: 18
Average Entry-Level Hiring: 4-5
Internships: No

CHASE MANHATTAN CORPORATION
One Chase Manhattan Plaza
New York, NY 10081
212-552-4503

Type: Corporation
Employment Contact: Fraser P. Seitel, Senior VP
Total Employees: 42,000 worldwide
Employees Involved In PR: 100
Average Entry-Level Hiring: 10
Internships: No

CHURCHILL GROUP/IPR
9575 Katy—Suite 390
Houston, TX 77024
713-781-0020

Type: PR agency
Employment Contact: Ms. Fern Congram
Expertise: Financial Relations, Marketing, Public Affairs—Regional, National, International
Total Employees: 1,097
Employees Involved In PR: 20
Average Entry-Level Hiring: 3-5
Internships: Yes

COLGATE PALMOLIVE
380 Park Avenue
New York, NY 10022
212-310-2199

Type: Corporation
Employment Contact: Robert A. Murray, Dir. of Corporate Communications
Total Employees: 40,000 worldwide
Average Entry-Level Hiring: ?
Internships: No

CONTROL DATA CORPORATION
8100 34th Avenue South—Box 0
Minneapolis, MN 55440
612-853-3850

Type: Corporation
Employment Contact: Sam Workman

Total Employees: 41,497 worldwide
Average Entry-Level Hiring: 10-20
Internships: No

CREAMER DICKSON BASFORD, INC.
1633 Broadway
New York, NY 10019
212-887-8010

Type: PR Agency
Employment Contact: Jean Farinelli, Chairman
Expertise: Full-service
Total Employees: 57
Average Entry-Level Hiring: 3-4
Internships: Yes

THE CREATIVE MARKETING NETWORK, INC.
70 Jefferson Avenue
Toronto, ON M6K 1Y4
416-539-0694

Employment Contact: Lynda Evans
Total Employees: 17
Average Entry-Level Hiring: 1
Internships: No

DALTON MACABE ALAOUZE INC.
64 Jefferson Avenue—Unit 6
Toronto, ON M6K 3H3
416-537-8493

Employment Contact: Mr. Michael Alaouze, President
Total Employees: 10
Average Entry-Level Hiring: 1-2
Internships: No

DOREMUS PUBLIC RELATIONS
120 Broadway
New York, NY 10271
212-964-0700

Type: PR firm
Employment Contact: Nina Palmer, Executive Vice President
Expertise: Corporate, Financial, Investor Relations
Total Employees: 50
Average Entry-Level Hiring: 4
Internships: Yes

DORF & STANTON COMMUNICATIONS, INC.
111 Fifth Avenue
New York, NY 10003
212-420-8100

Type: PR agency
Employment Contact: Ms. Sunhi Sockwell, Office Manager

Expertise: Consumer, Marketing, Industrial, Agricultural
Total Employees: 120
Average Entry-Level Hiring: 4
Internships: Yes

DOW CHEMICAL COMPANY
2020 Dow Center
Midland, MI 48674
517-636-1000

Type: Corporation
Employment Contact: Charles J. Moss, Personnel Coordinator
Total Employees: 53,000
Employees Involved In PR: 50
Average Entry-Level Hiring: 2
Comments: "We normally begin recruiting entry-level professionals December 1st for May-June hire."
Internships: No

DUDLEY-ANDERSON-YUTZY PUBLIC RELATIONS INC.
A subsidiary of Ogilvy & Mather
40 West 57th Street
New York, NY 10019
212-977-9400 or 951-5400

Type: PR Agency
Employment Contact: Dawn Dahl, Senior Vice President
Expertise: Marketing public relations
Total Employees: 180
Average Entry-Level Hiring: 1-2
Internships: Yes

E. I. DUPONT DE NEMOURS AND COMPANY
Wilmington, DE 19898
302-774-1000

Type: Corporation
Employment Contact: John R. Malloy, Sr. VP-External Affairs
Total Employees: 1,500
Average Entry-Level Hiring: 6-8
Internships: No

DANIEL J. EDELMAN, INC.
211 East Ontario Street
Chicago, IL 60611
312-280-7000

Type: PR agency
Employment Contact: Pam Talbot, General Manager
Total Employees: 365
Average Entry-Level Hiring: 6
Internships: Yes

EXXON CORPORATION
1251 Avenue of the Americas
New York, NY 10020
212-333-1000

Type: Corporation
Employment Contact: VP-Corporate Public Affairs
Employees in PR: 30
Average Entry-Level Hiring: 1-2
Internships: No

THE FINANCIAL RELATIONS BOARD
A division of FRB, Chicago
655 Third Avenue
New York, NY 10017
212-661-8030

Type: PR agency
Employment Contact: Managing Partner of Eastern Operations
Expertise: Investor and shareholder relations
Total Employees: 102
Average Entry-Level Hiring: 0
Internships: No

FORD MOTOR COMPANY
P.O. Box 1899—Room 930
Dearborn, MI 48121
313-322-9030

Type: Corporation
Employment Contact: R.L. Byers, Supervisor of Educational Affairs
Employees Involved In PR: 370
Average Entry-Level Hiring: 2-3
Comments: "We review and respond to all resumes. We do not interview without first reviewing resumes and writing samples."
Internships: No

ANTHONY M. FRANCO, INC.
400 Renaissance Center—Suite 600
Detroit, MI 48243
313-567-2300

Type: PR agency
Employment Contact: Richard M. Kelley, Senior Executive Vice President
Expertise: General PR counseling, investor relations, video services, special events
Total Employees: 70
Average Entry-Level Hiring: (Only hire people with 5-years professional experience.)
Suggestions: "Send brief letter and resume only—no phone calls, please."
Internships: No

GENERAL MOTORS CORPORATION
3044 West Grand Blvd.
Detroit, MI 48202
313-556-5000
Personnel: 313-556-2051
PR Staff: 313-556-2032

Type: Corporation
Employment Contact: John Muller, Head of Public Relations, 313-556-2028
Total Employees: 700,000+ worldwide
Employees Involved In PR: 65 on corporate PR staff, plus other professionals at GM divisions and subsidiaries.
Average Entry-Level Hiring: ?
Internships: No

GIRL SCOUTS OF THE U.S.A.
830 Third Avenue
New York, NY 10022
212-940-7500

Type: Corporation
Employment Contact: Bonnie McEwan, Director of Media Services
Total Employees: 625
Average Entry-Level Hiring: 5-10
Internships: No

DAVID M. GRANT, INC.
750 Third Avenue
New York, NY 10021
212-687-8600

Type: PR agency
Employment Contact: David M. Grant, President
Expertise: General
Total Employees: 20
Average Entry-Level Hiring: 2
Internships: Yes

GREYCOM INC.
A subsidiary of Grey Advertising
777 Third Avenue
New York, NY 10003
212-546-2200

Type: PR agency
Employment Contact: Mary A. Butler, Office Manager
Expertise: General
Total Employees: 52
Average Entry-Level Hiring: 1
Internships: Yes

GRODY/TELLEM COMMUNICATIONS
9100 South Sepulveda—Suite 200
Los Angeles, CA 90045
213-479-3363

Type: PR agency
Employment Contact: Susan M. Tellem, Mark S. Grody
Total Employees: 35
Average Entry-Level Hiring: 1
Internships: Yes

GTE CORPORATION
1 Stamford Forum
Stamford, CT 06904
203-965-2903

Type: Corporation
Employment Contact: Edward C. MacEwan, VP-Corporate Communications
Total Employees: 180,000
Employees Involved In PR: 200+
Average Entry-Level Hiring: 0
Comments: "We are downsizing staffs and do not plan to hire entry-level people."
Internships: No

HARSCO CORPORATION
P.O. Box 8888
Camp Hill, PA 17011
717-763-7064

Type: Corporation
Employment Contact: Herbert McIlvaine, Director of Corporate Communications
Total Employees: 11,600
Average Entry-Level Hiring: 10-15
Internships: No

HEWLETT-PACKARD COMPANY
3000 Hanover Street
Palo Alto, CA 94304
415-857-2067

Type: Corporation
Employment Contact: Ray Verley, Director-Public Relations
Total Employees: 84,000
Employees Involved In PR: 100
Average Entry-Level Hiring: 0
Comments: "We seldom fi'l public relations positions with people directly out of college. We prefer that applicants have at least some PR experience, preferably with a corporation similar to ours.

Among the skills we seek are a strong communications ability, both written and verbal, and, prefer-

ably, a college degree in either Public Relations or Journalism."
Internships: No

HILL & KNOWLTON, INC.
420 Lexington Avenue
New York, NY 10017
212-697-5600

Type: PR agency
Employment Contact: Joel Alan, Manager of Recruitment Services, USA
Expertise: Full-service
Total Employees: 2,000
Average Entry-Level Hiring: 5-10
Internships: No

INDEX COMMUNICATIONS LIMITED
512 King Street East—Suite 102
Toronto, ON M5A 1M1
416-862-0101

Employment Contact: Don Fenton, VP-Public Relations
Total Employees: 11
Average Entry-Level Hiring: 1-2
Internships: No

THE KAMBER GROUP
1899 L Street NW
Washington, D.C. 20036
202-223-8700

Type: PR agency
Employment Contact: Sherry Mohr, Director of Personnel
Expertise: Labor, Issue Management, Business, Politics, In-house art, Media
Total Employees: 92
Average Entry-Level Hiring: 5-6
Internships: Yes

KELLER-CRESCENT COMPANY
1100 East Louisiana Street
Evansville, IN 47701
812-464-2461

Type: PR dept. of ad agency
Employment Contact: Allen R. Mounts, VP Human Resources
Expertise: Marketing Communications/Public Relations
Total Employees: 550
Average Entry-Level Hiring: 3-5
Internships: No

KETCHUM PUBLIC RELATIONS
A unit of Ketchum Communications
1133 Avenue of the Americas
New York, NY 10036
212-536-8800

Type: PR agency
Employment Contact: MaryAnn Needham, Personnel Manager
Expertise: Full-service (best known for marketing PR, and food).
Total Employees: 700
Average Entry-Level Hiring: 5-10
Internships: Yes

LaMAR ADVERTISING
41 Britian Street—Suite 300
Toronto, ON M5A 1R7
416-362-8477

Employment Contact: Robert Snow, President
Total Employees: 12
Average Entry-Level Hiring: 2
Internships: No

AL PAUL LEFTON COMPANY
Rohm/Haas Building
Independence Mall West
Philadelphia, PA 19106
215-923-9600

Type: PR dept. of ad agency
Employment Contact: John Evans, Sr. VP
Total Employees: 155
Employees Involved In PR: 9
Average Entry-Level Hiring: 3-5
Comments: "Writing samples are always required with a letter of introduction."
Internships: No

LOBSENZ-STEVENS INC.
460 Park Avenue South
New York, NY 10016
212-684-6300

Type: PR firm
Employment Contact: Ruth Ost
Expertise: Full service agency with strong health, medical, consumer product and service organization experience.
Total Employees: 50
Average Entry-Level Hiring: 7
Internships: Yes

THE LTV CORPORATION
P.O. Box 225003
Dallas, TX 75243
214-979-7700 or 7941

Type: Corporation
Employment Contact: Charles M. Palmer, Dir. of Corporate Communications
Total Employees: 57,500
Employees Involved In PR: 100
Average Entry-Level Hiring: ?
Internships: No

McKINNEY PUBLIC RELATIONS, INC.
116 South Michigan
Chicago, IL 60603
312-372-1050

Type: PR agency
Employment Contact: Glen A. Hatzai, Executive VP & General Manager
Expertise: Business-to-Business, High Tech and Corporate
Total Employees: 30
Average Entry-Level Hiring: 1
Internships: No

MAKOVSKY & COMPANY, INC.
245 Fifth Avenue
New York, NY 10001
212-532-6300

Type: PR agency
Employment Contact: Bob Greenwald, Vice Chrman
Total Employees: 35
Average Entry-Level Hiring: 1-2
Internships: Yes

MALLORY FACTOR, INC.
275 Seventh Avenue
New York, NY 10001
212-242-0000

Type: PR agency
Employment Contact: Senior Account Executive
Expertise: Investor Relations, Marketing Communications, Travel & Tourism, Meeting Planning, Special Events
Total Employees: 35
Average Entry-Level Hiring: ?
Internships: Yes

MARSHALL FENN LIMITED
245 Davenport Road
Toronto, ON M5R 1K1
416-962-3241

Employment Contact: Debbie Butler, President

Total Employees: 25
Average Entry-Level Hiring: 1
Internships: No
Note: Other offices in Halifax, Montreal, Windsor, Ottawa, Winnipeg, Saskatoon, Regina, Edmonton, Calgary and Vancouver.

MEAD DATA CENTRAL, INC.
A subsidiary of The Mead Corporation
P.O. Box 933
Dayton, OH 45401
513-222-6323

Type: Corporation
Employment Contact: Scott Sherwood, Human Resources
Total Employees: 1,700
Average Entry-Level Hiring: 7-10
Internships: No

MEDIA PROFILE
579 Richmond Street West—Suite 300
Toronto, ON M5V 1V6
416-366-8464

Employment Contact: Patrick Gossage, President
Total Employees: 13
Average Entry-Level Hiring: 2
Internships: No

MELANIE COMMUNICATIONS GROUP, INC.
33 Niagara Street
Toronto, ON M5V 1C2
416-362-3900

Employment Contact: Susan Melmyk, President
Total Employees: 13
Average Entry-Level Hiring: 1
Internships: No

MONA, MEYER & McGRATH
8400 Normandale Lake Blvd.
Bloomington, MN 55437
612-831-8515

Type: PR agency
Employment Contact: Carol Cooksley
Total Employees: 100
Average Entry-Level Hiring: 3-4
Internships: Yes

NATIONAL M.S. SOCIETY
205 East 42nd Street
New York, NY 10003
212-986-3240

Type: Nonprofit corporation
Employment Contact: John Crevite, Personnel Mgr.

Total Employees: 120
Employees Involved In PR: 12
Average Entry-Level Hiring: 2-3
Internships: No

THE NEW YORK STOCK EXCHANGE
11 Wall Street
New York, NY 10005
212-656-3000

Type: Corporation
Employment Contact: Richard Torrenzano, VP
Total Employees: 2,000
Employees Involved In PR: 40
Internships: No

PHILLIPS PETROLEUM COMPANY
Bartlesville, OK 74004
918-661-6600 or 1215

Type: Corporation
Employment Contact: Dan B. Droege, Public Relations Director
Total Employees: 5,000
Employees Involved In PR: 75
Average Entry-Level Hiring: ?
Internships: No

PINNE, GARVIN, HERBERS & HECK, INC.
200 Vallejo Street
San Francisco, CA 94111
415-956-4210

Type: PR dept. of ad agency
Employment Contact: Stuart A. Matlow, Public Relations Director
Total Employees: 35
Average Entry-Level Hiring: 1
Internships: No

PORTER NOVELLI
1633 Broadway
New York, NY 10019
212-315-8000 or 8109

Type: PR agency
Employment Contact: Bill Novelli, President
Total Employees: 100
Average Entry-Level Hiring: 0
Internships: No

PORTLAND CEMENT ASSOCIATION
5420 Old Orchard Road
Skokie, IL 60077
312-966-6200

Type: Trade Association

Employment Contact: Martha Anderson, Senior Personnel Officer
Total Employees: 250 (with subsidiaries)
Average Entry-Level Hiring: 2-5
Internships: No

PRINGLE DIXON PRINGLE
245 Peachtree Center—Suite 1500
Marquis 1 Tower
Atlanta, GA 30303
404-688-6720

Type: PR and advertising agency
Employment Contact: Harry Hollingsworth
Total Employees: 40
Average Entry-Level Hiring: ?
Internships: Yes

REGIS McKENNA INC.
1800 Embarcadero Road
Palo Alto, CA 94303
415-494-2030

Type: PR/Marketing Consulting Agency
Employment Contact: Anita Emmorey
Expertise: Marketing Consulting, Strategic Positioning
Total Employees: 178
Average Entry-Level Hiring: 1-2
Comments: "We often grant informational interviews to entry-level people."
Internships: Yes

HEATHER REID AND ASSOCIATES
77 Bloor Street West—Suite 1903
Toronto, ON M5S 1M2
416-961-9331

Employment Contact: Paul Sero, Office Manager
Total Employees: 8
Average Entry-Level Hiring: 1-2
Internships: Yes

ROCKWELL INTERNATIONAL CORPORATION
600 Grant Street
Pittsburgh. PA 15219
412-565-2000

Type: Corporation
Employment Contact: Larry D'Angelo, Head of Personnel
Total Employees: 120,000
Employees Involved In PR: 200
Average Entry-Level Hiring: ?
Internships: No

THE ROWLAND COMPANY
415 Madison Avenue
New York, NY 10017
212-688-1200

Type: PR agency

Employment Contact: Peter W. Smith, Executive Vice President

Expertise: Corporate, Business-to-Business, Financial and Marketing PR

Total Employees: 120

Average Entry-Level Hiring: 2

Internships: Yes

RUDER FINN
110 East 59th Street
New York, NY 10022
212-593-6400

Type: PR agency

Employment Contact: Amy Bender, Executive VP Community Affairs & President of New York office

Expertise: Specialized departments in every field of public relations

Total Employees: 330

Average Entry-Level Hiring: 4-5

Comments: "The only way to be hired in an entry-level position is to go though our internship program."

Internships: Yes

THE SOFTNESS GROUP
3 East 54th Street
New York, NY 10022
212-674-7600

Type: PR agency

Employment Contact: Laura M. Russo, Manager of Operations

Total Employees: 40

Average Entry-Level Hiring: 1

Internships: Yes

SPECTRUM PR
49 Spadina Avenue
Toronto, ON M5V 2J1
416-599-8556

Employment Contact: Gerry Ofterholt, Office Manager

Total Employees: 9

Average Entry-Level Hiring: 2

Internships: No

UNITED DAIRY INDUSTRY ASSOCIATION
6300 North River Road
Rosemont, IL 60018
312-696-1860

Type: Trade association

Employment Contact: Marilyn Wilkinson, Senior VP of Communications & Public Relations

Total Employees: 99

Average Entry-Level Hiring: 2-3

Internships: No

WILSON PUBLIC RELATIONS
690-1155 West Georgia Street
Vancouver, BC V6E 3H4
604-681-7189

Employment Contact: Kathya Wilson, Managing Consultant

Total Employees: 10

Average Entry-Level Hiring: 2-8

Internships: No

Section 4

Appendices & Index

A

U.S. & Canadian
Trade Organizations

THE ADVERTISING CLUB
OF NEW YORK
155 East 55th Street
Suite 202
New York, NY 10022
212-935-8080

THE ADVERTISING EDUCATIONAL
FOUNDATION
666 Third Avenue
New York, NY 10017
212-986-8060

THE ADVERTISING RESEARCH
FOUNDATION
3 East 54th Street
15th Floor
New York, NY 10022
212-751-5656

THE ADVERTISING & SALES
CLUB OF TORONTO
P.O. Box 237, Stn. K
Toronto, ON M4P 2G5
416-483-5599

THE ADVERTISING & SALES
EXECUTIVES CLUB OF MONTREAL
#369, 900 Rene Levesque Blvd., West
Montreal, PQ H3B 4A5
514-866-1668

ADVERTISING WOMEN
OF NEW YORK
153 East 57th Street
New York, NY 10022
212-593-1950

AMERICAN ADVERTISING
FEDERATION
1400 K Street—Suite 1000
Washington, DC 20005
202-898-0089

AMERICAN ASSOCIATION
OF ADVERTISING AGENCIES (4A's)
666 Third Avenue
New York, NY 10017
212-682-2500

AMERICAN MANAGEMENT ASSOC.
135 West 50th Street
New York, NY 10020
212-586-8100

AMERICAN MARKETING
ASSOCIATION
250 South Wacker Drive
Chicago, IL 60606
312-648-0536

Alberta Chapter
P.O. Box 4143, Stn. C
Calgary, AB T2R 5M9
403-244-4487

British Columbia Chapter
1685 Ingleton Avenue
Burnaby, BC V5C 4L8
604-298-1123

Montreal Chapter
163 rue St. Paul, est. bur. 100
Montreal, PQ H2Y 1G8
514-867-3255

Quebec Chapter
1283 La Lorraine
Ste-Foy, PQ G1W 3Y5

Toronto Chapter
58 Yorkminster Road
Willowdale, ON M2P 1M3
416-921-4656

**AMERICAN TELEMARKETING
ASSOCIATION**
5000 Van Nuys Blvd.—Suite 400
Sherman Oaks, CA 91403
818-995-7338
1-800-441-3335

**ASSOCIATION OF NATIONAL
ADVERTISERS**
155 East 44th Street
New York, NY 10017
212-697-5950

BANK MARKETING ASSOCIATION
309 West Washington Street
Chicago, IL 60606
312-782-1442

**BUSINESS/PROFESSIONAL
ADVERTISING ASSOCIATION**
100 Metroplex Drive
Edison, NJ 08817
201-985-4441

**CANADIAN ADVERTISING
FOUNDATION**
350 Bloor Street East, #402
Toronto, ON K1P 5H9
613-236-6550

**CANADIAN ADVERTISING
RESEARCH FOUNDATION**
180 Bloor Street West, #803
Toronto, ON M5S 2V6
416-964-3832

**CANADIAN ASSOCIATION OF
MARKETING RESEARCH ORGS.**
1 Eva Road, #409
Etobicoke, ON M9C 4Z5
416-620-5391

**CANADIAN ASSOCIATION OF
PROFESSIONAL SALESPEOPLE**
#209, 1501 17th Avenue SW
Calgary, AB T2T 0E9
403-229-2090

**CANADIAN DIRECT MARKETING
ASSOCIATION**
1 Concorde Gate, #607
Don Mills, ON M3C 3N6
416-391-2362

**CHEMICAL MARKETING RESEARCH
ASSOCIATION**
139 Chestnut Avenue
Staten Island, NY 10305
718-727-0550

**THE COUNCIL OF AMERICAN SURVEY
RESEARCH ORGANIZATIONS**
3 Upper Devon—Belle Terre
Port Jefferson, NY 11777
516-928-6954

**THE COUNCIL OF SALES
PROMOTION AGENCIES**
750 Summer Street
2nd Floor
Stamford, CT 06901
203-325-3911

DIRECT MARKETING ASSOCIATION
6 East 43rd Street
New York, NY 10017
212-689-4977

**FINANCIAL INSTITUTIONS
MARKETING ASSOCIATION**
111 East Wacker Drive
Chicago, IL 60601
312-938-2570

**INSTITUTE OF CANADIAN
ADVERTISING**
30 Soudan Avenue
Toronto, ON M4S 1V6
416-482-1396

INTERNATIONAL ADVERTISING
ASSOCIATION
342 Madison Avenue
New York, NY 10017
212-557-1133

MARKETING RESEARCH
ASSOCIATION
111 East Wacker Drive
Suite 600
Chicago, IL 60601
312-644-6610

NATIONAL ACCOUNT
MARKETING ASSOCIATION
310 Madison Avenue
Suite 724
New York, NY 10017
212-983-5140

NATIONAL ASSOCIATION FOR
PROFESSIONAL SALESWOMEN
P.O. Box 2606
Novato, CA 94948
415-898-2606

NATIONAL COUNCIL OF SALESMEN'S
ORGANIZATIONS
225 Broadway—Room 515
New York , NY 10007
212-349-1707

NATIONAL NETWORK
OF WOMEN IN SALES
P.O. Box 59269
Schaumburg, IL 60159
312-673-6697

NATIONAL PREMIUM SALES
EXECUTIVES, INC.
1600 Route 22
Union, NJ 07083
201-687-3090

OUTDOOR ADVERTISING
ASSOCIATION OF CANADA
1300 Yonge Street, #302
Toronto, ON M4T 2W4
416-968-3435

THE POINT-OF-PURCHASE
ADVERTISING INSTITUTE, INC.
66 North Van Brunt Street
Englewood, NJ 07631
201-894-8899

PROFESSIONAL MARKETING
RESEARCH SOCIETY
2323 Yonge Street, #806
Toronto, ON M4P 2C9
416-480-1616

PROFESSIONAL SALESPERSONS
OF AMERICA
100 Maria Circle NW
P.O. Box 10285
Albuquerque, NM 87184
505-897-4568

PROMOTION INDUSTRY CLUB
P.O. Box 2098
Schiller Park, IL 60176
312-991-3285

PROMOTION MARKETING
ASSOCIATION OF AMERICA
322 Eighth Avenue
Suite 1201
New York, NY 10001
212-206-1100

PUBLIC RELATIONS
SOCIETY OF AMERICA
33 Irving Place
New York, NY 10003
212-995-2230

PUBLIC RELATIONS STUDENT
SOCIETY OF AMERICA
33 Irving Place
New York, NY 10003
212-995-2230

RADIO ADVERTISING BUREAU, INC.
304 Park Avenue South
New York, NY 10010
212-254-4800

SALES AND MARKETING
EXECUTIVES INTERNATIONAL
446 Statler Office Tower
Cleveland, OH 44115
216-771-6650

SALES & MARKETING EXECUTIVES
OF GREATER NEW YORK
114 East 32nd Street
New York, NY 10016
212-683-9755

**SALES & MARKETING EXECUTIVES
OF TORONTO**
2175 Sheppard Avenue East, #110
Willowdale, ON M2J 1W8
416-497-6272

**SALES & MARKETING EXECUTIVES
OF VANCOUVER**
1250 Homer Street
Vancouver, BC V6B 2Y5
604-681-3027

**SALES & MARKETING
EXECUTIVES OF VICTORIA**
P.O. Box 4214, Stn. A
Victoria, BC V8X 3X8
604-385-3032

**SOCIETY FOR MARKETING
PROFESSIONAL SERVICES**
801 North Fairfax Street
Suite 215
Alexandria, VA 22314
703-549-6117

**SPECIALTY ADVERTISING ASSOC.
INTERNATIONAL**
1404 Walnut Hill Lane
Irving, TX 75038
214-580-0404

**TECHNICAL MARKETING
SOCIETY OF AMERICA**
P.O. Box 7275
Long Beach, CA 90807
714-821-8672

**WESTERN BUSINESSWOMEN'S
ASSOCIATION**
1250 Homer Street
Vancouver, BC V6B 2Y5
604-688-0951

**WOMEN'S ADVERTISING CLUB
OF TORONTO**
P.O. Box 1019, Stn. Q
Toronto, ON M4T 2P2
416-481-5595

WOMEN'S DIRECT RESPONSE GROUP
224 Seventh Street
Garden City, NY 11530
212-744-3506

WOMEN IN ADVERTISING AND MARKETING
4200 Wisconsin Avenue NW
Suite 106-238
Washington, DC 20016
301-369-7400

WOMEN IN COMMUNICATIONS, INC.
2101 Wilson Boulevard—Suite 417
Arlington, VA 22201
703-528-4200

WOMEN IN SALES ASSOCIATION
8 Madison Avenue—P.O. Box M
Valhalla, NY 10595
914-946-3802

ℬ

U.S. & Canadian
Trade Publications

ADVERTISERS & THEIR AGENCIES
Engel Communications, Inc.
Mountainview Corporate Park
820 Bear Tavern Road
West Trenton, NJ 08628
609-530-0044

ADVERTISING AGE
Crain Communications, Inc.
740 North Rush Street
Chicago, IL 60611
312-649-5200

ADWEEK
A/S/M Communications
49 East 21 Street—11th Floor
New York, NY 10010
212-529-5500

AMERICAN ADVERTISING
American Advertising Federation
1400 K Street NW—Suite 1000
Washington, DC 20005
202-898-0089

AMERICAN DEMOGRAPHICS
P.O. Box 68
Ithaca, NY 14851
607-273-6343

B/PAA COMMUNICATOR
Business/Professional
Advertising Association
100 Metroplex Drive
Edison, NJ 08817
201-985-4441

BUSINESS MARKETING
Crain Communications, Inc.
220 East 42nd Street
New York, NY 10017
212-210-0100

CREATIVE
Magazines/Creative, Inc.
37 West 39th Street—Suite 604
New York, NY 10018
212-840-0160

DIRECT MARKETING
Hoke Communications, Inc.
224 Seventh Street
Garden City, NY 11530-5726
516-746-6700

**DM NEWS: The Newspaper
of Direct Marketing**
Mill Hollow Corporation
19 West 21st Street—8th Floor
New York, NY 10010
212-741-2095

FOOD & BEVERAGE MARKETING
Charleson Publishers
22 West 21st Street
New York, NY 10010
212-463-7770

INCENTIVE MARKETING
Bill Communications, Inc.
633 Third Avenue
New York, NY 10017
212-986-4800

INTERNATIONAL MEDIA GUIDE
Direct International, Inc.
150 East 74th Street
New York, NY 10021
212-983-0650

JACK O'DWYER'S NEWSLETTER
271 Madison Avenue
New York, NY 10016
212-679-2471

**JOURNAL OF ADVERTISING
RESEARCH**
Advertising Research Foundation
3 East 54th Street—15th Floor
New York, NY 10022
212-751-5656

JOURNAL OF MARKETING
and
**JOURNAL OF MARKETING
RESEARCH**
American Marketing Association
250 South Wacker Drive
Chicago, IL 60606
312-648-0536

MADISON AVENUE
Madison Publishing Assoc.
369 Lexington Avenue
New York, NY 10017
212-425-3466

MARKETING
777 Bay Street
Toronto, ON M5W 1A7
416-596-5858

MARKETING AND MEDIA DECISIONS
Act III Publishers
401 Park Avenue South—7th Floor
New York, NY 10016
212-545-5100

MARKETING COMMUNICATIONS
Lakewood Publishers
50 South Ninth Street
Minneapolis, MN 55402
612-333-0471

MARKETING NEWS
American Marketing Association
250 South Wacker Drive—Suite 200
Chicago, IL 60606
312-648-0536 (Association)
312-993-9517 (Editorial)

MEDICAL ADVERTISING NEWS
Engel Communications
Mountainview Corporate Park
820 Bear Tavern Road—Suite 302
West Trenton, NJ 08628
609-530-0044

MEDICAL MARKETING & MEDIA
CPS Communications Inc.
7200 West Camino Real—Suite 215
Boca Raton, FL 33433
407-368-9301

MOTIVATIONAL MARKETING
173 Waverley Road
Toronto, ON M4L 3T4
416-699-4890

**THE NATIONAL LIST
OF ADVERTISERS**
777 Bay Street
Toronto, ON M5W 1A7
416-596-5890

PERSONAL SELLING POWER
P.O. Box 5467
Fredericksburg, VA 22403
703-752-7000

PHARMACEUTICAL EXECUTIVE
Aster Publishing Corporation
859 Willamette Street
P.O. Box 10460
Eugene, OR 97440
503-343-1200

**PHARMACEUTICAL MARKETERS
DIRECTORY**
C.P.S. Communications
7200 West Camino Real—Suite 215
Boca Raton, FL 33433
407-368-9301

POTENTIALS IN MARKETING
Lakewood Publications, Inc.
50 South Ninth Street
Minneapolis, MN 55402
612-333-0471

PREMIUM INCENTIVE BUSINESS
Gralla Publications
1515 Broadway
New York, NY 10036
212-869-1300

PR REPORTER
PR Publishing
14 Front Street
Exeter, NH 03833
603-778-0514

PUBLIC RELATIONS JOURNAL
PRSA
33 Irving Place
New York, NY 10003
212-995-2230

PR NEWS
127 East 80th Street
New York, NY 10021
212-879-7090

PUBLIC RELATIONS QUARTERLY
44 West Market Street
P.O. Box 311
Rhinebeck, NY 12572
914-876-2081

SALES & MARKETING MANAGEMENT
Bill Communications, Inc.
633 Third Avenue,
New York, NY 10017
212-986-4800

**SALES & MARKETING MANAGEMENT
IN CANADA**
3500 Dufferin Street, #402
Downsview, ON M3K 1N2
416-633-2020

SPORTS MARKETING NEWS
Technical Marketing Corp.
1460 Post Road East
Westport, CT 06880
203-227-4140

**STANDARD DIRECTORY
OF ADVERTISERS/
STANDARD DIRECTORY
OF ADVERTISING AGENCIES**
National Register Publishing Co., Inc.
3004 Glenview Road
Wilmette, IL 60091
312-256-6067

TARGET MARKETING
North American Publishing Company
401 North Broad Street
Philadelphia, PA 19108
215-238-5300

TELEMARKETING
Technology Marketing Corp.
One Technology Plaza
Norwalk, CT 06854
203-852-6800

TELEMARKETING INSIDERS REPORT
470 Main Street—Suite 108
Keyport, NJ 07735

TELEMARKETING MANAGEMENT
CMC Publishing
200 Connecticut Avenue
Norwalk, CT 06856-4990
203-852-0500

TELEPROFESSIONAL MAGAZINE
Box 123
Del Mar, CA 92014

Index

MARKETING & SALES Career Directory

The Career Press

America's Premiere Publisher of books on:

- Career & Job Search Advice
- Education
- Business "How-To"
- Financial "How-To"
- Study Skills
- Careers in Advertising, Book Publishing, Magazines, Newspapers, Marketing & Sales, Public Relations, Business & Finance, the Travel Industry and much, much more.
- Internships

If you liked this book, please write and tell us!

And if you'd like a copy of our FREE catalog of nearly 100 of the best career books available, please call us (Toll-Free) or write!

THE CAREER PRESS
62 BEVERLY RD.,
PO BOX 34
HAWTHORNE, NJ 07507
(Toll-Free) 1-800-CAREER-1 (U. S. only)
201-427-0229
FAX: 201-427-2037